ETHICS AND THE URBAN ETHOS

Ethics and the Urban Ethos

An Essay in Social Theory
and Theological Reconstruction

Max L. Stackhouse

Beacon Press   Boston

BT
738
.S695
1972
61686

Copyright © 1972 by Max L. Stackhouse
Library of Congress catalog card number: 77–179155
International Standard Book Number: 0–8070–1136–3
Beacon Press books are published under the auspices
of the Unitarian Universalist Association
Published simultaneously in Canada by Saunders of Toronto, Ltd.
All rights reserved
Printed in the United States of America

*Dedicated to my lovely
and beloved wife*
JEAN

CONTENTS

ACKNOWLEDGMENTS

The sources of one's ideas are often unknown. But some sources are well remembered: James L. Adams, Paul Tillich, Reinhold Niebuhr, Paul Lehman, James Gustafson, and Robert Bellah were most influential and diverse teachers; Jacques Ellul, Harvey Cox, Gibson Winter, and Herbert Richardson among my senior colleagues in theology are the most significant "religious" authors who have dealt with fundamental conceptions of the city in ways that both trouble me and evoke admiration. A grant from the Harvard–M.I.T. Joint Center for Urban Studies and another from the Danforth Foundation for an intensive summer seminar at M.I.T. provided the time for the initial research. The people of St. Mark Congregational Church in Roxbury, Massachusetts, were a continuous source of inspiration and sustained exposure to an urban experience different from my own. Invitations to speak at the Society for the Scientific Study of Religion, Bluffton College, the United Church of Christ Conference on the Urban Crisis, the Chautauqua Institution, and Huron College of the University of Western Ontario offered opportunities to formulate specific parts of this material. And the opportunity to write up some notions on Constantinian theology provided by T. Sizer's book on *Religion and Public Education* (New York: Houghton Mifflin Co., 1967) from which parts of Chapter VI are taken was most helpful. I am grateful to these many people and organizations.

My deep appreciation also to Doralee Denenberg and Dolores Kronberg for critical and sensitive typing and reading.

Max L. Stackhouse
Andover Newton Theological School
July 1971

Christianity began its course as a doctrine of itinerant artisan journeymen. During all periods of its mighty external and internal development it has been a quite specifically urban, and above all a civic, religion. This was true during Antiquity, during the Middle Ages, and in Puritanism. The city of the Occident, unique among all other cities of the world—and citizenship, in the sense in which it has emerged only in the Occident—has been the major theater for Christianity.

MAX WEBER
*The Economic Ethic of
the World Religions*

ETHICS AND THE URBAN ETHOS

Chapter I

AN INTRODUCTION

The modern setting of man is an artifact. It is made, it was not given. It is invented, built, and contrived. It was not found or discovered. It is a product of human projects, even if the projects are made from the givens. Societies consist in the interplay of givens and projects. The city has tipped the balance: projects far outweigh the givens.

When society is governed by givens, nature or tradition determine actions. Questions as to what "I" or "We" ought to be or do are not raised. Duty is given in the very structure of things. Everybody knows. The means of adaptation to the givens are also given. Conceptually and emotionally man draws his models and metaphors from that which is given. Psychologically, sociologically, physically, and intellectually, he survives and succeeds as he integrates himself more deeply into the given system, making it a part of him, making himself a part of it. Life is already organized; the problem is to find its patterns and laws and to fit in. He who most authentically represents the pregiven structures is most honored.

When society is governed by projects, life is not so conceived. New forms are imagined and invented; intentional creation of new social and psychic worlds is common. People construct and are expected to construct life anew. The possibilities are not seen as being given in nature or tradition. They are seen as technical ones: how can we bring nature and the routines of the past into line with our new horizons? He who reconceptualizes and reorganizes for the construction of new patterns is most honored.

There are dangers in such a situation: the psychological needs of individuals can become divorced from any overarching patterns. Liberated from the tyrannies of natural and traditional necessity, individuals are plunged into the anxiety of not knowing what they ought to do. The cues to proper action are not given and instead have to be constructed with art and imagination. It is frightening to be called upon to create new worlds, and it bears temptations to the strong to pretend to be gods. At the same time, the city as an artifact is made possible in part because of the triumph of certain rational processes which direct precise means to the accomplishment of desired ends. In order to build bridges, skyscrapers, communications media, and subway systems, in order to develop educational curricula, set up political parties, and let contracts, relatively precise use of reason is required. Yet the triumph of these forms of reason does not provide the purposes and ends of action; but only the how, the means, of action. And whenever ends or purposes are justified by appeals to reason, it is because the boundaries and the context of that specific end are already established on nonrational grounds. In such a context, the specific purpose can be called reasonable because it is rationally consistent with what is not examined.

Frequently, in an artifactual context, the individual is cut off from more coherent patterns of meaning. The primordial harmonies of nature and tradition are broken. Man is called upon to exercise imaginative and relatively free construction of his own life, but he is often given only the tool of reason to do so. Reason is both necessary for and inadequate to the task of creating a new ethos. When accepted as sufficient, man willingly or willy-nilly becomes a cog in his own machine. He has no guidelines or boundaries for action.

When reason becomes linked with the ecstasy of imagination, separated from any reality but its own fabrications, madness or fantasy reigns. Totally new and ordered worlds are dreamed. The artifactuality of the urban ethos produces, in this case, both psycho- and social pathology and the creative exploration of the recesses of personal and social consciousness. The line between them is narrow. And when a society becomes governed by such pathologies or fantasies, it is demonically possessed. It becomes organized chaos as one can see, for example, in the novels of Kafka. We have seen the symptoms in urban nations of the twentieth century—in Japan, Germany, South Africa, Russia, and to a considerable degree, the United States—and have seen the systematic destruction they have wrought. But linkages of imagination and reason have also freed man from holding to things "as they have always been," and produced modern democracy, modern socialism as well as Freud, Einstein, Martin Luther King, Jr., and a host of other breakthroughs.

But when persons and groups, without dominating society, each develop a link between their own imagination and their own reason that serves their *own* ends, and are not fundamentally concerned with the overall shape of the society, fragmentation ensues. Everyone emotionally or intellectually, politically or economically grabs his fragment, which is partially real, and creates a total reality with it. It has no enduring foundation. This, too, has been seen too often in the modern world. The splintered identities, the competing ideologies, the fractured parties, and the glaring, cluttered advertising of competing businesses assault the person and the society from a thousand sides. The overwhelming number of people in modern society think one of these four things about the city: a given to be endured, an art to be designed, a madness separate from reality, a fragment that cannot endure. They flee it, condemn it, ignore it, try to live in it without guidelines, reject it, or just use it to create their own fragments.

At least such is the case in developed societies and among urbanized peoples. Around the world, urbanization is taking place at increasing rates. Those, apparently, who celebrate the return to preurban forms of life are not those caught in them. And, in one sense, they have already been indelibly stamped by the city and cannot return. Thus, whether intellectuals like it or not, modern man lives in the city, and in the urban ethos it produced, the epitome of all man-created social order with its distinctive forms of existence.

The artifact of the urban ethos, however, is no longer confined to or neatly identifiable with the city. Ironically, cities are sometimes less "urban" than other areas. On the one hand, the city proper has often become the place where many are trapped in preurban society by racial, class, and ethnic models and metaphors that have forced them to exist in solidified "orders of nature." Literacy, industrialism, citizenship, complex patterns of organization, mobility—all marks of urbanization—are often denied to those in the center city. On the grounds of rather negligible natural "givens," such as skin color or gender, frequently reinforcing traditional master-servant relationships, the society is constructed. Pressures are on these oppressed groups to fit into the preexistent artifact, and not to try to reconstruct it. They are told to be preurban in an urban setting. Those groups are struggling to shatter the preurban residues of nature and tradition that still bind them and their oppressors so that they too may gain control over the massive artifacts constructed by their fellow man. Yet the preurban states of existence wherein minority peoples are forced to live in the center city are what most people think of when urban matters are mentioned. They are right in one sense, of course, but they are wrong in thinking that the inner city is the norm for urban life. It is a problem precisely because people there are forced to be preurban.

On the other hand, the urban ethos has burst the bounds of the city. It is not long since all people had to move to the city to encounter it as the immigrants still do. From settings in which the political, economic, religious, and family life were all of a single organic tissue that moved, if at all, like an amoeba, they crossed a boundary and saw the change in style of life, in pace, in complexity, in personality, and in the ascendancy of dominant institutions in differentiated spheres of life. Frequently, they stayed and in two generations became a part of that differentiated change. Neighbors belonged to different parties, ate different ethnic foods, worked in different occupations, worshiped at different altars. And the roles of Mama, Papa, and children became more and more diverse. People still move to the city—all over the world, at an unprecedented rate. But the city itself has spilled over the countryside in sprawling developments. It has spread yet more widely through communications, more significantly through a vast reorganization of finance, markets, and jobs, and its impact is felt most profoundly through a rearranging of values, expectations, and concepts of self and society. The urban ethos now goes to the people. Indeed, the urban ethos now dominates the society and world development at nearly every level.

The artifact of the urban ethos is the decisive characteristic of modern society. This artifact has taken on a life of its own through the very pervasiveness of its dynamism. Its intensity creates new personality structures and new collective structures, both creative and destructive, that in turn shape new aspects of the artifact. Yet the very plasticity of what is fabricated—so necessary for intentional reshaping—raises questions of the survival of civil society in any recognizable form. The artifact's complexity frequently demands and nearly always allows new institutions and groups, both ameliorative and pathological, to form and dissipate in a cascade of diversity. Yet there is an essential unity of the urban ethos that demands a reduction in conflicting loyalties and provides the basis for a new worldwide interaction of quite similar cosmopolitan persons and organizations.

An ethos is as difficult to understand as the structure that supports it. It is the subtle web of values, meanings, purposes, expectations, obligations, and legitimations that constitutes the operating norms of a culture in relationship to a social entity. And when the undergirding structure is as complex as the city, the task of merely defining the ethos is monumental. Yet one of the distinctive tasks of ethics is to define the ethos; that is, to identify, to evaluate, to arrange or rearrange those networks of norms that obtain in a sociocultural setting. Both social analysis and the utilization of specifically ethical categories are integral to such an effort. The task thus stands between sociology on one side and philosophy or theology on the other. To deal with this task, one must try to find the operative norms that are built into the structure and functioning of the society in the midst of urbanization. Ethicists must try to identify and evaluate these operating norms according to the best standards they can find. Their task is a special variety of political sociology: they must seek, as it were, the *logos* in the *socius* of the *polis*. And the "logos" part is often religious. Every urban center in history has had a theological principle at the core of its ethos. This can be seen physically if we think of the ziggurat, the temples of the Incas, the cathedrals of the medieval town, or the village church on the green. In each case the ethos is understood in terms of a more universal force. The question is whether the modern city is different. Is it fundamentally secular and pragmatic or is there here also a theological core, invisible and diffuse, but identifiable? And if there is some identifiable core, how are we to evaluate and judge it from the standpoint of the most profound theological tradition of the West, the Judeo-Christian tradition? Indeed, does it force some reinterpretations of that tradition itself?

Why, it might properly be asked, should one attempt to link up those fading speculative sciences, theology and ethics, in their prescriptive dimensions, with the problems of the urban ethos? Why not only treat the city descriptively as would an anthropologist or sociologist? Those most deeply engaged in urban planning, urban theory, and practical urban politics see few specific connections between their most profound spiritual commitments and what they do every day. And even if one could come to some conclusion about the question as to whether there are hidden values at the core of the urban ethos that are or are not valid from a Judeo-Christian perspective, would it really have direct and practical consequences?

My answer is that I do not know. But there are a set of converging concerns that appear to make such an enterprise worthy of the effort:

Among many observers of the religious scene, there is a growing belief that organized religion is on the brink of a new reformation, or, as I prefer, a new formation. No one is sure that it will occur. There are no known Augustines, Thomases, Luthers, Calvins, Loyolas, or Xaviers on the immediate horizon. But the seminaries, the university departments of religion, certain parts of the church bureaucracies, the ecumenical symposia and conferences, and increasingly some segments among the pastors and laity are engaging in a searching, no-holds-barred reappraisal of the tradition, of the church, of the meaning of the biblical heritage, and of the role of religion in a secular world. In debates that cut across denominations and congregations, confessions and conservative-radical splits, a new spirit and a new enthusiasm for the ecumenical and prophetic possibilities are in the wind.

This new movement is not so new as many think. It is rooted in the critical and reconstructive efforts of the last dozen decades. For several generations a significant minority have recognized that the religious social philosophies of both Catholicism and Calvinism, the only two ever fully developed in the West, were incapable of dealing with the modern world. The new movement derives from Schleiermacher, Troeltsch, Rauschenbusch, the Niebuhrs, and hosts of others who anticipated many of the contemporary motifs and this movement finds new resources and resonance in the newer churches of the developing countries. It has been given existential meaning in this country by men like Martin Luther King, Jr., who tried to bring the heritage to bear on the problems of the city through direct action, who was driven by his faith to move from the myth-dominated culture of southern piety to the northern urban metropolis in a way that joined prophetic action with a redefinition of a conserved tradition.

The new movement in the church, however, has also, at its strongest, been informed theologically and intellectually by its concern for continuity with the Catholic tradition struggling to update itself and also by the great reaction of neoorthodoxy which has now put the closing brackets on the Protestant Era. It is deeply concerned about the relationship with Jews and with ethically concerned humanists. It is shaped by the post-Kantian criticism of Christianity by Weber, Nietzsche, Marx, and Freud, all four of whom it has posthumously baptized as previous eras did pagan or Renaissance humanist sources. In this context, it is becoming recognized that it is the responsibility of every churchman to be a pre-reformer or a pre-revolutionary to support and participate in those efforts that reconstitute life and thought so that the cause of truth, justice, and righteousness may live. The Judeo-Christian tradition in this newer perspective is not to be understood as a set of eternal truths, nor as merely private conviction, nor as belief in miraculous events. It is first of all an historical movement with an interpretation of sin and salvation, a view of the realities of evil, and the vision of overcoming them. This realistic-visionary movement shifts and turns as it encounters successive societies and cultures, specifying the marks of destruction and the possibilities of hope that are peculiar to a given epoch. And this movement must continually develop fresh conceptual and institutional frameworks if man's conception of life and history is not to decay into chaos or leap to the fantasy of totalitarian illusion. Thus, it is the responsibility of a scholar who sees continuing promise in this movement to try to develop the frameworks by which the movement can be sustained and to present his case for inspection also by the cultured despisers of religion. In this generation, that responsibility demands examination of the pertinence of theology and ethics to the urban ethos.

As one who tries to be sensitive to the contemporary directions of thought, I could not avoid hearing the injunction among contemporary theologians of secularity to listen to the world, to take it seriously, to hear what it has to say.[1] The coming of age of religious man means that the world is to be understood on its own terms. Listen to the facts and figures of the world, gain a technical competence in charts and graphs. The world is increasingly an urban world, and the city is the place where significant noises are made. I religiously, and I mean religiously, listened to the hearings, the rallies, the revolution in Black consciousness, the riots, gathering all the facts I could digest about the deep divisions over public education, urban renewal, slum housing, welfare programs, city management, and especially the impact of planning on the city, urbanity, and civic values.

Yet despite serious attempts to listen, the attempt to understand the city became more and more complicated during the last decade. The most urbanized nations were confronted with a range of protests which were both localized in and dependent upon city life, while simultaneously echoing, at their most profound levels, several centuries of antiurban intellectual protest. Ideas sharply critical of urban existence that had been generated in the poet's study or the scholar's library or the monk's cell over the past two centuries burst into general public consciousness in the form of hippies, astrologists, drug cults, neomystics, and Jesus freaks.[2] And they become legitimated in slightly more sophisticated form as a new kind of consciousness that will bring salvation to the decaying and destructive worlds of unreconstructed consciousness.[3]

Simultaneously, these calls for new antiurban consciousness have become mixed with other and still vigorous antiurban voices of a more substantial nature. Minority power advocates sometimes see the city as a subtle form of detention camp and attempt to form a community within the metropolis that is both a part of and separate from the dominant structures of urban life. Revolutionary militants seeing the hidden forms of oppression willingly accepted by segments of the urban underclasses celebrate Lin Piao's or Che Guevara's views of the cities as being the seat of imperialism, but find themselves adopting styles of life and modes of organization that are only available to urban man. Somehow taking to the Catskills to launch an attack on New York doesn't make sense in our environment. Ecologists portray the city as the continuous symbol of man's violation of mother nature, but call for recycling and similar new technologies that will of necessity increase man's urban control over his environment. And women's liberationists cite the city as the primary example of aggressive and rationalistic male dominance while arguing that attitudinal and intellectual capacities are not gender-based and demanding equal access to technological-managerial skills and employment.

The result of this cacophony of antiurban voices, each oddly dependent upon the city, is a strange coalition of counterurban forces. Those prophetically sensitive to the pathologies of the city are allowing the future of urban civilization to be decided by those with less profound sensibilities. For when the poets and reformers fail to relate their ideology to the actual conditions in which they live, in this case the city, but actually undercut the foundations of their own existence, they both discredit their efforts and become unwitting allies of those who have used the city for private benefit and now abandon it. The prospects for the city of the future, if these lines are pursued without reserve, is Calcutta.

Yet these voices betray in their concern for the city, even in their negative concern, that the questions at stake in the shape of civilization are fundamentally religious and moral. It is meaning and righteousness, in their ultimate dimensions, that are sought. And their antiurban bias stands as a judgment upon contemporary civilization, for it has not offered either a convincing case for and vision of the promise of complex cosmopolitan existence or the actual life experience of its benefits over a broad base. Nothing will compromise this bias but a compelling vision and a real experience that can provide a religious and moral conviction. Until that is met, the city will continue to be the prime target of ideological attack.

The city during the last decade has also become aware of a deeply rooted, more literal attack. The Military-Industrial Complex is in many ways the most advanced, if distorted, form of urban civilization. It is advanced in that it is no longer dependent upon a specific geographical base as is a metropolis, but can transport nearly the whole of a city halfway around the globe in a matter of hours. It is urban in that it has all the technological and organizational interdependencies of a modern city; it is rooted in the social history that generated also the contemporary megalopolis, and it is deeply dependent upon a near-religious commitment to a specific version of the ethical predispositions required for urban life. It assumes that it is man's God-given role to protect one's own territory, to maintain a quality of nondissident citizenship, and to engage in the planned mastery of the political environment. This complex is designed to protect and extend our relatively democratic, urbanized society by cosmopolitan involvements. But it is distorted in that it cannot defend the cities from nuclear attack, prevent the decay of urban communities at home, or provide the impetus for democratized civility abroad. Indeed, it seems locked into a pattern of reciprocal international targeting of cities; it diverts the sense of urgency from domestic urban problems; it threatens civil liberties by its own methods of surveillance and intimidation; and it engages in policies toward nonwhite and poor countries that often reinforce the exploitative structures within those nations. The complex has become the chief custodian of the values and virtues of American civil religion. It is the secularized "church" of national piety, promising its own variety of "eternality," and "salvation" from demonic forces. In all these areas, the Military-Industrial Complex frustrates, while simultaneously exemplifying and trying to protect, the fragile moral possibilities that exist in contemporary urban society. And it does so in part because of the quasi-theological sense of its own calling and its mission in the country and to the world.[4]

In such a context, urban listening and urbane thought find themselves in difficult straits. The old concepts of conventional wisdom do not seem to hold, and new ones are not forged. One turns, in such a situation, to the urban theorists, for one becomes aware that urban facts do not speak for themselves, nor do charismatic voices or institutionalized pieties seem to give self-authenticating visions. Indeed, piles of facts are gathered regularly for general consumption and then passed onto the dungheaps of history; prophetic voices rise temporarily above the din, drawing attention to some genuine condition or some profound human hunger only to be swallowed again into the entrails of the city; and somehow, new cities rise on the burial grounds of those destroyed in war. Perhaps the theorists can help, for although life cannot be interpreted contrary to the facts nor fly in the face of profound human passions nor ignore the probability of imminent destruction, only theory will tell us how to evaluate, weigh, and interpret them—and subsequently, how to act wisely.

Urban theorists tend to agree on many things: urban civilization is more differentiated than other forms of life, such as the tribe or the farm or the town. It allows greater specialization of function and increased participation in voluntary activities. It requires effective rationalization and bureaucratization of routine activities, but allows more direct participation in certain mass political activities that have large-scale and long-term significance. Urban civilization involves complex organization and increased interdependence which some see as extending the range of human responsibility and others see as adding undue forms of impersonal stress. Patterns of community identity become diffuse under the impact of urbanization, a phenomenon which some see as providing freedom and mobility, while others see as bringing anonymity and rootlessness. Relationships tend to become pragmatic or functional, which some interpret as demystifying and liberating and which others see as mechanizing and dehumanizing.

Urban theorists disagree on many things also. As we shall later see, they tend to focus on one or another specific dimension of human experience in the city as the point from which to evaluate the whole of urban existence. And many of these disagreements are fundamental. But perhaps more profound than even these is the sense of unity that they sense in modern urban existence, even in the face of fragmenting controversies tearing at the soul of particular cities. The theorists who write about the city evidence a reverence, an awe toward the ultimate values that are sought by urban life. The city becomes an object of respect and a subject of commitment even if they disagree as to the significance of particular characteristics of urban life.

How is one to react when one is enjoined by theologians to listen to the city and finds there piles of facts that render no meaning, the discord of voices protesting it on religious and moral grounds, a distortion of it at the command center of American military and industrial power finding its legitimacy in a quasi-theology of American destiny, and a relative agreement among theorists as to what the patterns of urbanization entail and a profound awe toward them; but a fundamental disagreement about what to make of it? A clue is provided in a critique of Talcott Parsons by Barrington Moore, Jr. Moore accuses Parsons of being a theologian. The tone is such that the accusation is tantamount to condemnation. Moore is right. Parsons is a secular theologian. In fact, Moore is one himself although he worships at a different altar.[5] Armed with philosophical, scientific, and historical sensibilities too rich to become a part of contemporary religious "rapidation,"[6] the social theorists are in many ways the secular theologians of our time. It is they who are trying to come to grips with the fundamental forces that shape man's existence and provide promise of his salvation. It is they who are trying to find the forms of power and worth that give shape to meaningful and moral existence. That power and worth people used to call "God."

It is ironic that by following the injunction to engage in secular listening and reflection, one is driven back to the theological questions presumably abandoned by secular theologians as passé. Meanwhile, the theologians who themselves saw everything dependent upon secular listening have now apparently decided to develop another journalistic jag. They unfortunately cannot agree, this time, as to what it shall be. Some speak of a theology of celebration, some of hope, some of revolution, some of ecology, some of neomysticism. In view of such theological fascination with ripples that hardly touch the deeper tides and currents of contemporary life, it becomes possible to suggest that it is not rigorous empiricists, the death of God theologians, nor the neoromantics, nor the cryptorevolutionaries, nor the official custodians of civil religion who are the significant secular theologians of our time, even though they command attention because they speak in forms of language of the nineteenth century vaguely familiar to the cultured despisers, and are therefore presumed to be profound. Instead it may be the social theorists who are the more secular and more radical and more theological theologians of today in the senses of dealing with the real world, trying to get to the roots, and raising the ultimate questions. Thus, our trek must initially be from theology to the city to the deeper relations of social theory and theology and ethics.

Now if the social theorists are doing the job once done by theology, how are they doing? And what are their fundamental presuppositions? If one is fundamentally concerned in aiding the reconstruction of a religious social philosophy for a new formation, and if one begins this by serious attention to the real world and its theorists, what elements of significance can be drawn from secular experience and the secular theologians? Perhaps this question can be best answered by accenting three aspects of cybernetic theory upon which several social theorists today depend. Cybernetics is the study of systems, their construction, communications, and control.

The first element of a viable system, so goes the theory, is a relatively precise coherence between the specific parts and the whole. Of course, there can be, indeed must be, high levels of differentiation and individuation, and a viable system must be capable of dealing with a wide multiplicity of variables; but channels of information and power flow must be relatively unobstructed so that the various parts can relate to others and to the whole. Translated into felt problems of the city, there is today a loss of moral cohesion that gave shape to the whole and to the proper relationships of the parts to each other. But as Robert Nisbet pointed out some time ago, "The real problem is the failure of our present democratic and industrial scene to create new contexts of association and moral cohesion within which the smaller allegiances of men will assume both functional and psychological significance."[7] The fault for this is usually hidden at the feet of technology, science, and the city itself. But, as Nisbet continues, "the attack on these elements of modern culture is ill-founded, for no one of these is either logically or psychologically essential to the problem at hand."[8] It is quite possible for these to exist with coherent patterns of social relationship and moral definition without being oppressive or monolithic. But such a possibility is as yet only a theoretical one. We frankly do not have a blueprint or even a vision of a modern large-scale social system that is holistic and coherent and that is neither an apology for the present nor burdened with threats of tyranny.

A second cybernetic element that allows us to identify certain of the contributions of the social theorists is the principle of feedback. No viable social system can today operate without definitions of goals that are continuously monitored and modified by the parts of the system that are most affected. In urbanized culture, this means the construction of appropriately complex mechanisms to register, evaluate, and respond to the unanticipated effects of action toward particular goals. Contemporary social theory, whether in the Marxist tradition of demanding control by the controlled, in the republican traditions of celebrating voting procedures to legitimate government by consent of the governed, or in the "new left" camp of "participatory democracy," all recognize that "feedback" is a fundamental requirement of modern, large-scale social systems. Without it, society is destined to calcification and collapse or to engender dissensus and revolution.

The third feature of cybernetic thought, however, is the most interesting for our purposes, even though it is less often accented as a basic concept. Cybernetic theory presupposes symbolic control. Computer people have a negative way of stating this: GIGO—"garbage in, garbage out." Of course, in computers the symbols are primarily numbers, but the principle holds also in social systems where symbols are more subtle combinations of concepts, valuations, and emotive meanings. No matter how coherent a system one has and no matter how effective feedback mechanisms are, wrong, mistaken, or confused symbols fed into the operations will render only incoherence and foolishness. The implications of this feature of cybernetic thought is in some ways the most wide-ranging and the least explored. Rightly and clearly ordered symbols must be continuously fed into the whole apparatus of modern society, or we get only GIGO. In short, there is a necessary place for "right doctrine"—hopefully not imposed dogmatically or coercively. Indeed, there is something of a bias against such a thing in some segments of both contemporary theology and its secular correlates in social science. But the presuppositions of both disciplines finally require it.

This implies also that the urban situation may be out of control in part because we have lost symbolic or conceptual control. Such an observation will strike many as a new appeal to dogma or a new invitation to betray fundamental human questions by resurrecting idealistic philosophy. And it is surely the case that those who have tried to do either theology or social theory by merely clarifying the symbols and concepts have often abdicated the responsibility to relate this feature of cybernetic thought to the actualities of the human tissue of life by feedback or the construction of a new coherent whole. In consequence, many theologians and social theorists have turned to other forms of reductionism—forms that see all symbols and concepts as projections of psychological or social needs and unmitigated historical relativism, granting only marginal importance to symbolic or conceptual integrity. Again, the result is GIGO.

To identify the problem as one of symbolic or conceptual control also runs counter to the conventional wisdom of today's self-proclaimed prophets. The problem, according to many of my students and friends, is precisely that there is too much control, too many rules, too much management, too much authority, too much thought, too many symbols in the hands of the establishment, too much programming of personal identity. Not enough feeling, not enough physical contact, not enough unstructured expression. Therefore, liberation from control in favor of human spontaneity is the issue. But they are, I believe, wrong in their identification of the problem. Close attention to their rhetoric reveals new symbols, new disciplines, new patterns in the making that are not acknowledged for what they are.

On the one hand, control today is hardly a problem of quantity. Literally no one has control over the life of the modern urban ethos, or even any major sector of it. Yet, the entire life of the city is founded upon human control over environment. The sense of powerlessness is widespread as much because no one controls as because some do a lot more than others. Day and night are blurred into a single stream of human activity because of human engineering. Seasons come and go without major shifts in styles of living. More people participate in political activity, having some say in their destiny, choice of friends, ideas, churches, and marriage partners than in any other society in history. Businesses, schools, unions, voluntary association, families, and individuals make more decisions affecting their futures without permission from anyone than is conceivable in preurban society. The very possibilities of countercultural experimentation are only available on a larger scale in a cosmopolitan society. Except for the poor and the Black and women, who are often denied extensive participation in these choices, quantity of available control is enormous, but diffuse. The problem, then, is quality and distribution of control, not quantity.

On the other hand, the notion that liberation involves overthrow of structured, institutional life does not take account of the historic tendency of man to spontaneously devour his neighbor when there is pure spontaneity. Gunslinging, pogroms, adventurism, ruthless destruction of the weak, exploitation are as much a part of spontaneity as love and harmony. The Altamont murders were as real as the Woodstock frolics. *The Lord of the Flies* is as real as *Walden Two*. In short, there is always the need for kinds and degrees of control. The kinds and degrees that presently obtain may not be desired or necessary, but we are not thereby relieved of the requirement to understand man in society. And society inevitably implies some conception of controls for the sake of human fulfillment through rules, management, authority, institutionalized structures, and roles.[9] The secular theologians who try to find the grounding of those that people choose, agree to, live by, or tolerate are the true radicals of modern thought, for they seek a society with its laws written on the hearts of men and not the abandonment of society and law.

Today we are engaged in an intensive cybernetic conflict that is also, at its deepest levels, theological conflict. That is, we are witnessing a quality of confusion that derives from the feeding of mutually conflicting symbols into the programming end of incoherent complex systems with insufficient patterns for feedback. In such a situation, the question is what kind of vision of coherence, what kinds of patterns of responsibility, and what symbols are deep enough, profound and far-reaching enough to render meaning to personal, social, and cultural life. This requires the joining of religious and sociological materials. In previous ages, these questions have been dealt with explicitly in religious terms, such as "God," "salvation," or "grace." Today, in part because of the trivialization and prostitution of religious terms, explicit religious terms are suspect. Nevertheless, urban society and social theory are caught in a conflict of the gods, gods which the secular theologians presuppose and endorse or deny, often without acknowledging that they are dealing in theological-ethical—indeed, ultimate—matters. In short, the fundamental commitments of the age, the culture, and the civilization are what is involved in both religion and in contemporary social theory, and the critical reflection on these is inevitably one of the tasks of theological ethics.

It may seem odd to deal with matters in this way precisely at a point of history when many see religion on the retreat. And, indeed, in certain overt ways, there is a shift in religion toward privatization and away from societal concerns, a decline in church support, and a movement of the church away from engagement in urban life. Nevertheless it is quite clear that some public institutionalization of religion has taken place. Church organizations and leaders speak out on public issues constantly, although this is now less prevalent in schools and catechisms in direct and coerced ways. Clearly the removal of prayer from the public schoolroom, the abolishment of required chapel in universities, and the decline of notions of heresy from seminaries and ecclesiastical courts indicate the relative absence of coerced belief, and the clearer separation of throne and altar. But in highly indirect ways, fundamental and unprovable assumptions rooted historically and logically in theological loyalties have been built into the control systems of modern institutions. Often demythologized and secularized for export beyond the boundaries of parochial religion and popular cultus, metaphysical assumptions about the nature of man, the good and evil of man, and the structures needed to save and assist man have become a part of our laws, our ways of selecting leadership, our images of the self, our distribution of power and the kinds of majesty we attribute to these. In these locations, the underlying assumptions have often been divorced from any overarching sense of divine origin, intention, or destiny. They have become broken myths, containing fragments of meaning but without coherence or compelling purpose. Each fragment becomes radicalized into reductionistic ideology. Several fragments become woven together into "party" or "school." And those who try to stand back to see the whole picture drift into relativistic purposelessness. Yet some attempt to see the whole is required.

Finally, the theological ethical treatment of the urban ethos is required by very practical considerations. The voting of urban funds by state and national legislatures for urban priorities and investment in urban problems by corporate interests will never be accomplished unless there is a fundamental recognition of the legitimacy of urban forms of life. And while it is manifestly clear that people vote and invest their lives or their money according to self-interest and direct financial or power returns, it is not so clear that they do only that. People also vote or invest according to what they believe is right, good, and fit. And people always both perceive this, and perceive their self-interest, in terms of assumed general ways of looking at the world. The common sense of one age is often the theological or philosophical breakthrough of a previous one now plowed into the fabric of common assumption. And the pervasive antiurban perceptions of life among those who hold the moneybags will only be compromised when a more significant set of interpretive filters are developed for them to see new connections between their interests and their obligations to do the right, the good, and the fit. Then, perhaps, urban fiscal problems will have only technical hurdles to overcome.[10] At present, however, debates about new federal-urban ties, by-passing the states in large measure, or federal-state ties bypass-ing the cities, or new "metropolitan states" bear fundamental value commitments as to which styles of life are ultimately *better.*

From this set of concerns and with these hypothetical con-nections between the social theory and theology, it is necessary to pose a series of questions to that confusing artifact, the urban ethos:

Why does urban, suburban, and exurban man, all infected by the urban ethos, scurry so compared to all the nonurban peoples of the world? He acts as if life is going somewhere, and not only toward death as everybody else knows. Yet he refuses to engage in speculation about or at least claims disinterest in matters beyond the predictable. Urban man is thought to be so materialistic, so consumed by the possibility of consumption. Is his interest in money really a lust for power or greed, or does once-filthy lucre now represent something nonmaterial to him? He does not seem to enjoy consumption and visits his sharpest contempt on profligate consuming. Man in the urban ethos is thought to be so individualistic and so calculative, but what he really calculates about is his children's future, his corporation's survival, his party's victory, and his nation's security. These are only partly explainable through categories of self-seeking, for they are also outpouring. Why is he so confident, or is it arrogant? Why is he so defensive, or is it vulnerable? Why so competent, or is it flimflam?

And why is the city itself, for all the peoples of the world, so seductive, that all feel its pull and feel the sensuousness of its attraction? Why so repugnant that the image "Whore Baby-lon" is ever attached to it? Why so exciting that every human with life wants to go there; and so frightening that it evokes terror to the newcomer? Why so self-destructive that its destiny is the archaeologist's shovel, and so self-generative that ever-new structures and civilizations rise from its ghettoes and ashes? Why at once so supportive that the urban ethos is characterized by the multiplicity of services, and yet so demanding that only the strong survive? Why so grand and why so awful?

The flood of questions cannot be answered. But precisely the flood demands at least the construction of a raft, if not an ark, out of the best timbers that can today be mustered—social theory and theological ethics.

Through the impact of the several concerns and questions so far discussed, I have been led to the conclusion that the crisis of modern urban society is substantially an ethical crisis, one that has clear social and theological dimensions. On the one hand, contemporary man finds himself in the midst of vast patterns. On the other hand, he has few tools to deal with anything but bits and pieces.

The consequence has been a theological-ethical or social-psychological retreat to "micro-ethics." What are the morals of the relationship between employer and employee, man and wife, student and lover, parent and child? What are the techniques of building interpersonal sensitivity through small group training, or of new private styles of life through communes? The intensity of attention to these problems has obscured the problems of "macro-ethics." Not only do people have problems, but urban society as a systemic reality is fraught with divisions among groups of people and with structural maladies that threaten the very existence of civil society, and that inhibit whole segments of the population from developing employable skills, stable families, capacities to sexually relate, and responsible mothering and fathering. No speaking of "micro-ethical" maturity and love can solve the problems of urban design, transfer of power, racial conflict, urban-versus-farm-preference legislation, the divisions between the rich and the poor, or the institutional impact of the Military-Industrial Complex, all of which effect micro-ethical patterns. It is the "macro-ethical" structures that very often prevent the possibility of maturity and love, that deny manhood, womanhood, and the viability of maturity and love to whole groups. And the great structures of society are inevitably supported by theological-ethical claims to their legitimacy.

In three areas of contemporary life, the concern for "macro-ethical" analysis is widely acknowledged. All are intimately connected with problems of the city, and are deeply influential in the present study. The problem of poverty groups is widely acknowledged as a problem for classes of people, and not just for individuals. We have not yet decided as a nation what to do about it, but we recognize the problem.

Secondly, racism can no longer be viewed as personal prejudice or the failure of interpersonal communications. The legacy of both the social institution of slavery and the theological-ethical understanding of the "orders of creation," racism threatens urban existence by perpetuating a caste system involving political, economic, and cultural isolation. Or, if the victims of racism wish to overcome their isolation, they are forced to deny significant dimensions of personal and social identity. Economic, educational, political, and religious structures perpetuate the social and theological-ethical legacy in ways that the individuals in them cannot always acknowledge. Social and cultural forces are at work here that are not malleable to personal and interpersonal stratagems, although ironically their transformation requires personal commitment. Yet they threaten the life of the cities and the well-being of urban people.[11]

A third area is the role-definition of males and females in our society. While individuals or families may reach tolerable or even personally delightful modifications of or adjustments to their assigned roles and expected behaviors, the cultural and social constraints often developed in preurban societies prevent some vocational possibilities from being realized, impose enormous and unnecessary psychic burdens, and prevent actualization of basic norms of equity between male and female at numerous points. These cultural and social constraints are often rooted in and reinforced by conceptions of how the world was made at the hands of God. Even where the conscious awareness of the symbolic and mythical sources of such ultimate legitimizing of role-definition is lost, the hidden theological dimensions shape the boundaries of human perceptions of the proper and the possible. Micro-ethical solutions such as finding a tolerable harmony with one's spouse, therefore, only reinforce the macro-ethical patterns if there is not the simultaneous concern for the social, cultural, and hidden theological patterns which shape both partners, neighbors, and the unmarried.[12]

Thus, it is a presupposition of this book that no man can today consider himself morally responsible if he is not engaged in some significant way in dealing with "macro-ethical" problems. In a sense, I only echo a basic principle of Aristotle and of the Bible. Aristotle held that to be human is to participate in the ordering of one's society. Anyone who does not is defined as "idiot." And the biblical view is overwhelmingly in favor of understanding the life in relationship to the life of God through the upbuilding of a community. And these are theological-ethical problems precisely because they ask what kind of ultimate frameworks of meaning and responsiveness, worth and power, sin and salvation, good and evil are necessary to legitimate and reconstruct various large-scale dimensions and structures of the ethos.

My attempt in this book is directly related to these problems, but in a way that is somewhat different from contemporary theological and ethical writing on the city. Most of it has been either exhortation or tactics. I am more burdened by the fact that even exhortations to direct and immediate involvement, so necessary for genuine and professional education, may, and recently have, become the occasion for avoiding the hard intellectual work of analyzing and reconstructing fundamental assumptions for secular and sacred theologian alike. In short, I hope to take one step, at least, toward the development of a depth-sociology, to plumb the symbolic roots of large-scale systems, to counterbalance and to supplement the enormous strides of depth-psychology over the past generation.[13]

Chapter II

PERSPECTIVES ON THE CITY

As a beginning we should identify the major alternative perspectives of the social theorists, the secular theologians of the city. Each of these perspectives lifts up a crucial segment of the meaning of the urban ethos, and examination of these perspectives reveals a fragment of urban consciousness that is valid. Yet, as we shall see, closer inspection also shows two unexpected things: fundamental distortion of the urban ethos by too earnestly constructing a world view on a valid but restricted basis, and an unacknowledged dependence upon a theological commitment at the core of the social theory.

At the first level of urban analysis, we find three perspectives that are common in ordinary experience and worked out by some theorists in a systematic way. The first, we may call personalism. It understands the urban ethos according to its impact on the self. Positively, it is often stated in the proposition, "The city is people." Negatively, "The city is depersonalizing." The second, we will call morphologism. This position understands the city according to its geographical and geometric shapes, its use of space, its population densities and flows, its heights, its widths, and its breadths. The third, we call naturalism, for it attempts to understand the city according to primordial patterns of nature which it believes the artifact of the urban ethos cannot or ought not distort. Each of these views has a long and deep philosophical history that has taken on new vibrancy during the past several decades in Western intellectual life. We need to look at each of these in some depth.

The Personalists

The *personalists* tend to see the center of an ethos in terms of interpersonal and intra-personal relationships. The character of a society and a culture can be identified through the quality of the I-Thou relationship and of the I-Me relationship. The transcendent importance of the single person or of the authentic interpersonal relationship to this analysis makes maturity, integrity, and love predominant values that are applied not only to persons, but to the whole of society.

Personalists appear in many forms and assorted sizes. They appear in the popular literature that shows the oppression of the gray flannel rat race, in the celebration of personalized cultus of the "counter culture" (which is in fact more conformist than it acknowledges), and more seriously in the romantic journalists who preach some agrarian nostalgia. More sophisticated varieties, from which the popularizers draw, can be found in the thought of Jung and his disciples, and the personalisms of psychoanalysis, phenomenology, and some existentialism, whatever their intramural disputes. All attempt to offer a definition of the ethos in its normative aspects from the standpoint of a concept of integrated personal experience.

The urban ethos, according to this coterie of views, can best be seen in the fragmenting of character induced by modern economic and political life. The transition from status to contract, from primary to secondary group relationships, from organic life to division of labor, has brought into question overarching and culturally supported faiths, social structures, and creeds that provide a clear and holistic definition of the self. The present situation promotes the differentiation of personal relationships and accents the tangential and compartmentalized aspects of life. The product of these developments in the urban ethos is a threat to personal meaning. There is a loss of any coherent sense of the self, a loneliness in the crowd, an atomizing of human relationships. The person is split into a series of roles and masks into which he slides and from which he departs without involvement. All relationships are relations of limited liability. In this view, the artificiality of the urban ethos produces a hoax, inauthentic personhood.

The chief forces of evil in this devastation of personal integrity are derived from or identified with the institutional or sociocultural order which itself is without integrity. Frequently, the society is seen as a machine, manipulated by unidentifiable and irresponsible exploiters who allegedly control the destiny of society. At other times, the very complexity of social existence itself has become the impersonal exploiter of human resources. Still others see any focus on societal matters as purely mechanical and contrary to proper accent on the inwardness of the self—on subjectivity. And, since urban society even more graphically than others demands conscious attention to the forms and structures of existence, it is more alienating and dehumanizing. In any case, the urban ethos is depersonalized.

One underlying assumption of the personalists is that there is an inviolable and constant human nature—a given personhood. And whatever disagreements there may be on the quality of that nature, there is agreement that, whatever it is, one can move from its description to normative prescription. The personalists charge that man was a person once or that society was personalistic once, or at least we once knew what personhood was. For the society had space for and supports for inwardness, or integrity, or maturity, or love. But man in the urban ethos is now somehow being deprived of that reality. The personalists do not, however, specify when the golden age of persons was. Nevertheless, there is often the hint of nostalgia for previous periods of "authenticity." Under examination, the "golden age" it turns out, is not an historic period, but a philosophical principle. Ironically, that principle itself is an artifact, a construct.

Although it is not a necessary aspect of personalism, the protest against depersonalization is often laden with the reactionary notion that the spread of the urban ethos implies the leveling of men. The city makes common certain dimensions of experience and entails the destruction of distinctive claims of personal status. The loss of particularistic, localistic, or provincial values and privileges, whether of class, race, region, or religion, has plunged many who invoked unique authority into the insecurity of the relativity of the urban ethos. There is nothing special about "me." "I" am replaceable, expendable, one of many. The moral appeal to a natural elite or a divinely sanctioned superiority is shattered in the cosmopolitan ethos of modern society, as is the unified objective pattern which assures one of his inherited uniqueness. Forced to be men and women among men and women without prerogatives, many have found the position intolerable. Ideas once sheltered by esoteric language become the grist for the mass communication mill. Taste and style that were the fashion of the few become the fad of the many. And choice once restricted to the aristocrat becomes the option of the man on the street. But it is a moral judgment of a very dubious sort that suggests that these trends are destructive of personhood, unless one wishes to restrict personhood to certain classes. Indeed, one can argue just the opposite: these patterns may be viewed as the extension of personhood beyond elite control. It is actually a process of "personalization," not "depersonalization." The problem is that we do not know how to integrate and relate mass personalization into a social cohesion that sustains the newfound personalism. Nevertheless, in this view it is possible to hold that whatever inhibits the further extension of that kind of "personalization" may be judged as a danger to the city.

It is true, of course, that precisely the processes that make personality available to the masses create other problems for the person. On the one hand, since choices are made by the many instead of by a few, the immediate impact of a single person's choice is not so great. The choices of one immediately bump up against the contrary choices of others, requiring the cooperation of others in particular decisions or the calculation of others' reactions and responses in private choosing. When routinized, as in modern production and consumption, there is the unconscious interlocking of multitudes through impersonal social mechanisms. On the other hand, the multiplicity of choices being made by many, in such a diversified environment offers few clues as to what choices ought to be made. The cues from the society seem vague or contradictory, with no rhyme or reason. And when the cues seem relatively clear and direct, as in advertising, political speeches, or preaching, they are recognized as manipulatory, seductive, and divorced from the subtleties of life where persons live it. Thus the individual is drawn into a vortex where it is both necessary to have his antennae out, to be sensitive to the mass of others in new ways, and, at the same time, to stand alone, to acknowledge the dim visibility of the general shape of things, to make his own judgments. Urban personality is simultaneously more interdependent with others and more alone, at once affected by pervasive trends and radically free.

Psychoanalytically oriented personalists see these pressures as inducing a neurotic syndrome in modern man. Compulsive, caught up in rationalization, insecure, and alienated from his own feelings, urban man is sick. Symbolic reinterpretation of private history or exercises in "polymorphous perversity" are prescribed to recover the lost organic ties to one's emotional roots.[1]

A more radical variety of personalist response to this condition is found in the existentialist affirmation of the need for authentic subjective decision. This view sees the fundamental structures of man as internal to his psychic structure and to the quality of the interpersonal relationship. The proper life-style of urban man is the resistance, living in a network of personal risk and decisions and actions that are only negatively or tangentially related to governing structures. The accent on radical freedom and the capacity of man to develop subjective, non-socially determined patterns of meaning has opened dimensions of the self that had long been obscured. And this view has freed individuals from conventions that were unexamined, and passivities that were untested. But such personalism tends to draw brackets around the self or the small group so that the person is considered in himself or discovered in a one-to-one relationship. These conceptions are incapable of dealing with such problems as the organization of the city and are necessarily confined to the micro-ethics of ego and alter ego.[2]

Analysis based on psychoanalytic or existential personalism is not dangerously reactive; it is basically irrelevant, although it provides the illusion of ultimate relevancy to those caught in what appear to be merely personal crises. It cannot provide the patterns of constructed convention necessary to civil society. And if the identity of the self is integrally related to the structure of the society, no view that omits reference to society can deal with personality. Thus, there are fundamental dangers in the irrelevancy. Concentration of focus on the problems of intra- and intersubjective relations prevents serious reflection on larger, structural problems and allows the institutions to become more tyrannical or to collapse, eventualities that could destroy both the self and the relationships to others. Subjective and intra-personal relations, after all, are only interstitial. They exist in the midst of and in between larger structures that sustain, protect, encourage, or inhibit them. Unless these structures are shaped to encourage or permit them, they can easily be driven underground where they play havoc with selves and face-to-face relations. A massive artifact like the urban ethos does not maintain itself as does nature where whatever happens—even volcanoes, lightning storms, forest fires, packs of wolves devouring deer—can be said to be "natural." The city requires constant attention and an analysis that does not offer insights for maintaining the structures that protect personhood is self-contradictory.

Thus, the personalist position does not fulfill its own intention; it does not deal with the whole person or the new shapes of personality developed in urban life. The isolation and absolutization of the concept of the person extracted from the actual social matrix is a fundamental distortion of what it means to be a self and what it takes to promote authentic self and small group relations. The personalists not only isolate the theory of persons from the complexities which shape personality and among which persons actually live but they distort the matrix by seeing it only in interpersonal terms.

It cannot be denied that the personalists have identified and continue to accent a dimension of reality that is of fundamental significance. How can one deny it? We cannot bring about structural change to bring about new personal possibilities without transforming the horizons and filters by which people view the world. And that involves personal transformation, personal affirmation, and personal decision-making. Yet that is gained not by focusing on individuals alone but by opening new perspectives on society. It is a cliché to note that each individual is different from all others and makes his own response to what he finds in his environment. But it is a cliché of modern origin. It is not at all clear that the statement is true in so striking a degree of tribal, peasant, or even town life. In the urban ethos, however, literally thousands may live in conditions that are quite similar; and yet not two will be alike. Circumstance, education, common laws, and customs have tremendous power that might well be expected to overwhelm the individual. Yet the self is often able to resist that power without being aware of a battle to preserve himself. No man is completely socialized, although those persons who find the same image of themselves being projected onto them at the hands of multiple institutions by virtue of their race or sex have the most difficult time. Yet precisely in the city where the person lies open to the manifold influences of his environment, he finds more standpoints from which to shape his environment both by direct action upon it and by selective perception of it. No urban man is ever fully the victim nor the master of his setting. But there is a wider possibility of not becoming a victim in the urban ethos, for there are always alternative patterns of meaning, authority, obligation, and purpose to which one can turn.

If, however, we wish to evaluate the adequacy of the personalist perspective on the urban ethos, we may ask whether it reveals the actual matrix in which persons live their lives and find meaning and purpose.[3] Does it describe the norms of the ethos? And we may ask whether it can provide a fundamental point of constructive reordering. Does it legitimate or disconfirm the operating norms through its interpretive conceptualization and its practical consequences? Does it normatively prescribe norms for the urban ethos? Is its definition of reality adequate either to where people actually live or could live? Since the personalist view functions both as a description of what the condition of the urban ethos is and as a prescription for consequences of that condition, we question its descriptive and prescriptive adequacy.

The way in which the various personalist positions are presented already suggests their inadequacy. And there are empirical reasons for skepticism. The personalists pass over wide ranges of material concerning the persistence of intimate personal relations in the city and the construction of new forms of intimate group life where personal life comes into bloom. They neglect the continuing importance of nuclear and even extended family patterns, of political, professional, and voluntary association, of peer groups, and of church centers of identity. To be sure, such centers of personal identity and interpersonal patterns have modified or superseded certain personalized relationships found in previous extended family, guilds, towns, and neighborhoods, but it is not immediately clear that the latter is more "personal" than the former. The personalists bypass the fact that mass communications are only partially effective in manipulating what are supposed to be atomized and fragmented personal lives.[4] And they discount or avoid the wider range of uniqueness in personality found in the modern urban ethos than in primitive societies or in previous stages of recent Western city life. The data on the frequency of personal pathology within the contemporary environment are so ambiguous that they are not useful and are not at all convincing about the increase of sickness in the urban ethos as compared to previous or other cultures.[5] At best they reveal shifting definitions of pathology and changing social awareness of it.

The fact that these large segments of human experience are ignored raises the question as to whether the personalists are providing an *analysis* of society or an *ethical critique* based on a partially valid assumption. And if the test of adequacy is to rest on ethical assumptions, we must examine the adequacy of the conceptual framework from which they derive their judgments as well as the empirical question itself.

It is quite possible that the urban ethos allows the development of new personality types and demands a redefinition of personality, both in its descriptive and normative dimensions. Simple appellations of "depersonalization" may only reveal a fixed, preurban notion of personhood. Thus, what we have found is not merely a perspective for social analysis; but a *credo*. We have found a set of believed presuppositions that have all the marks of major theological systems but which cut across ordinary secular and religious distinctions. They provide a doctrine of sin in social repression and/or fragmentation; the dogma of redemption by personal affirmation; and a theory of ultimate worth and power. God is implicitly understood as transcendent personhood, now secularized from its theistic origins to anthropological grounds. We have discovered a quasi-theological language, within which the disputes take place, and to challenge it is blasphemy.

The core of this *credo* is that ultimate reality consists in the existence, the being or the becoming of the self. Leaving aside those highly salable forms of the *credo* which are egoism or individualism wrapped in piety or rationalized self-justifications, we must look analytically at those person-oriented assumptions that are serious. And the hard question is, "What is one to be or to become?" The conventional answer is "His true self." Tragically, that is the problem and not the answer. It is the problem because the urban ethos evokes it more profoundly and more widely than other varieties of social arrangement, giving fewer cues as to what you are and yet demanding each to decide. Hence the very consciousness of the problem is related not only to the self, but to the fabric of the society into which one is socialized and to which one is called upon to contribute. It is not the answer because, as V. Gordon Childe pointed out in his study of the rise of complex civilizations, "Man Makes Himself" in significant measure.[6] While the psychoanalytical varieties of personalism accent that the self is given in primordial and unavailable ways, the existentialist personalists also properly accent that man decides what he really is in the fact of his doings in existence, and in the "now" of it. In the former case, a fundamental doctrine is required in order to say what man really is and therefore ought to be. But that doctrine is not itself primordially given; it has to be constructed out of the artifactual myths and languages of societies and cultures. Oedipus, Electra, and the archetypes to which psychological theory appeals are cultural symbols. And in the latter case, one is continually confronted with the problem of *how* one therefore ought to exist. The existentialist answer "authentically" is of necessity continuously filled in with the furniture of cultural artifacts and social experience. And when the immediacy of "now" is accented, one continuously is forced to ask how big a "now" is— the sweep of the second hand, the life of a self, or a period of cultural history? Is the former divorced from the latter?

What the self really is, what it ought to become, how the person is to exist, and how to justify the answer to these questions, then, remain the unexplained, ungrounded problems of the personalists. And to deal with them in our day separate from the inevitable citizenship of the person in an existent, becoming, and existential urban ethos of social-cultural history is impossible.

The *credo,* unexamined as a *credo,* is nevertheless utilized in an ethical fashion: it attempts to offer a vision of ultimate reality by which one can define the ethos and distinguish good and evil, interpret the signs of the times, and offer the means of righteousness unto salvation. Personalism is a secularized theological ethic of the urban ethos. It calls for an ethically based revolution against the urban artifact—against the jungle of machines, the impersonal corporate units, the institutional church, the constant shift of loyalties, by recovery or affirmation of spontaneous personhood and total interpersonal relationships. But the resources for such a revolution must, in the final analysis, depend upon the urban ethos itself.

The Morphologists

In contrast to the personalists, technical and professional urban analysts often tend to see the center of an ethos in terms of the shape of *impersonal* "systems" of urban development. The decisive patterns of meaning are found in the morphology of collective artifacts. The normative importance of "ecological systems" is applied to the interpretation of the urban ethos. These "morphologists" see the city in terms of overarching patterns. As Leonard Reissman points out, "questions of purpose, motivation or human will could, in a sense, be set aside so long as it could be shown that they yielded patterned consequences in spite of the diversity and the supposed unpredictability of human volition. . . . This did not deny that people were in fact motivated by or that societies were organized according to other, more complex principles. Instead, the ecologist was to argue that motivation and social organization were not of first order of priority for urban study."[7] These "collective morphologists," like the personalists, represent a variety of positions that appear to be quite contradictory. Some see the pattern of concentric circles as the best analytic tool for urban growth and see the kinds of norms by which people live as identifiable in terms of their location within these circles.[8] Others see urban structures in terms of grids of interlocking small centers.[9] And still others speak of segmental patterns in which modes of transportation from outlying areas to the center of the city are, and should become, the defining characteristic or urban development.[10] In each case, one of several layers of the morphological development of the urban collectivity is identified as the critical layer. Patterns of ethnic succession, transportation flows, structural differentiation, are seen as the decisive "level" of analysis not only to solve a particular problem but to understand the city and the urban ethos itself.

The ultimate morphology may be seen in organic terms, demanding that an adjustment of urban life be made by learning from the "natural" patterns of growth of a city. Often the concentric circle motif not only functions in analysis, but is adopted as an ideal and is set forth as a utopian model of the future, if we only arrange it so that it will be "natural."[11] Sometimes parallels are drawn to natural patterns of growth in cells and tissues.[12] The ultimate morphology may be seen in terms of the patterns of communal life in lower animals; and the pathologies of those communities under certain conditions become the mode by which one interprets the pathologies of contemporary urban existence.[13] The morphology may be drawn from factors of density and distribution, so that the crucial factors of the urban ethos are determined by demographic patterns.[14] In any case, there are certain common assumptions that run throughout the various schools of collective morphological thought. The first assumption is that the objective morphology of the megalopolis of the future will determine the survival of the urban ethos and the civil values and virtues that are involved. The second assumption is that man must be oriented toward the future: that man is called to speculation on the shape of the future and to engage in present planning for it.

Many of the studies based on morphological assumptions shift from the descriptive to the normative treatment of the morphology of the city at only one point, even though it is clear that the entire motivation of their efforts are human values and human community. They are concerned to maintain the patterns that are necessary for urban survival—traffic flow, refinement of structural differentiation, disposal of the vast wastes accumulated by the city, and other such housekeeping chores, in efficient and harmonious fashions. The ecological studies thus provide significant data upon which such decisions can be made.

Under the impact of "systems analysis" modes of ecological research, however, there has been a growing awareness that many decisions made, presumably, as to the viable structures of

61686

the city are also made in such a way that structural pathologies of the city are also preserved. The primary values built into morphological analyses of this sort—systems maintenance of the efficiency and harmony of the whole—may not be sufficient. The crisis of the modern urban ethos, it is felt by many systems morphologists, is that man has lost control of the shape of the urban structures by concentrating far too much on pattern maintenance and on harmony and efficiency. The urban ethos, in its ecological manifestations, is demanding transformed, not polished or oiled extensions of present morphological structures. Our failure to provide such a transformation allows us to slide into the evil of uncontrolled shapelessness. What is needed is rapid technological and technocratic reordering of priorities through such techniques as the reallocation of land use, development of new transportation patterns, controlled suburban sprawl, "scatteration" of ethnic groups, and centrally planned new towns in order to regain control.

The remarkable thing about the urban ethos to this coterie of views is not its fractured character but its interdependence and its systematic interlocking. Hence, the failure of one subsystem to be fully coordinated with the others inhibits the transmutation of the whole into the new shapes that modern life demands. And, one cannot transform one subsystem without transforming the remainder. In contrast to the personalist understanding of the city as fragmented and fragmenting, the new systems analysts see the overwhelming character of integration and interpenetration of parts in the whole fabric of urbanized life.

The morphological schools of thought identify a number of analytically relevant matters. They see the city as a necessary tool for the concentration of resources to attain civilizational achievement. Thus they are sensitive to the idea that such a tool must be efficient and accessible and, further, that there must be a degree of relative harmony among the highly differentiated parts of the urban organism. These are functional prerequisites of the urban ethos. But, the interlocking systems of modern existence must also express and reveal the shifting sensitivities of modern man and his values. If collective morphologists intend to speak to such issues and not merely to report or make technical suggestions as they indeed do, they are led to concepts of intentional planning and control *for the good life.* They arrive by technical and descriptive procedures at the threshold of ethics.

But at this point the morphological perspectives can provide little insight. If we agree that we must transform, what do we transform toward? The answers tend to be of three kinds: some reply that we attempt to reestablish patterns natural to man. But what is natural? There is a hidden metaphysic of natural law that seems at least on the surface to be contrary to injunctions to intentionally transform. And there is little consensus as to what would be natural even if the apparent contradiction is overlooked. Some reply that we must allow the people to define the new goals. Let the people decide. But in the context of the city, it is not clear what that means. Shall we use present economic and political structures for decision-making? But they are not themselves transformed. What we have is a result of such procedures. Shall we construct new models of citizen decision-making as is apparently intended by the slogan "All Power to the People!" How shall the people be organized to arrive at general and not merely localistic decisions? Whence do we draw the models for that? The presuppositions of the morphologists do not provide for questions of "purpose, motivation or human will" as Reissman pointed out,[15] nor, therefore, for the kinds and shapes of institutions that allow "purpose, motivation or human will" to become operative in large-scale systems.

By accident or arrogance, then, a technocratic ideal emerges. The morphology of the future must be left to those who best understand the problems. Thus, there is the implicit notion that there can be a shift from the registering, codifying, interpretation, and coordination of morphological change to the intentional initiation and programming of that change. It is a shift of monumental proportions.

The entire practice of urban renewal, regional planning, coordinated zoning, and transportation development as a *vocation,* a calling or a profession—having all the overtones that one is called to profess something by which one improves the lot of humanity and civilization—raises questions that have not yet been answered. What is the planner to profess? What is his controlling value as that of the lawyer is justice, that of the doctor is health, that of the teacher is truth, and that of the clergyman is faith? Is he the doctor of a social order? What is a healthy social system in an industrial urban society? If he attempts to answer these questions on the basis of the organic models that generated the schools of morphological research, he runs into difficulty. Belief in intentional planning implies an ethic that is willing to impose ever new forms of constructed existence upon the given ones rather than attempting to recover the "givens." Is it possible to impose a natural concept on an artifact to make a more radically intentional artifact in the name of nature? Civic "health" is not so clear as physical "health." Is the planner to be controlled by justice? Advocacy planning is a very significant attempt to develop a planning ethic in the direction of justice but it is still rooted in undeveloped institutions and possesses no processes of finding adjudication. Ought it? On what grounds? What would "advocacy courts" look like? Is the profession of the planner to be truth? Ought we, for example, to build transportation systems in such a fashion that the forgotten ghettoes and the centers of decision-making are made graphically visible to the passing public, so that the truth of the disjunctions between political and economic affluence is revealed? Still further, should not the points of reference, the distinctive character of buildings, areas, and regions be so contructed that the essential patterns of the community are exposed? Men would then have a point of visual reference that would educate them to the structures and processes that are operative, through which they can evaluate, and then shape politically, the essential morphology of the city. But which structures are the truly decisive ones? Which aspects of human experience are essential to the primary analysis and construction of the morphology? In short, the morphologists have to come to grips with two questions: what are to be the integrating values of the professionally urban man and what is to be the shape of the urban artifact with which he has to deal?

Efforts to ask questions about the good society and to find a basis for vocational profession indicate a necessary quest for a new variety of ethic in the urban ethos. And in both its objective and subjective dimensions, the ethic has to be based on ultimate commitments as to what a good order is, and on what ultimate values one should govern his profession. Such decisions are necessarily based on a *credo*. The modern morphologists, thus, are best compared to the anonymous constructors of the medieval cathedrals who tried to express in aesthetic terms the fundamental commitments of common, corporate forms and belief patterns that were determinative for the culture. They differ from the medieval designers, however, in two ways. To the morphologist, the entire city is not dominated by a monumental expressive structure but becomes itself the expressive monumental structure. And the *credo* is by no means agreed upon.

It is very significant in this regard that collective morphologists want to make the morphology of the city apparent so that the people may become participants in the process of reshaping it. Such a desire indicates that at least one aspect of the *credo* is settled in principle: the decisions as to what values are to be dominant in the process of intentional transformation are to be determined by the interaction of democratic and professional values. Their position, thus, rests upon a faith that is especially manifest in the programs, more in its promises than by its effectiveness, of community participation in planning processes.

The upshot, then, of the morphological approach to urban analysis is, like the personalist one, a *credo*. It holds an underlying doctrine of sin—a fall into formlessness, and a concept of redemption—the physical, structural articulation of underlying and hidden interdependencies and systematic linkages by transforming the objective shape of the city. Still further, the position is rooted in an ethic that has full confidence in the ability of man technically and politically to shape his destiny and articulate his values if the structure of the urban ethos is laid bare. The *credo*, however, has not told us what that destiny looks like. And in the absence of such a vision, the possibilities of a neat, clean, and efficient tyranny or an egalitarian chaos wallowing in its own filth because nobody wants to take out the garbage, reduce consumption, or pay to have urban services supplied, haunts us all.[16] The means are provided for determining what the ends should be, but the means do not themselves imply the ends. The collective morphologists thus have brought to vivid consciousness the ability of man to use the urban ethos as a tool, the intricate relationship between man's ability to be ethical—to define the ethos by finding meaning and purpose in the objective shape of things—and the necessity of democratic political processes and professional commitment for determining the end toward which man the maker and transformer can use the tool. But it has not answered the question—transform toward what? Nor, it must be said, has it provided much help in suggesting the kind of polity by which a massive artifact like the city can reconcile the need for technological and technocratic control, to maintain and transform itself, and the democratic values presupposed in the more advanced forms of the quest for a healthy, just, and truthful collective morphology.

The Explicit Naturalists

The personalists, we have seen, either reject the importance of polity and objective morphology or merely ignore them. Hence, they are irrelevant to the definition of the urban ethos, even though we must acknowledge the partial validity of their presuppositions about the transcendent significance of persons. The morphologists lead us to the importance of vocation and polity and raise questions of transformation toward future structures, but cannot on their own presuppositions answer those questions. Both the personalist motifs and the collective morphological orientations to the urban ethos can be best understood as *credo*. It is interesting to note that at least one presupposition frequently appears among both those protesting against the "depersonalization" urban ethos and those involved in technical analysis and transformation of the urban artifact. That is "naturalism." With the necessary abandonment of the simplistic "given" metaphors for the normative interpretation of the massive artifact of contemporary urban life, some have begun to feel that urban man has made the wrong choice. Are there not "natural" balances and orders in both personal and collective life, which, if trespassed upon, will ultimately destroy us? Can man use nature against itself, continually transforming its shape with abandon, as the entire urban ethos is geared to do, or will he thereby undercut his own foundations? Is not, in the long run, the artifact so dependent upon the given that more artifacticality of personal or morphological sorts will deplete the given and all will collapse?

This motif of contemporary urban analysis has been dealt with by many writers covering a whole range of views. Sociology as a science was in fact born out of the agony of transition into an urban-industrial society and the attempts to develop a science of society comparable to the natural sciences. If one recalls the great dichotomies that characterize the major operating assumptions of many of the great classical sociologists, he can see the skepticism about the shift from "natural" to "nonnatural" bases of social organization and human relationship. Maine described the shift from a status society to a contract society. Tönnies saw the organic natural will of *Gemeinschaft* being superseded by a destructive rational will of *Gesellschaft;* Durkheim sought to find the structures of collective conscience and social interdependence that could hold together a society changing from "mechanical" to "organic" solidarity; Redfield worked with a folk-urban continuum that sometimes seems to presage disaster for the urban end of the spectrum; Weber was driven to much of his vast research by an attempt to find out what caused and what sustained the new form of rational society that he saw emerging from traditional society; Sorokin contrasts the solidarities of familistic relations to the segmental ones of contractual relations, and Marx sees the development of urban-industrial society as the epitome of bourgeois alienation. All suggest that unless there are new ways of recovering the natural roots of existence, modern civilization with its "nonnatural" structures of existence will destroy itself.

More recently, naturalism has become almost a popular movement as ecologists warn that a "natural" backlash is mounting feverishly due to pollution and population, and psychologists warn of social pathology induced by repression and rationalization. Attempts to put areas of exterior nature into a "deepfreeze," to prevent any human manipulation of it, are widespread. And sensitivity groups and therapy groups are being organized all over the country to overcome the urban man's presumed reticence to allow his truly "natural" feelings to emerge. Communes attempt to reestablish harmony with nature and recover the more "natural" life-style of extended families in close-knit experimental communities. Among masses of population, interest in astrology indicates a cultic interest in finding the ways in which social events, personal identity, and the natural forces of the cosmos are interlocked. And President Nixon said in his State of the Union address, "Restoring nature to its natural state is a cause beyond party and beyond factions. It has become a common cause of all the people of the country."[17]

The foundations for the new naturalism, however, are perhaps best summarized in a brilliant and much-quoted work by Lynn White, Jr.[18] Many of the contemporary efforts are superficial, he points out. If we are going to get to the roots of the issue, says White, we need to clarify our thinking by looking in some depth at the presuppositions that underlie modern technology and science, and upon which urbanization rests. White points out that the imposition of human ends upon nature in the degree that allows transformation of nature to become a cultural presupposition is based in several developments. First,

> Science was traditionally aristocratic, speculative, intellectual in intent; technology was lower class, empirical, action oriented. The quite sudden fusion of these two towards the middle of the nineteenth century is surely related to the slightly prior and contemporary democratic revolutions which, by reducing social barriers, tended to assert a functional unity of brain and hand. Our ecologic crisis is the product of an emerging, entirely novel, democratic culture. The issue is whether a democratized world can survive its own implications.[19]

Thus, he has identified one of the problems that confronted us in the personalists, the extension of the powers of the elite to many, and he has identified a problem that is posed by the morphologists—the conflict of democratic and professional values. But he presses the roots of the question further. The fundamental developments in the area of technology and science which shape the urban ethos are fundamentally Occidental—they imply a peculiarly Western conception of the relationship of man to nature. Where does this motif derive from, this motif that is now exported throughout the world? In part it derives from the influence of Arabic and Greek scientific works on Western life. The controversies that developed out of this influence implanted criticism as a cultural principle. "Out of criticism arose new observation, speculation, and increasing distrust of ancient authorities."[20] Further, advances in agriculture profoundly changed man's relationship to the soil, and hence to the whole of nature. But what people did with this critical stance and about these relationships depended upon their beliefs about human nature and destiny. In a very real sense it was the religious tradition that revolutionized the West. "The victory of Christianity over paganism was the greatest psychic revolution in the history of our culture," and the dominant patterns of daily action and common cultural pattern are "rooted in, and . . . indefensible apart from, Judeo-Christian teleology. The fact that Communists share it merely helps to show what can be demonstrated on many other grounds; that Marxism, like Islam, is a Judeo-Christian heresy."[21]

The essential ingredients from the Judeo-Christian heritage which have had fundamental import are the linear interpretation of history, the most anthropocentric religion the world has seen, and the concept of creation. The linear conception of history presumes that events in history are not repetitive and that meaning can be found in the changing patterns of history: action *within* history toward a transformed order is one of the signs of sainthood. The anthropocentric nature of Western religion is expressed through the belief that God created Adam, who is in the image of God and is to establish dominion over the whole of physical creation. In some branches of the tradition, it is believed that man should exploit nature for his proper ends. And the notion of creation indicates that nature is not itself to be regarded as a given but as a fashioned artifact. Hence it is subject to use. Still further, there is the notion that He who was most fully man was also fully God began a new creative process to transform heaven and earth. It is not accidental, points out White, that "from the thirteenth century onward, up to and including Leibnitz and Newton, every major scientist, in effect, explained his motivations in religious terms."[22]

White has recognized, as the personalists seldom have and

the collective morphologists almost never have (although it is here claimed that they must), that the foundations of the modern technological urban culture are laid in an ethically legitimating *credo,* and that understanding of the urban ethos must involve a theological-ethical critique.

White makes such a critique, and it is for that reason that I have utilized him as a spokesman for the naturalist position.

Since both science and technology are blessed words in our contemporary vocabulary, some may be happy at the notions, first, that, viewed historically, modern science is an extrapolation of natural theology and second, that modern technology is at least partly to be explained as an Occidental, voluntarist realization of the Christian dogma of man's transcendence of, and rightful mastery over, nature. But, as we now recognize, somewhat over a century ago science and technology—hitherto quite separate activities—joined to give mankind powers which, to judge by many of the ecological effects, are out of control. If so, Christianity bears a huge burden of guilt.[23]

In short, the ecological disruptions that modern man is beginning to experience—such as water pollution, air pollution, and the denudation of forests—are primarily due to a theological ethic which White sees wanting. For example, the whole concept of a sacred grove is alien to Christianity which tends, instead, as he points out, to see giant redwoods as timber to house humanity.

White poses an alternative. If we are not to bear the revengeful wrath of the ultimate powers in the universe, we must mute present dominant motifs in our *credo* and accent subdominant ones. For example, we might imitate Saint Francis of Assisi who "tried to depose man from his monarchy over creation and set up a democracy of all God's creatures. With him the ant is no longer simply a homily for the lazy, flames a sign of the thrust of the soul toward union with God; now they are Brother Ant and Sister Fire."[24]

White draws parallels between Francis' movement, the cabalic developments in Western Judaism, some movements among the contemporary exponents of a counterculture, who have all developed a profound reverence for life. (He might also have added, the liberal theological stance typified in Albert Schweitzer's philosophical-theological reverence for all living things.) White comes to the conclusion that these attitudes are protests against the dynamic forces of technology and science that have gotten us into the present mess. And we will not get out of it until we adopt an explicit naturalism. No new set of basic values has been accepted in our society to displace those of Christianity. Hence we shall continue to have a "worsening ecological crisis until we reject the Christian axiom that nature has no reason for existence save to serve man."[25] The fact that few recognize the underlying attitudes and values as rooted in a *credo,* much less a Christian one, is irrelevant.

Since White's article appeared, a veritable explosion of naturalist social theory about the urban ethos, its technology and its effect on persons and general morphology has taken place.[26] It may take the form of predicting inevitable consequences from population increases, such as extrapolations for man based upon experiments such as Calhoun's now famous work with rats.[27] It may involve postulating the origin of hostility in the "territorial imperatives" built into animal kind, of which man is one.[28] It may involve accenting the natural limits of the biosphere that demands a return to "health foods" farming as the normative mode of production. Divorce, delinquency, riots, and other sundry ills all are explained by such theses. Indeed, at present it is taking a hundred forms. But the fundamental presuppositions are quite similar: man is first of all a creature among creatures, and his society is best ordered when naturally ordered in harmony with the rest of creation. The urban ethos puts us over, against, or above nature. And the pretense that we can be other than natural is rooted in fundamentally wrong Western values. We must change our values and again take up what is genuinely natural to regain our sanity, our society, our salvation.

This position is not without difficulties, however. Few of the more recent nontheological writers have recognized as White did that "human ecology is deeply conditioned by beliefs about our nature and destiny—that is, by religion."[29] Such an admission forces acknowledgment in principle that nature is not in fact the only source from which our destinies are determined. Indeed, it suggests that the way we conceive our relationship to nature is perhaps as important as the given relationship. The realm of idea evidently has consequences. But at this point, one confronts a dilemma. Are conceptions that place man over, against, or above nature natural? If they are, then why ought we not be obedient to them in our naturalism? If not, and nature is the real power, whence comes their potency?

The problem, of course, is that naturalists at their strongest see the power of supra-natural principles and ideas; but precisely because they are naturalists, they cannot in principle allow supra-natural possibilities to dominate. They fail to recognize that the most natural thing about man is to transform nature to his own ends, to humanize what is pregiven and not just fit into it, to use nature against itself, most dramatically in building societies and cultures. The urban ethos, fundamentally an artifact and as such non-natural, is in view of this failure automatically suspect. The only way to deal with it is to force it back into a natural model. Hence, "natural human scales" and "natural human densities" are talked about by architects, while the intelligentsia disillusioned with the urban ethos for a myriad of reasons, try in a thousand compulsive rituals to recover the purity of naturalism, to prevent "artificial" economic or racial integration of neighborhoods, to preserve "natural" male and female roles, and to inhibit "artificial" institutions that transform the environment.

The full irony of the situation, however, is only seen when it is recognized that the naturalism rests itself finally in a *credo* that is not naturally given. Natural laws of population densities do not determine social behavior as much as does social organization as we can see comparing Southeast China to Southern England, or Calcutta to Chicago. Territorial imperatives in Homo sapiens may be limited by laws and custom. The natural limits of the biosphere are frankly not known, even if some shrewd guesses exist, and we have not yet set up the institutions nor committed the funds to find out. Further, as Harold Visotsky recently wrote, surveying some of these beliefs, "no support exists for the claim that there is an optimum size for the human group, nor can it be stated with confidence that there is any particular space requirement for an individual. Living arrangements tend to be highly culturally relative. . . . Where physical distancing becomes impossible . . . people seem to make use of psychological distancing mechanisms."[30] These involve value choices that do not depend on nature except that it is part of the nature of human kind to have to make them. Thus, artificial social institutions, laws, research institutions, and psycho-cultural variations become necessary supplements to any naturalist argument. If this is the case, then urban man has to develop models as to what is culturally, socially, and psychologically beneficial on grounds that cannot simply be inferred from nature, for every ostensible natural model is rooted in a non-natural *credo,* is informed by the relativities of culture, and requires a humanly planned and designed effort to attain it. Every naturalist effort requires the construction, artificially, of doctrines and institutions to sustain their convictions and to establish new controls over human efforts. The naturalist positions, then, can only warn us as to the limits of our present supra-natural pretensions, but it cannot deny the necessity of them nor hold to its own tenets in an unqualified way. They too will have to rely on a *credo* that involves a normative definition of personhood beyond the fact of the natural givenness of individuals, and a definition of morphology that cannot be limited by natural, pregiven patterns. The question is not, then, as White posed it with half his argument, a question of nature, but as he stated it with the other half of his concern, a question of *credo* and control, and the way in which *credo* and patterns of domination—political as well as technological—interact. And, more precisely, it is a question that directly challenges the primary religious-cultural tradition of the West—and in less explicit forms, the urban ethos in all modern and developing societies.

Chapter III

URBAN POWER

I n the failure of the personalists to account for the power of social, cultural, and political forces, even as regards the self, in the gaps of morphological assumptions about political powers and structures, and in the inability of naturalists to accomplish their aims without constructing supra-natural political and cultural machinery, the whole question of urban political arrangements comes to the fore.

At a different level of conceptuality from that just explored, a quite distinct, terribly important, second range of social theory has also focused on the city. Although at marginal points this second set of perspectives is related to the previous motifs, it more often stands isolated from such concerns, and sometimes against them. Reflecting an interpretation of social reality that concentrates on the political dimensions of existence, this body of thought takes quite seriously the supra-natural, social-decision aspects of urban life that deeply affect the structures of urban personality and morphology. The dominant political interpretations of urban life, however, seldom accent the more philosophical issues that are built into the assumptions of the positions explored in the previous chapter. Indeed, they reflect an impatience with all such talk of authentic identity, normative shape, and harmony with nature. It is political punch that moves the urban world, and that comes from money, rewards and punishments, votes, or whatever else can be marshaled to get things done with minimal overt violence. There are several subvarieties of this general approach. But, as we shall see, such "realisms" involve competing interpretations of urban experience, each of which depends upon unacknowledged *credo* no less than does each of the previous analyzed views.

The critical issue in the political structure of the urban ethos is that of power. The urban ethos does not rest only on and in an artifact, but on and in an artifact that is used. The way in which the resources of city life are used and the direction in which the urban ethos is to be transformed is a question of power. The power of man to manipulate his natural, and to a certain degree, his social and cultural environments has compromised his reliance upon both divinely sanctioned political orders and any "natural laws of history." Indeed, when it is known which human group has power it is possible to predict which kinds of resources will be allocated. And that in turn determines what varieties of human character will be sanctioned or celebrated, which personalities will be honored or despised, what will be invented or designed, what kinds of flows and structures will be inhibited or facilitated, and which levels of nature will be lifted up as normative, and which "natural" patterns will be transformed. The question as to who has the power in the urban ethos is therefore not only a question of practical political consequence, but of human destiny. If man is substantively deciding on his future, who among men is making these decisions?

Modern urban power consists in intentional, organized action that shapes the artifact. Urban power is a part of the urban artifact; it is not discovered, it is constructed. Hence, it is a system-related property and both the amount and the distribution of it are variable. As such, urban power is, in several respects, prototypical of the structures of power that are emerging at other levels of complex society.[1] The metropolitan systems of power are no longer autonomous systems, as compared with classical definitions of urban power; but are instead subsystems of larger cultural forms, forming institutional and conceptual bridges to other subsystems through *ad hoc* authorities and by common participation in higher, more comprehensive social systems.[2] Intercity agencies in metropolitan regions dominate transportation, water, and waste disposition, and often police functions without a direct chartered constituency or democratic controls.

There are a limited number of basic interpretations of power in urban life. Each interpretation rests upon a basic interpretive model, a *credo*, which it attempts to relate to the technical data at its command to a larger conception of social reality. Further, each model tends to choose a level of experienced meaning and interpret the entire power constellation on that basis. The data can, in part, confirm or negate the model. But beyond the factual reference of the model, there is a "meaning" reference of the model. That is, each model is seen as an appropriate way to see urban life if one is going to act purposively in it. Thus, each model surreptitiously or manifestly bears the image of an ideal social organization, a vision of how things ought to be.

The Power Elite Model

The usual, or "conventional-wisdom" discussions of urban power focus on the term "community power structure." In its early use by political science, this term referred to the particular mode of political arrangement such as the contrast between city-manager and mayor-council types of city government. During the last generation, however, it has come to apply specifically to the forces behind the visible phenomena of law and politics. Further, this term has become identified with a particular set of presuppositions about the forces which determine the political decisions that are made irrespective of the formal structures of political organization. Still further, this view is freighted with considerable philosophical baggage.

In this "power structure" model, the fundamental features of social experience and meaning are identified as socioeconomic stratification. The model assumes that there is a hierarchical, pyramidal social arrangement with those at the apex being a "power elite" or "set of influentials" who, by virtue of their social position, benefit at the expense of the "masses." There are, of course, some "mediators," politicians, government bureaucrats, et al., but they are primarily puppets of those at the top. Thus the decisions they make are "in reality" enactments of decisions made elsewhere.[3]

The crucial question is, then, who is at the apex of the hierarchical and hidden social pyramid; for it is assumed that a person or a clique is the determinative force in urban policy. In short, the economic elite is equated with the political elite, or the latter is at least seen as the agent of the former, and it is assumed that history is determined by a conspiracy of a few economic interest centers. The "power structure" model is not only a sociological model, it is a social-ethical model. That is to say, the chief defenders of the model view social analysis as intimately related to social criticism, and the main impact of their work is frequently to show the discrepancy between democratic values and the way things are. While one interested in social ethics may applaud the intention, several awkward questions continually recur.

Nelson Polsby, in a devastating methodological critique, has shown that the studies which are most frequently cited to support the power structure contention have ideological assumptions built into both the instruments for gathering the data and the conceptual frameworks for interpreting the data.[4] Power elite theorists ignore or explain away countervailing evidence. By internal analysis of eight major writings of the "power structure" school, he points out the attempt to "save the stratification theory despite what appears to be contradictory evidence" in their own presentations. By definition, Polsby points out, a "power structure" is only recognized as genuine when it contains big businessmen; thus other centers of power are discounted or are interpreted as being really controlled by a "hidden elite" that no one can see. Polsby does not take into account the fact that this view has had a functional power in promoting several significant efforts to organize in a democratic way people for whom there is in fact a ceiling on possibilities for action, but his statement of the problem exposes the reliance of this school of thought on a *credo*.

The "power structure" view has also been criticized on external evidence. William Jennings, using many of the same tools of the "power structure" writers, has restudied Atlanta, the scene of two "power elite" studies.[5] He concludes that "the findings tend to reject the notions of monolithic power structures of a ruling elite and the pervasive influence of economic dominants. Instead, they show a multiplicity of power centers and polylithic power structures with economic dominants only one of several kinds of influential in the community."[6] The kind of evidence he presents points to the conclusion that there is a whole range of factors affecting urban power which are not taken into account by this view.

More recently, a modified version of stratification theory has come to attribute extraordinary power to the mass media, which are seen as manipulating the individual. This view involves the recognition that decisions are in fact made on a much broader basis than by a few at the apex; but it also suggests that the decisions are "fixed" by the cynical manipulations of programmers and advertisers. Leon Bramson, however, in a notable but neglected little book, has collected a wealth of material to show that people are not so easily manipulated. "Any given person in the [mass] audience reacts not merely as an isolated personality but also as a member of the various groups to which he belongs and with which he communicates."[7] Thus, the thesis that urban change is controlled by a "hidden elite" through the instrument of mass communication is seriously compromised; there is a "filter of reception" which is supported by group membership—family, friendship, class, church, vocational, voluntary associational, recreational, etc.—and which formally and informally establishes interpretive frameworks for perception. Mass communication has not only failed in many highly publicized commercial efforts, as Bramson has shown, but more recent attempts to prove the success of American strategy in Vietnam by selective release of elite-controlled information through the mass media has in fact produced a moral resurgence that aids critics of the policy. Mass communication techniques are further only relatively successful even among people who are not active participants in groups.[8] Add to this evidence the suggestions by Daniel Lerner that the growing practice of audience research is a means whereby the programmers and publishers themselves become subject to the *vox populi* to such a degree that they cannot control standards,[9] and add again the perceived necessity for urban renewal authorities to cultivate neighborhood groups for feedback and to modify vast programs to accomplish desired ends. It becomes highly questionable whether mass communications' "hidden elites" do in fact manipulate the directions of urban change in any exhaustive manner in spite of considerable influence. Indeed, the fact that mass communications can gain more attention by focusing on dissident minorities who strategically use dramatic techniques to gain audiences means that smaller groups can get wider coverage than at previous periods of history. Minorities are not always so well served by such visibility as they hope, for selective reporting may evoke premature hostility among many.

Nevertheless, mass communications may be potentially more democratic and needful of protection and extension than of attack.[10]

In two ways, nevertheless, the communications variety of the stratification theory model does contribute to the understanding of urban power in a direct manner. Mass communications media have brought about the conscious construction of artificial personality images to a degree previously unknown in political life. It is quite possible to suggest that the process is not merely a gimmick to manipulate the public, although that is clearly present. The portrayal of candidates in terms of images and symbols and slogans, rather than of sharp debate on particular issues, lamentable as it may appear, can also be seen as an attempt to specify "value sets" that a particular juxtaposition of symbols represents. When candidates for mayor accent "Law and Order" against a "Law, Order and Justice" candidate, or "He will stop crime on the street" against "He cares," or "concern for the elderly" against "concern for the needy," the urban voter reads quite precise messages as to what problems will be attacked from what perspective even if he knows little about how government actually works. Thus, in a basically pragmatic setting such as the modern metropolis, normative and symbolic factors are being introduced in surrogate forms. Through the set of cues evoked by the images, the voter has in fact a rather clear-cut value choice to make: he can decide between value-sets which will affect many policies and, indeed, which determine the selection of problems that are to be addressed officially. This leads to both a positive and a negative consequence. The artificially defined image serves as a control over the whimsicality of decision-making by persons in positions of authority and makes them subject to popular value-sets. It also produces a studiedly ingenuous leadership, a priesthood of urban power that exists by manipulation of images drawing its support from a subtle combination of what the people want to hear and what they ought to hear.

Thus, one of the chief forms of power, leadership, is defined by symbols, artificially created images, designed to represent the widest and most meaningful support among the population while leaving specific policy questions open for debate. A classical theological distinction between person and office is radically and concretely affirmed.

Secondly, the stratification points to the fact that people on the lower rungs of socioeconomic life continually bump into very real blocks when they attempt to alter the social system for their own advancement. It appears from the bottom that there must be people at the top manipulating things to keep them down. Yet the blocks are much more subtle than the present theory represents. Rather than seeking individuals joined in conspiracy, one must ask what norms are built into the various institutions that select leadership, define priorities, influence the judgments of those in positions of responsibility and power. Communications concepts recognize that highly significant cues continually convey images that define cultural expectations of good and evil. There are principles of legitimacy that pervade the web of the social system in such a way that no matter where one turns, one finds similar responses to question, critique, or confrontation—not because the leaders have agreed on a common response; but because there are pervasive assumptions about "reasonableness," "propriety," and "appropriateness" pervading all the major institutions because they are shaped by the same cultural history. Cultural, legal, religious, philosophical, and social definitions of what is "normal" become institutionalized in the many subsectors of society where, divorced from ideological roots, they function irrespective of the intentions of participants, whether leaders or followers. The power structure is, in significant measure, governance by the dead who routinized the cultural values of previous days. Such governance both prevents wild fluctuations in society, thereby providing the relative continuity and stability needed by all to find meaning for their lives, and inhibits the creative reconstruction of the urban ethos as it must respond to new problems. Yet, although tainted by inevitable self-regard, the individuals who represent and the institutions that operate out of these cultural values are often less malicious conspirators for egocentric aims than public-spirited servants who rise to ascendancy because they have, by the social-cultural system, been given the time, the energy, the skills, and the money to work for "the public good." They also arrive at positions of leadership because they in fact do fulfill "most adequately" the felt needs of the society and represent the vision of the good man as decided by previous leaders when they were on the way up. The power structure analysis, then, may be judged to be quite unsubtle in their analysis, although driven to it by a profound ethical concern to empower those without such resources. Thus, while they often want to be "tough-minded" in a sense that trivializes the import of ethics, they are in fact advocating on rather obvious, even prophetic, ethical grounds the redistribution of time, energy, skills, and money so that they can be used in a broader understanding of "the public good," and a fundamental redefinition of what "the public good" really is.

If either of the two models of "power elite theory" were believed to be substantially correct, practical ethical concerns also come into play. If there is a power elite that determines most policy, and it is judged ethically wanting, the strategy of transformation must be through the conversion or deposing of the decision makers. In fact, taken alone neither is likely. Or, if they are accomplished by some quirk of circumstance, conversion or deposing are not necessarily of much consequence. In numerous cities the presumed power elite was overtly converted on the question of discrimination against Blacks in housing, job opportunity, education, and political participation and some significant gains were made. But the fundamental patterns of racism have not been decisively altered from the standpoint of the ghetto. Indeed, having been converted on the point, the presumed members of the power elite were quickly abandoned as "white liberals." Because things did not immediately change as the theory required, it was widely felt that the elite must have cynically betrayed the cause. Hence, some militants move increasingly toward revolutionary options. But what if the theory was wrong in the first place? What if one held that patterns of social and cultural expectation built into the web of institutional life were more powerful than presumed elites and that what elites there are, are themselves products of larger sociocultural forces that they do not fully control.[11] Then one could understand why the conversion of elites without alteration of social and cultural patterns is only marginally important, and why moves toward deposing of decision makers may only assure more subtle "urban security" and repressive controls at the hands of others playing the same roles. Yet these are, if the power elite theory is accurate and pushed to its conclusions, the only choices, for other attempts, such as the always painfully slow organization of the people or the construction of new social-cultural "filters of reception" could easily be truncated by those firmly in control. If, however, the unstated moral concerns of "power structure" research are valid, the practical moral strategy involves providing leaders with significant rather than trivial symbols and images, conscious recognition of the moral symbiosis of communications media and popular wish, clarification and redefinition of fundamental social "norms," and the forming of groups responsive to new moral sensitivities. These would produce alternative patterns of leadership and the ascendancy of alternative personality types.

We see, then, in power-structure theorists a moral drive toward right, just, and equitable order that reflects deep ethical commitments. But the ethical *credo* around which the model is constructed neither entails accurate analysis of the way things in fact are nor provides a program for action that would lead to the fulfillment of the moral vision.

The Pluralist Model

A parallel development to the urban "power structure" theory based on analyses of influentials or elites has been "urban-decision" research. This approach, rather than presupposing that there is a single stable power structure with a clearly defined apex, asks how public decisions are in fact made.

Research of this type, already hinted at in the earlier reference to Jennings, has been carried out in Chicago by Rossi and Dentler,[12] and by Banfield and Wilson,[13] in New York by the massive research under Kaufman and Sayre,[14] by Dahl and Wolfinger in New Haven[15] and Martin and Munger in Syracuse,[16] to mention a few. These efforts, studying the process of decision-making in relation to community structure, have shown that there are differing groups that exercise notable powers with regard to differing areas and issues. Each group may well have its internal elite. Most groups operate by the "iron law of oligarchy." But the powers of one group are not easily trans-

ferred to the issues beyond its own boundaries, and the influence of one set of elites does not carry much weight in
another group.

The basic state of affairs in this model is one of a multiplicity
of groups engaged in restrained conflict. In the formal power
arrangements of the modern city, those groups having most
power are agencies, institutions, and bureaucracies. And it is
conflict between these that accounts for the pluralism of urban
power arrangements. Indeed, some analysts, such as Sayre and
Kaufman, show the fantastic variety of power nodes existing in
a city such as New York. They come to the conclusion that one
of the great difficulties is that things are so diversified that it is
hard to get anything done at all. When something does, in fact,
get done, it must go through a maze of proposal, counterpro-
posal, hearings, negotiation, compromise, and implementation
procedures. And these are accompanied by legal moves and
policy directives that clarify and limit the possibilities at every
point. Power is not found by looking for the arbitrary will of
hidden elites, but by analysis of the rationalized patterns of
bureaucracy, procedure, public scrutiny, and law. Progressive
change is not blocked as much by elite veto groups as by the
fact that present patterns of urban organization are disjointed.
The fundamental problem for urban man is not monolith seeking diversity, but rampant multiplicity seeking unity.

What unity there is is found by political leaders. Those in
political office are themselves, however, not the decision makers
—nor are they characteristically puppets of hidden power elites.
Of course, they select, sometimes under pressure, the issues
upon which they want to concentrate, but decisions on those issues are not finally made by them. They are brokers who mitigate the inherent conflicts between agencies, institutions, and
authorities by negotiating proposals through a process of decision-making with many checkpoints. At their best they are
statesmen; but even at their worst, grubby, small-minded, or
self-seeking urban politicians hold together some semblance of
political order by managing and compromising the claims and
interests of competing groups.

Citizens may effect the decision process by developing competence in one or another area of urban organization, by elect-

ing officials who choose the problems that concern them, by making their views known to the proper authorities, and, through representative processes, changing the laws that govern the various bureaucracies and leaders. These channels are relatively open, even if seldom used wisely.

The conflicting interaction of multiple power nodes, the dynamic processes of political brokerage, and the potential effect of citizen action on decision processes all, in this view, contribute to a view of the structure of urban power that sees it as dynamic, changing, and relatively open, even where it moves slowly because of its disjointedness. Out of this mix flows a continuous stream of programs, activities, and operations. Dynamic change, not fixed stability, characterizes the organization of urban power. Insofar as urban power is problematic, it needs focused structures of accountability so that the pluralism does not get out of hand. Without visible structures of accountability, corruption and stupidity can go undetected and uncontrolled. For the most part, however, the political power of the urban ethos is democratic. People get pretty much what they want.

What the pluralists lack is a *credo* that can sustain, extend, and make accessible and comprehensible to the people the values of a dynamic, pluralistic, and democratic arrangement of power, values that the pluralists have proved to be present in principle in the formal structures of power in the city. Only a *credo* that legitimates these structures *and* gives them a sense of direction *and* connects them to the possibilities of ordinary informal human activity prevents the collapse of pluralism into directionless chaos or the alienation of formally democratic structures from the will of the people.

It is ironic that the power-elite theorists and the pluralists both take their point of departure from democratic theory. The power-elitists, however, focus on the disjunction between ostensible political procedures and nondemocratic economic structures, while the pluralists focus on formal political procedures, sometimes to the point of neglect of the inequality of accessibility to those procedures for economic reasons. Their debate, thus, represents a world historical struggle between economic visions of democracy, often using quasi-socialist perspectives, and political procedures of democracy. Neither in their current forms offers the grounds for holding their view as normative. They do not deal with the wider context of power wherein structures or procedures occur. And both are limited by the failure of their underlying *credos* to combine accurate analysis and ethical vision, even if they rely on unspoken ethical presuppositions.

A Supplementary Theory

It may be that we shall have to turn to other areas to find the crucial models for the analysis of the urban ethos. One such alternative is traced out by William Kolb.[17] It is founded on the premise that the "value sets" of both leadership and the institutionalized collectivities of modern urbanity are rooted in a specific, historic, cultural, and religious system. Kolb makes a rather strong case for a moral order that is built into urban life, shaping the directions of change, legitimating the principles of leadership, and defining the rules of the game that inhibit open conflict between competing persons and groups.

Violence and chaos are constrained by cultural patterns that provide negative checks and positive outlets for this wolfishness that is man. Violence, force, and destruction are thus caused less by the false repressions of society and civilization, as the personalists claim, and less by the conflict between poorly articulated parts of a differentiated social system, as collective morphologists claim, and less by a natural rebound in response to unnatural manipulation of nature, as the naturalists claim, than by the absence of those values that induce civilization. Where institutionalized forms of cultural values are not present, violence erupts.

Kolb's thesis is compromised, unfortunately, by a problem that he seems to neglect. Cultural values that give shape to civilized control are not self-sustaining, and must be supported and implemented constantly by community formation— the creation of new artifacts and social centers of identity for people standing on the boundary of violence and power. Value orientations do not seem to be able to sustain themselves, even in their institutionalized state, without reinforcement, support, nourishment, and repeated rearticulation, redefinition, and respecification. If they are to have the kind of efficacy that Kolb attributes to them, there must be community organization and community formation at concrete societal levels to articulate and support urbane cultural values against other personalist, morphological, naturalistic, or elitist varieties of cultural values. These unofficial groups refine the cultural values of each generation anew, make competing values a working part of peoples' lives, and provide the context for the potential exercise of power. And the cultural values, especially as present in religious orientation and thought, become normative perspectives that are also lived realities.

If this modification of Kolb's analysis is correct, the patterns of power will be intimately related to processes of group formation around cultural values. But these processes do not appear overtly in either power-structure or decision-process studies, for both tend to concentrate on formal institutions of a political or economic character without pressing the boundaries to ask about the context in which these power structures or decision processes occur. And, as we have seen, it may well be that more pervasive, but less direct forms of power are determinative for the city than the *credos* of the power-elite theories or the pluralist theories allow.

Where might we look? What alternative patterns of power are available? Max Weber, upon whom Kolb partially depends, points out in his classic study of the city that urban man forms intentional groups and develops a sense of membership.[18] His contemporary and colleague, Ernst Troeltsch, pointed out the decisive character of the formation of multiple intentional communities in modern society.[19] Wide-ranging observation of urban man has revealed that he is a "joiner," entering into multiple voluntary associations that exercise influence in public affairs. And particular contemporary studies show the enormous significance of such participation in modern society.[20]

These authors hold, in various ways, that the indirect contributions of voluntary associations shape the dominant ethos in highly significant ways even where the direct linkages with power structures or official decision-making processes are not clear. The voluntary associations generate potential political power and build up reserves of influence that are inordinately difficult to trace in a short-run empirical study, but which, over longer historical periods, seem to have great significance. Voluntary associations generate an apperceptive mass among the people and among the decision makers. They allow people to become familiar with issues and to develop kinds of sensitivity that resonate to one or another value set. They engender competence or at least senses of competence that allow people to enter into political dialogue, to form pressure groups, to set forth plans, and to declare actions legitimate or illegitimate. This seems to be the case whether the voluntary association is politically oriented or not—bowling leagues and music societies evidently have this result as a latent function as do unions, guilds, parties, do-gooders, and interest groups that function in non- or semiofficial capacities manifestly.[21] Such groups become, in the urban ethos, the arenas wherein consensus is worked out on the basis of some conception of what ought to be. These groups often evoke or provoke the emergence of issues and acceptable images into the public arena. And, when the issues do come to the fore, one finds a relatively competent, discerning, and discriminatory, if not technically trained, constituency that can ask hard questions and can respond favorably or negatively to proposals. Further, these associations become the vehicles whereby personal life-styles are tied into a social fabric and public issues. Very deep questions of personal identity are involved in the committing of oneself to a voluntary association even if most of them operate on the basis of "limited liability."[22] And, since voluntary organizations do not, in the final analysis, hold the coercive powers of formal political structures, they must hold their constituencies by appealing to concepts and symbols, patterns of authority and polity that people acknowledge as proper in themselves for governing social ends and means. On the basis of these presuppositions about "good order," people legitimate, tolerate, or are horrified at the use of all the more overt forms of power from persuasion, to arm-twisting, to blackmail, to tanks or bombs by official or unofficial groups in the urban ethos.

Such a suggestion that the core of urban power lies in voluntary associations, through its indirect forms of influence, needs considerable further exploration. Especially important is the fact that no voluntary association nor coalition of voluntary associations exercises direct forms of power over a long period of time. They become nonvoluntary as soon as they take up the sword of coercion. Also, no single voluntary association or coalition of voluntary associations can in themselves exercise decisive influence, the more subtle, indirect form of power. Counterinfluences can always be generated by other associations. What is required in a theory of urban power, then, is a pattern for understanding pluralistic voluntary associational systems on a large scale, for that is the unique contribution of urban life to the social organization of power.

The problem with the pluralist position in its more pervasive or, even in this alternative, tentative form is that they, with rare exceptions, reveal a pluralist preference without giving the grounds or specifying the normative shape of that preference. Having proved that, indeed, there is some kind of pluralism, they tend to rest their case. Is it really "any old kind" of pluralism that is desired? What if the ethos is so pluralistic that the parts cannot articulate into a viable whole? And what if the pluralism operates within a set of boundaries in such a way as to prevent other or new centers of potential power from emerging or ever gaining ascendancy on issues vital to their survival or well being? And what if the pluralism operates with a common set of cultural apperceptions that prevent new kinds and qualities of projects for the future from ever getting into the multi-centered process of decision-making? In these cases, the frustrations and moral sensibilities of the power-elite theorists come back into play, even if they have sometimes defeated them by their own fallacious analysis. There must be some standards for pluralism in polity, else the prevailing norms that already exist in the images of leaders and in the cultural drift are not accessible to challenge.

Such standards depend upon belief systems, upon *credos*, that themselves become plowed into the fabric of institutional life. But as with previous perspectives on the city, the way of justifying such *credos* is not given in the analysis itself. And we are again confronted with the problem of *credo* and its foundations.

Chapter IV

SOCIAL THEORY AS SECULAR THEOLOGY

What is the relation of social theory and *credo?* Such a problem poses the question of the relationship of interpretive models and data and necessarily moves us toward a social-ethical perspective. It also requires that we ask about the characteristics and background of a conceptual framework, a *credo*, that is more adequate than the ones we have examined.

Interpretive Models and Technical Data

Technical data are inevitably used in the making of ethical judgments about large-scale social systems. All of the positions described refer to innumerable studies to show that they are dealing with the decisive level of urban organization and that therefore there is an intrinsic obligation to move in one or another direction. It is presupposed that rational empirical attention to data will provide a normative perspective, even where there is considerable suspicion of any explicitly moral perspective. Closer attention to "what really is," in contrast to "what appears to be," will render what "ought to be." Ethics is inevitably present, and legitimated by appeals to "what really is."

From the side of professional moralists, however, we often get what would seem to be a different view of how ethical positions ought to be grounded. Man derives, according to many varieties of ethical method, the ethical norms from a methodologically dogmatic source such as an absolute philosophical principle, a "necessary" concept, or scriptural sources. And, in order to make them pertinent, proponents apply those norms to a given situation, a process that entails technical definition of what the situation is. Technical data are seen as significant but secondary. Philosophical or religious-ethical norms are seen as "superordinate" factors; they are not empirically present in the present order of things. The "ought" cannot be gained from the "is." Hence they have to be kneaded into the mix of history.

"What ought to be" is, for the moralist, "what really is," and "what emperically is" is subject to that reality.

Ironically, however, both of the above ways of relating data to ethical norms presuppose a distinction between "really" and "apparently," "ought" and "is," religion and life, sacred and secular, which they are trying to overcome. The real heart of ethics takes place in the relation of these two levels. Failure to recognize the presence and interaction of these two levels allows some moralists to accept uncritically what some social scientists would have us believe, namely, that the social-scientific enterprise is "purely scientific" and hence "value-free," while some social scientists are allowed to presume that morality deals in absolutist abstractions not pertinent to the real task of understanding social reality. We have already seen, I think, that the relationship between values and data is much more subtle.

Of course there are kinds of dealings with facts that are relatively value-free. Literally hundreds of studies of urbanization point out that in the early 1800s the world contained some one billion persons, that a hundred years later the number had at least doubled, and that by 1960, it had tripled. It is further often pointed out that the organization of this population into urban complexes has proceeded apace with the population growth. There were only seventeen towns of more than 20,000 at the beginning of the nineteenth century, and now we are living in a situation where some seventy-five percent of the much-enlarged world population resides in urban areas of at least this significant size.

But once these "plain, unvarnished facts" are stated, it is impossible to go much further without introducing ethical matters. What do these facts mean in terms of quality of life, styles of living, valuations of what is worthy and powerful in existence? Whenever interpretive categories are introduced, valuational elements begin to creep in. And, indeed, often the flat figures themselves are cited in order to urge more concern for urban problems, in order to evoke senses of obligation in researchers, policy makers, and the citizenry. It is assumed that mere recognition of the magnitude of urbanization will bring about alterations in attitude and policy.

Nor can "pure" values be stated apart from the context in which they are perceived. It is a truism to note that every discussion of ethical norms is bound to a cultural condition in some measure. The data that are selected, the modes of interpreting data, indeed, the presuppositions as to what should be studied are dependent upon deeply rooted models as to what reality ultimately is and *ought* to be. Data do not select themselves, interpret themselves, or group themselves into systematic studies.[1] Nor do values leap to the foreground, become codified into a *credo,* and applied to particular situations on the power of their own existence. The ways in which data and values interact is thus in part dependent upon prevailing operational norms that are in force in a particular ethos. And to deal with this interaction, it is necessary to be self-conscious about the models implicit in the operational norms of the ethos and in efforts to interpret it. It is necessary to be simultaneously self-conscious about the data, for the data of the urban ethos are still vast and uncharted. But the presuppositions used in selecting and ordering the data are the actual points of dispute and are, more often than not, neglected in contemporary social science. While it is often necessary to remind moralists and ethicists to attend to the technical character of the data they use, the public influence of unexamined values in social scientific perspectives is today more enormous. And it becomes necessary to point out how deeply rooted in values and how related to the operational norms of the ethos these perspectives often are.

The contemporary picture is complicated by the fact that there are conflicting and competing values built into the structures of the urban ethos and governing the various perspectives on that ethos. Thus, to provide an accurate interpretation of the urban ethos it becomes necessary to articulate and arrange these. Such an effort requires that at least one of the tasks of ethics becomes an attempt to make social scientists conscious of the ethical roles they actually play, and to offer to both the ethicist and the concerned citizens in general the tools whereby the assumptions of interpreters may be exposed and evaluated. This requires what may be called "an analytical ethic."[2] By combining the terms analysis and ethic in the same phrase, the term "analytical ethic" implies that social analysis and social theory are intrinsic parts of any ethical perspective and the relationship therefore is best made explicit. The terms also suggest that it is normative concerns that govern even the scientific enterprise in large measure, and that this ought to be acknowledged.

But how, more precisely, would an analytical ethic work? What are the assumptions of such a position? At the outset, we should have to say that one of the principal purposes of social theory thus understood is to bring the hidden models of the ethos, and the historical conditions that influenced its development, under critical scrutiny. What are the competing norms of meaning, purpose, and righteousness that already exist? We must, in short, look around in the ethos. But man does not just respond to everything he finds; rather, he critically attempts to discern those structural and functional moral principles, or norms, that are in operation in the widest and deepest reaches of a particular human activity and to see how they hang together. In the final analysis, these are veiled in mystery, but precisely for that reason, the social theorist who is of necessity also an ethicist must have an analytical model, a *credo*. Every attempt intentionally to interpret, act, communicate, or organize assumes that distinctive tendency of humankind to depend upon a *credo*. Man does, and indeed must attempt to put his findings in a wider context, ask what the antecedents and causes of such operating principles were in the past, whether these principles are appropriate in the present, what gives them legitimacy, and ultimately, whether they can function in the future. Usually in a society there are several principles in operation, there are various groups behind the various principles, and there are various evaluations of these competing principles and models within each group. One must ascertain the circumstances under which these competing principles can be brought into conjunction or, alternately, one of them may be shown to be superior to another on the basis of its intrinsic merit, its appropriateness to the context, and its probable consequences.

There are several problems attached to such a view. First, such a method would appear to make the social analyst who is concerned about his hidden values dependent upon prevailing models. To a degree, clearly, it does—but only to a degree.

The concepts, ideas, and sensitivities by which a social analyst defines the norms of an ethos, are borne by existing patterns of life and institutions even if there is radical disjunction between the pattern's or institution's *raison d'être* and its actual performance. It is only by the analysis, articulation, and comparative evaluation of these that an ethic intrinsically related to the ethos can be built. A social analyst is, in short, dependent to a large extent on what is going on in history to provide a starting point. It is the internalized operating norms of his profession, for example, that forces him to engage in an analysis of controversial issues. And if he exposes the dastardly operating norms in a particular institution of the ethos, such as a school or prison, and comes under attack, he takes recourse in the operating norms of reform groups or professional groups that exist on the basis of alternative operating norms. But it is not enough to build a portrait of the conflicting operational norms as they now work. How are some to be validated against others? Do we study patterns or trends merely to know better what inevitabilities govern us or in order to gain some mastery of them and thereby, perhaps, change our course? The historically sensitive social analyst not only inevitably does, but must become an ethicist. The personalist and the morphologist, the power elite theorist and the pluralist, the socialistic and the bourgeois social analyst, not only disagree as to the way things are, but also how they *ought* to be and what we *ought* to do about it. Each rearranges the available norms in specific directions, based on fundamental conceptions of history, life, and meaning. This crucial ethical reordering is far too often undertaken uncritically. Yet the task remains to rework what has been derived, redefining, rearranging, critically castigating, and vindicating some operational norm and calling explicitly or implicitly for commitment to and actualization of other norms.

Both the processes of analyzing the way things are and of rearranging the derived norms demand the construction of a *credo,* a purposive, explicit, critical conceptual apparatus of interacting specified norms. The effort to construct such a model is the meta-ethical dimension of analytical ethics—a dimension that requires use of symbols.

Most forms of social analysis operate within a framework

where the "meta-ethical" assumptions are given or believed to be given. Thus, most selection and interpretation of data in the social sciences are merely a tidying up, and a making consistent, of the details in a specific area in terms of a school of thought. Social science in this mold can be cumulative within limits and provides a systematically arranged body of data without which any depth analysis of social phenomena is impossible. However, it is social theory that attempts to provide a compelling model by which to select, order, and interpret. Yet, as we have seen in the previous two chapters, theoretical perspectives raise decisive ethical questions, at the point at which they depend upon a *credo*, which they cannot answer. They are dependent upon meta-ethical models that are incapable of elucidating the way things are and rendering a compelling vision of how they ought to be. Nevertheless, it is the peculiar point at which the descriptive and the prescriptive elements of theory join in a meta-ethical model that we have identified as *credo*. And we have come to that point precisely because the urban ethos poses a context where the meta-ethical assumptions are in apparent conflict or dispute. Neither the technical social scientist nor the ordinary citizen sees adequate clues as to what in fact his condition is or what he ought to make of it. The meta-ethical models for the urban ethos are confused, contradictory, and, in some cases, small.

In developing an adequate meta-ethics, or *credo*, ethics itself plays a crucial role in social analysis, for it continuously asks three questions: what is right, what is good, and what is fit. By the first, ethics wants to know what is of intrinsic worth. Is there anything that is in and of itself commendatory? Ethics recognizes that cultures define what is right differently; but it continues to press the question by use of symbols that transcend the multiplicity of definitions empirically present. By the second question, ethics asks whether the ends and probable consequences of a trend, a policy, a position, or a perspective are, so far as known, relatively consistent with the best purposes man can project. Of course, projections vary, but the whole dimension of future projection seems always to be present, even if it is serial rehearsal of the past. And, the third question asks whether the "rights" and "goods" actually pertain to the present

conditions, the genuine tissues of life, the actual fabric of existence, wherein people and societies find themselves. These
peculiarly ethical questions demand attention to dimensions of
existence that are not given in the empirical world of man, but
are only given in *credo*.

An adequate *credo* is formed, then, by weaving together a
supra-natural and a supra-historical combination of the elements
of right, good, and fit in such a way that the intrinsic meanings,
ultimate purposes, and appropriate matrices of life and history
can be seen as having some coherence with regard both to what
is and what ought to be.[3] Such a *credo* would also, presumably,
direct analysis to decisive levels of social existence. To be fully
adequate, an analytical ethic would have, then, to supply a
credo that the social theorists have not been able to provide on
their presuppositions, in spite of their considerable contributions. And one of the tests of such a *credo* would be the capacity
to evoke recognition of *credo* assumptions on the part of social
analysts and their participation in the construction of meta-
ethical models that are more adequate than those presupposed
by the positions already presented.

The next step is to show the relationship between the meta-
ethical interpretive model and the operational norms of the
ethos, the actual claims and obligations laid upon man and
built into the institutional arrangements in a specific setting.
At this point technical data are again highly pertinent. The
credo must be shown to make more sense out of wider ranges
of data and the competing claims regarding that data than
alternative perspectives. And in relating the *credo* to the data of
the empirical situation, there is the possibility of disconfirmation,
redefinition, and criticism of *both* operational norms and dimensions of the *credo*. One is, therefore, continuously pressed to
reexamine the meta-ethical models.

In short, while a *credo* can presumably render a model of
the right, good, and fit, it cannot be validated on ethical, philosophical, or theological grounds alone. Instead, its adequacy
and the legitimacy of using such a *credo*, must be confirmable
or disconfirmable according to its relationship to technical data
about the structures, projections, and functions of human life
and institutions in a given ethos. Thus we are partially depend-

ent on what "is" to find our "oughts." But the explicit "oughts" are not, or need not be, mere reflection of the present "is"; they can be rearranged consciously into new meta-ethical "ought" patterns and tested against the historically changing situation.

Such a method, of course, presupposes that there is change in history, that norms are bound up in the very fabric of history, and that norms partially built into the structure of history are precisely those that can most effectively affect history. But such a method also presupposes that these norms can only be grasped symbolically. Our problem, seen from this perspective, is not to hold symbols as a judgment over the head of history from the outside, but to use symbols to discriminate between better and worse from within our historical perspective. On the one hand we cannot transcend our historically conditioned perspective except by *credo,* and on the other a *credo* unrelated to our context has no power to deal with the data of life.

A second problem follows immediately from the first. How may we rearrange the norms derived from within history without appealing to exterior, nonhistorical standards? The answer lies in part in the recognition that there are levels of human existence that necessarily bind man into human societies. And, in societies, certain problems arise that must universally be addressed. Every human group has to come to some resolution of the problem of the relationship of the individual to the collectivity, the one and the many. And every human group has to develop ways of coping with its environment. And every human group has to deal with authority and freedom. To deal with these, every human group generates a definition of right and of obligations to uphold those rights. The content of that definition may differ; but the universality of its occurrence means that such phenomena have to be a touchstone of social theory. Further, every society recognizes that the right is not constantly the case, that it cannot be discerned in empirical life entirely. Hence generalized or symbolized statements of the definition of right with its *prima facie* obligations must be articulated. Thus, out of the necessities of historical experience, nonhistorical, symbolic articulations must be generated. But once articulated, they are presumed to have some continuing and decisive relationship to actions and institutions in the society. If they do not, they are considered not, in fact, to have been right, although everyone thought they were and can be reconceived, or the actions and institutions in the society are judged to be "not right" and they are protested or altered.

The answer lies also in part, however, in the realization that history involves change as well as constancy at the very abstract levels of the definitions of rights and obligations. If there is change in fact, then one may attempt to rearrange the various dimensions of life to account for the future probabilities. No simple predictability is ever claimed, but frequently some possibilities are more probable than others, some are more desirable than others in terms of the already existing operational norms, and some provide a nexus for meaningful historical action toward a significant end. But these ends are held to be valid only insofar as they fulfill or allow redefinition of symbols of the ultimate ends of the society and of the people in it. Yet these ends are not immediately given. The significant ends are those capable of actualizing ultimate purpose captured only in symbol through persons and institutions. The analytical method under discussion is an attempt to see the implications of such sensibilities in terms of social function. People undertake social analysis not only to articulate the way things are, but to induce ends. And one must have at least a crude vision of future possibility to act. Yet the final end is not immediately visible. Our thinking about the future, whether oriented toward particular problems or toward some universal state or event that fulfills and transforms our operational norms into a unity, is necessary to the meta-ethical construction of a *credo* and directly pertinent to immediate historical reality. Ethicists speak of this in terms of the "good." But the data of history are not in, the future is not fully upon us. Thus the meta-ethical model of rearranged, analytically derived norms is always provisional. It must be subject to the confirmation or disproof of historical data. Claims based on natural law, *Blut und Boden*, the natural superiority of a racial or sexual elite, the natural law of history that shall prove the proletarian or bourgeois class superior, or the inevitable natural growth and decay of civilization, are "unethical," precisely because they do not allow themselves to be corrected by the historical level of human experience, the ethos. Their appeal is not to the ethos but against it, even where they function to transform the ethos. Similarly, moral claims based on a *credo* ostensibly derived from pure spirituality, mystical experience, transcendental divine revelation, or eternal truths are suspect on the same ground, although these may have emotive significance of some sort and are less destructive in the short run than the racist, sexist, and class claims. No claim concerning our specifications of norms has the right to such final legitimacy so long as man is an ethos-bound creature. Our *credo* is provisional, subject to correction by life and history.

The charge may be made in view of what has been said that while freeing the ethical dimension of social analysis from being an unexamined assumption of or a mere implication of science, natural or social, on the one hand, or of dogmatic theology on the other the present view has made this into a branch of sociology. As indicated above, there is some truth in the charge, but only some. Classical ethics has been closer to politics than to physics or metaphysics. And the motivation of American social science to develop a "natural" concept of human affairs was grounded in both social protest on the one hand and the concerns of the churches to analyze the situation in which they found themselves in order to form better strategies for church building, mission, and evangelism on the other. Several generations of American sociologists were recruited from among socially sensitive pastors defrocked because they did not believe in the Virgin Birth, and from acculturated minority groups who had to try to make moral sense out of their adopted religious and social environment. Perhaps because of this heritage, and certainly also because of the theoretical support morally sensitive sociology received from Max Weber and Émile Durkheim, not to mention Karl Marx who was, most strikingly, a moralist redefining the ethos,[4] a good bit of sociology has been social ethics in disguise. Thus it may be necessary to acknowledge that analytical sociologists are at the cutting edge of ethical sensitivity. And this acknowledgment occurs at a time when theological-ethical sensitivities on social matters have been blunted because of the influence of a new form of propositional revelation[5] or a retreat to subjective decision-making,[6] in spite of the rather recent burst of religiously motivated social criticism.

But there is a fundamental inadequacy in the crypto-ethical positions taken by urban social theorists. The lives and institutions that constitute the urban ethos are shaped by parameters of thought and meta-ethical models fundamentally influenced by Western theological and moral traditions. Because the basic patterns of these traditions have been so long accepted, they have become a part of the conventional wisdom of scholar and citizen alike. And, in their conventional forms, the dependence upon explicit theological and ethical *credos* of the past has been ignored. In such a context, the urban theorist is impatient with apparently speculative matters of a theological sort. The situation is further complicated by the hard-won secularization processes that separated church and state, that demanded argument and evidence and not merely appeals to supernatural authority in scholarly dispute, and that allowed pluralism and skepticism in theological matters. But it can be argued that these secularization processes are themselves dependent upon fundamental theological shifts that redefined the decisive meta-ethical models, and that the failure of theology as a churchly or academic pursuit to keep pace with its own implications as a fundamental way to portray social reality through *credo* does not mitigate its importance. While church and state may well be separated, *credo* and politics are not. While appeals to supernatural authority may not overtly appear in planning, academic, or policy questions, what covertly is understood to count as evidence and argument depends upon a common meta-ethical model among the disputants. And while pluralism and skepticism are widely acknowledged and celebrated in the urban ethos, it is a pluralism within the constraints of a belief that truth better surfaces in such a setting and it is a skepticism within a context of fundamental trust about there being some viable pattern of rights, goods, and fits in the common life.

We know that individuals are acculturated over a relatively short time into some tolerable commonality in an urban family. And we know that large groups, such as immigrants, are acculturated into wider ranges of value orientation commensurate with urban styles of life when they live in that context. In both cases, a level of maturity is said to be reached when there is the clarification of and critical evaluation of the *credos* of those who shaped the acculturation process. It surely is also the case that urban theory might well mature to a point where it consciously comes to grips with that which has shaped it.

Further, it is perfectly possible to argue that the development of the urban ethos, on such a massive scale as modern society portends, indeed, demands, self-consciously selecting and reinterpreting elements from the past that have shaped the present. Not all are beneficial, not all are important. Some elements are frankly pathological in their effects. Yet pious citizen, consciously if superficially, and skeptical scholar, less consciously, but often more profoundly and nearly always in nonreligious form, depend upon them when confronting new social phenomena.

The first responsibility is to show the creedal streams from which the major *credos* of urban analysis derive. Having gained some familiarity with the fundamental meta-ethical models by which people view the urban ethos, we can begin to construct a more whole, more integrated one by a reconstruction of creedal history pertinent to the urban ethos.

Background of the Models

Now, if the development of an adequate social analysis for the urban ethos depends upon the articulation of a meta-ethical interpretive model, a *credo,* that bears intrinsic connotations of being or symbolizing "right," that bears explicit normative direction toward the "good," and that is appropriate, or "fitting," to the actual tissue of life as experienced, we need to investigate the major alternative models in some detail. We also need to look more explicitly at the nature of symbols, since the argument heretofore points so much to their importance. Further, we need to ask whether there is an available conceptual model that grasps the several dimensions we have been speaking of thus far.

On the basis of what we have found, we are inclined to look for the models in theological realms. Indeed, each of the perspectives investigated earlier had all the marks of a partial theological-ethical system, and we have just seen that this was necessary.

It should not surprise us, although it may astonish some and alienate others, that we should look to theology for the models. There is a resistance to using theological models, occasioned by the trivialization of theology in many religious circles and the theological illiteracy of cultured despisers. Nevertheless, both historically and systematically, theological symbols have had certain features that are highly pertinent to the discussion. For one thing, theology has been one of the most elaborate forms of systems analysis ever engaged in by man.[7] The ways in which parts relate to wholes, changes in subsystems affect other subsystems, the decisive significance of underlying models, and the intricacies of the relationship between objectivity and subjectivity, description and prescription, are all part of the legacy of theology.

Theology at its strongest organizes its systematic thought around the symbol of "God." In working toward an urban theology, the symbol "God" does not necessarily focus on the question of a theistic being. Both "theism" and "being" carry metaphysical connotations that some periods of history have seen as the best way to point toward that which is deemed to be of ultimate worth and power operative in history. But these may not be the best way to do so in an urban ethos. "God," as a symbol, focuses our attention around two loci: it is first of all around power (dynamic) that theology organizes its thought. What is it that has that highly elusive power to sustain and transform life? Second, the power must be from some persons' or groups' perspective *worthy* power, capable of making urban constructs work for human good. And while urban analysis recognizes the fundamental shifts that take place in the transition to an urban ethos, urban meta-ethical models organized around worth and power presuppose that urban man is not different from men of other ages in this respect at least: he worships, and insofar as he is able is obedient to, what he thinks is ultimately worthy and powerful. Theology is in this view, therefore, the critical and systematic study of that which man worships. It involves the explicit articulation, criticism, and reconstruction of fundamental *credos*. Whoever asks the question of what is ultimately worthy and what is ultimately powerful as it relates to contemporary existence is asking the theological question about the urban ethos.

Assertions about the ultimate importance of personhood are neither natural phenomena nor self-evident. Marxist scholars, particularly, have shown that it is a bourgeois concept that has been given legitimacy by theological grounding. They properly see the implicit connection between the development of personalist loyalties, city citizenship, and attendant concepts of private property—all reinforced by theological developments of an ideological sort. The absolute value of personhood does not occur in situations where man's primary reference is nature (in spite of the claims of early Rousseau), nor in tribal settings where the plethora of natural gods reign. And in spite of metaphysical concepts of a human spirit in many of the world's religions, the actualization of personality, individuation of choices, and concepts of personal liberty have developed most extensively in the Western city under the impact of specific theological ideas.

The common features of the diverse concepts of person derive from a major stream in the Western theological tradition that has become manifest today in several ways. The early Greek concept of *persona* that referred to the mask which one wears in a drama, and ancient Hebraic concepts of the *nephesh,* the unity of mind and body governed by will were wedded in the medieval tradition to the Roman notion of *individuum* that had legal roots. In the latter tradition, the "person" was self *or a group, a persona ficta,* that had status before the law. Throughout the medieval period, the person was an objective concept that referred to one's status in an organic sociopolitical system vertically organized into a "great chain of being."[8] The interpretation of serf, lord, prince, spiritual prince, vicar of Christ, angels, archangels, and the Trinity were cosmic personalist motifs seen as built into the orders of creation. These are the sources of personalist *credos.* And in these periods, each knew his place. Identity was understood as cosmically founded and of transcendent importance.

In the Catholic ecclesiastical mystics, for the spiritually elite, and in Lutheran reformation, for the masses, these concepts were not undercut but were internalized and made subjective because under the impact of an apocalyptic interpretation of history and a nominalist theological assumption the objective order was thought to be in rapid decay or to be a human construction and hence of little positive significance. The concepts of justification by faith and priesthood of all believers shifted the emphasis from the objective manifestations of *persona* and status to the subjective will. And real man's status was defined internally rather than externally.[9] From this root came two divergent traditions which have reconverged in contemporary analysis of the urban ethos. The pietist tradition, on the one hand, accents the importance of individual decision-making—a tradition that has produced the "revivalism" of the frontier and ultimately the populist motifs in American life, subverting certain Calvinist beliefs in the positive importance of laws and structures (including the neopopulism of antiurbanization and criticism of urban artificiality). On the other hand was the bourgeois intellectual tradition of German theology and, when secularized for export, philosophy which can be traced from Luther through Kant, the neo-Kantians such as the highly influential Wilhelm Dilthey, to the contemporary phenomenologists, existentialists, and psychoanalysts. The wedding of these traditions has produced a secularized and semipietistic personalism that pervades many contemporary interpretations of the city.[10]

The difficulty with this movement, as suggested before, has been its inability to provide a serious social philosophy in a situation when persons feel enormous anxiety, for their social worlds appear to be dissolving before their eyes. This is due to the prevailing tendency to relegate all objective concerns to a second level of priority. While this view properly recognizes that no individual is perfectly socialized or acculturated, so that a relative gap always exists between self and society that allows some critical distance, the view makes the gap more absolute than is the case. Thus, a gap between the self and the social system is made so wide that there is no accent on the dependence or the necessary engagement of the self in the society. Creative reconstruction of society to reduce personal strain engendered by the society is seldom seen as crucial. This gap is not an accident or incompletion but a constitutional deficiency derived from a particular theological or ideological, if you will, way of looking at the world.[11]

The contemporary morphological collectivists are also rooted in theological precursors. From the Jewish and the Christian adaptations of Greek and Roman thought derives a utopian tradition based on vigorous transformationist motifs.[12] Where the influence of Greco-Roman natural law theory has been strongest in the theological tradition, the transformation has had the notion of return to the lost paradise, the golden age when man once again would establish his harmony with nature. Where Hebraic notions of linear history have dominated, the transformation has been futuristic and aggressive.[13] In both views there has been a tendency to see the major developments in terms of a succession of epochs in which new objective shapes are formed. The contemporary manifestations of this tradition derive from two sources besides those mentioned in Chapter II:

(a) Joachim of Fiora, whose importance is being increasingly recognized, spoke of the several ages of man, and saw man emerging into a new age of creativity and efficiency in which poetry, social organization, religion, indeed all of life would be transformed in the creation of a new humanity. The early utopian literature such as Campanello's *City of the Sun* and More's *Utopia,* which discuss in detail the objective morphology of the city, and the "new towns" of the nineteenth century and the new communal utopian experiments are deeply dependent on this tradition. When they became linked with more scientific and technological orientations such as those in Comte or Mannheim, one finds the technocratic, transformationist ideas coming into their own.

(b) But the collective morphologists are also dependent upon another theological root that has derived from a quite different stream. The Calvinist Revolution in England is a primary source, in constrast to many popular notions, of modern revolutionism. It sanctioned the killing of the king and consciously recognized that the social-political order is an artifact subject to transformation for the service of man and the glory of God.[14] There had been tyrannicide before, but this revolution was programmatic and provided both a proto-democratic concept of political participation in decision-making and morphological attempts to make society subservient to good order. The Calvinist drive was, as Lord Acton once pointed out, not to create a new church but a new world, to remodel not only doctrine but society. These notions are related to the bourgeois revolutionism of urban design and management today, for these merged in the nineteenth century with a new burst of "liberal-progressive" thought and became divorced from the explicitly theological roots. The morphologists are creating a new synthesis out of the old fabric as one can see by examining the basic concepts of urban planners today.

And what is the source of the notion of radical and progressive transformation of nature as it is criticized by naturalistic assumptions? Ernest L. Tuveson has shown, in a very significant study, that the roots are in millennial literature that conceives of the creation of a New Jerusalem. And that new order was to be implemented by understanding and acting according to the laws of nature. In nature, it was thought, one found the great thoughts of God. From the revival of chiliasm which generated the emergence of the new science "the Western Christian world took the first step away from the ideal of world transcendence toward that of world-reform."[15]

Still further, the question of contemporary political organization derives from theological beliefs. The ancient cities were overwhelmingly dominated by temples,[16] and their political leaders by priestly accoutrements. The theocratic regimes of Israel and the organization of the gods and the priesthood in Greco-Roman civilization were the fundamental patterns that shaped the ancient Mediterranean world. It is not accidental that Socrates was poisoned for profaning the gods and threatening civil order or that "King of the Jews" is reputed to have been the sign on Jesus' cross. The theological order was the basis of political order. Fustel De Coulange in his famous, although dated, study of the ancient city indicates the shift in political and legal life as influenced by the shifts from family-centered piety to organization of religion at other levels of society.[17] And the well-known contemporary theologian–political analyst Reinhold Niebuhr pointed out that "every extension of community in history embodies some contrivance of priest, soldier and statecraft. . . ."[18] He went on to suggest that while every form of piety is tainted by the lust for power, no lust for power exists nakedly. And to understand why this is so requires a theological perception of the human community.

But while a case can be made for the *historical* impact of the theological tradition on the urban ethos, the more important question for our purposes is whether or not there can be any constructive, *systematic* relation between the major motifs of the tradition and the contemporary urban ethos. Many have seen the forsaking of the explicitly theological roots of these perspectives as indication that secularization is an inevitable, and beneficial, process that has attended the development of the modern urban ethos. Theological perspectives are interesting archaeology, but hardly necessary and often dysfunctional.

The claim made here is that there are, and must be, if we are to understand a theological "meta-ethics," *credos* which many social analysts pretend to avoid, but in fact use, because *credo* is necessary to the analysis of the urban ethos.

Differences in *credo,* says the tradition, are not merely matters of private opinion, but are alternative conceptions of ways that life is to be patterned. What, when the pressures mount, is to be given precedence? Theology, and especially theological ethics, has attempted to gather in diverse motifs and tie them into a single bundle by symbolic language and operational organization. It has claimed that symbolic language is the only language capable of performing this task. Symbolic language can gather into itself diversities and contradictions that exceed rational analysis, although it is not anti-rational. Symbolic language lays out dominant themes to form an explicit or an implicit *credo* by which we select and interpret our environment. It captures and articulates primordial decisions about our attitudes toward life, and thereby represents the decisive precipitates of a culture or subculture. Symbolic formulations are imaginative constellations of terms in relationship that identify meanings and purposes, that provide an angle of vision on life, and that make conscious and dominant certain crucial features of life in a way that neither ordinary rational discourse nor coercive power can ever fully provide. Symbols evoke responses at the emotive level as well as at the intellectual level. Symbols combine personal loyalties and cultural patterns in a society. Men and societies may be said to live by self-interest, or even by enlightened self-interest: but men and societies interpret their interests and their neighbors' in terms of clusters of symbols that illumine, evoke, and motivate—even if the interests always taint the perception and the use of symbols. And even if, as cynics claim, symbols are but masks to hide their interests, symbols have a potency which often exceeds and sometimes forces sacrifice of interests. The cynic must somehow account for the fact that people and societies feel compelled to justify their interests by appeal to symbol.

Symbols are more efficient than realities. Reality is too bulky to carry around. So people plan, program, evaluate, and organize production, distribution, and consumption by symbols. Governments issue declarations or carry on negotiations in symbols, and these shape and select reality. Psychiatrists sort out in a year or two what became confused in a lifetime of reality, through the use of symbolic exchange.

But precisely because symbols are, in one sense, not real while having enormous potency, they can obscure rather than reveal reality. And when they do, destruction ensues. When vibrant, accurate ethical symbols are used, the ethos is sustained and positively reconstructed. When not, life decays. Thus when urban analysis does not attend to symbolic dimensions, the bits of information, styles of operation, and complexities of purposes become viciously destructive. Each fragment preserves the claim of being true to the wholeness, and conflicts between perspectives become a veiled conflict between the gods.

Now if the gods are in conflict, if there are antiurban *credos* that represent the worship of nonurban models of ultimate worth and power standing against prourban ones, or if within the gods of urbanity there are some standing against others, how do we judge between them?

On the broad scale, we know that fundamental religious and symbolic orientations are adopted according to their capacity to give constructive shape to personal and social existence. We know that ancient Israel turned to Jehovah for he made a people out of no-people. We know that Christianity triumphed over paganism in the ancient Mediterranean world because it gave a more compelling interpretation of life than did its foes, and that it gained influence even when all other forms of power were in the hands of its opponents. Similarly, the adoption of Therevada Buddhism in South East Asia was due to its capacity to gather up and organize disjointed dimensions of life more profoundly than the alternatives. So also Islam in what are now the Arab countries, and so also a multiplicity of lesser-known cults and sects in particular locations.[19] In each of these instances there were patterns of life that had affinity with the historical traditions and there were choices of partially new symbol systems that reorganized personal and social existence. New symbols gained influence accordingly as they rendered both a compelling account of why things are the way they are and a portrait of how they ought to be. Precisely why people and societies came to these conclusions is not fully known, but it is possible to suggest that one crucial reason was the ethical function of the symbol systems. That is, the meta-ethical models adopted were perceived as being intrinsically right, as giving shape to good ends, and as being fitting to the context of life. By analogy, it is possible to assume that the *credos* of urban theorists are serious attempts to do the same thing.

The Use of Theology in Urban Analysis

Now if meta-ethical models are in competition in the urban ethos, and if people tend to choose them according to their rootage in an historical tradition and according to their ethical function, which shall we choose in our context?

It would appear that the Judeo-Christian *credo* would be more pertinent to the urban ethos than any other, in spite of the aberrations that have appeared under its guise. There are several reasons for such a claim.

Most obviously, the modern urban ethos was developed under the impact of the Judeo-Christian heritage. Max Weber's massive corpus of work indicates that the technological, economic, administrative, and political capacities of non-Western cultures were at various points in time highly developed. If these were decisive alone, these cultures should have moved toward modern, industrial, urban culture. In fact, they did not. And that is because the *credos* operating in those cultures inhibited rather than served as a catalyst for such development. The conjunction of material forces and "spiritual" forces are necessary for fundamental alterations in history. It was under the influence of specific meta-ethical models in the Judeo-Christian tradition that such movements took place.[20]

Similarly, it is argued in different ways that those countries which have recently adopted the patterns of urbanization with varying degrees of reluctance or enthusiasm have found it necessary to develop meta-ethical models of life that have fundamentally analogous elements, even where they are not explicitly Judeo-Christian.[21]

The objection may, of course, be raised that the urban ethos was in fact produced by factors other than the theological ones, and that the *credos* developed are merely mythical objectifications of the social, political, or technological factors that shaped the environment and the ethos. Such an objection raises an important debate that is evident not only in the literature already cited but in a wide range of literature on the development of urban civilization.[22] But I hope it is clear that no single cause is suggested. When we suggest that there is an integral relationship between the Judeo-Christian *credo* and development of the urban ethos, we mean that the *credo* expresses the essential precipitates, the core commitments, of the culture that guide the perception of and the response to "material" forces. The material forces have, of course, a kind of independence and autonomy when looked at alone, but when it comes to the human response to these forces, *credos* become highly influential. Not all urban analysts have recognized what Durkheim did two generations ago: that a belief system, once produced, if it is, by the social matrix, becomes itself a moral and social fact of primary importance that is decisive for the development of the culture.[23]

But, more particularly, when we place these broader observations in the more limited context of this study, we find that the particular modes of interpretation of the urban ethos by contemporary social theorists are dependent on streams of thought derived from the Judeo-Christian heritage. Their capacity to discern and accent valid elements of the urban experience can be said to be rooted in the fact that both the elements which they see, and the *credos* by which they discern them, are rooted in a near-forgotten stream of theological influences. And, one can suggest that their incapacity to present a more holistic interpretation is due to the fact that the elements they depend upon are no longer systematically related to the other elements. The partiality and fragmentation experienced by urban man and the incompleteness of urban theory are due in large measure to the breakdown of previous syntheses, and the separation of the secular theorists and ordinary citizens from the roots of their own thought.

In a very profound sense, one might celebrate the breakdown, for previous syntheses often had elements that inhibited the realization of their own implications. But that does not relieve contemporary theory from the effort to reconstruct.

There is a second major reason that the Judeo-Christian tradition is pertinent to the urban ethos. The Judeo-Christian tradition has had in nearly all its forms three decisive ingredients that are necessary to urban existence. It is, in principle, peculiarly future oriented. While the tradition affirms that man was given a garden, the tradition affirms (even if popular piety does not always) that once the boundaries of "dreaming innocence," to use Paul Tillich's phrase, are broken, man does and must look toward a divine future that is not heaven nor return to the paradise once forsaken. No uncompromised otherworldliness, and no myth of eternal return is involved in the Judeo-Christian tradition as it is in every other world religion. Instead there is hope of a new creation, an urban re-creation in a New Jerusalem, that stands normatively as the hope of the faithful.

Similarly, the forms of Judeo-Christian symbol-system have been *theologically* treated. That is, they do not exist merely as piety. Instead, there is a built-in dimension of critical evaluation of piety. None of the other world religions, except Marxism if one may so classify it, has developed critical and "scientific" tools to deal with the fundamentals of the meta-ethical models. And where there are developments of Hindu, Buddhist, Islam, or other "theologies," they appear under the impact of Christian influence or as an attempt to make the indigenous religious traditions of a region capable of sustaining and extending the urban ethos developing in these locales. Thus, the fact that the Judeo-Christian traditions, and here the accent must fall on the Christian side, are peculiarly theological, equips them for the kind of critical and reconstructive interpretation of the fundamental precipitates of the culture that the urban ethos demands.

Also, the peculiar conceptions of the future, and the peculiar way in which *credos* are treated theologically, are related to the way in which the Judeo-Christian tradition works through an artifactual social institution. The church is not natural. It is an intentional community that tries to base itself on the fundamental power and worth of "covenanted" existence which it claims is not found by race, clan, sex, nation, class, or other "natural" divisions among men. The conceptions of the future and the critical way in which it tries to perceive its own loyalties, then, are related to an attempt to give structure to a highly artificial social construct, and to discriminate between good and bad social constructions in life. The Judeo-Christian tradition is, thus, both within itself and vis-à-vis the operating power arrangements in society a social-political structure for intentional community.

There is danger in such a social concern: power gets separated from conceptions of worth and celebrated for its own sake. Such has been the experience and the temptation of the tradition among politically concerned theologians since the ancient Hebrews. There, the temptations led to "false prophecy." And some more recent forms of Zionism border on such dangers.[24] Christians have had their full share of such distortions also: the Constantinian party in the fourth century, the Erastians of the late medieval and reformation period, the German Christians who supported the Nazis, the comfortable and very pious racists of South Africa, and the American religious chauvinists.[25] The very closeness of these positions to the main line of theological development in the churches has made it hazardous to attempt constructive social and political theology, and has contributed to the confusion of observers of the theological traditions. But the hazard does not detract from the fact that intrinsic to the Judeo-Christian tradition is a drive to define and construct artificial social systems that are right, good, and fit.

The Judeo-Christian tradition, then, has three elements that are crucial to its history and to the urban ethos. In traditional terms, they are usually called: eschatology, doctrine, and ecclesiology. We will shortly have to look at these in considerable detail to see if these elements can render the foundations of a *credo* for the urban ethos. And one test of their adequacy will be their capacity to link together the partially valid, but conflicting and fragmented motifs that we found in the analysis of the secular theologians, the urban theorists.

But before we do so, we need to summarize and extend our preliminary observations about the general character of theological reflection. We need to recognize that theological motifs did not come full-blown from heaven. They are themselves human constructions, forged with great care because the authors felt they were dealing with the fundamental powers and values of human existence. If we recognize this, we can make two further observations. On the one hand, the theological systems that have been forged over the ages are not different in kind from those which we found in the contemporary interpretations of the urban ethos. Theologies were forged in times of social, political, and ethical crises, and they were forged precisely with the end in mind of providing conceptual tools by which man could both understand and operate responsibly in his environment or so that he could legitimate his protest against the environment or his urge to transform it. They, too, involved questions of ultimate loyalty and of the limits of man's transgression of ultimate boundaries. The drawing of one's primary terms from the realms of personality, morphology, nature, or political life does not exempt one from being theological. One is still asking which fundamental forces determine existence; one is still asking the why of existence, the why of its sometimes emptiness or tragedy; and the means of redemption from them; one is still asking as to the nature of ultimate good power and the proper kind of polity to support it; one is still asking what "trees of knowledge" in the gardens of primordial nature may not be violated without expulsion from the present environment; one is still asking as to the ultimate value of the person in an artificial, highly structured environment; and one is still asking how the present structures should be transformed to find fulfillment of the right, good, and fit. The point, in short, is that if these are the sorts of questions that need to be asked—and are in fact being asked—we are foolish to cut ourselves off from previous efforts to deal with such questions. The modern artifact of the urban ethos that is now the predominant pattern of life did not give birth to itself at the advent of the twentieth century. Although it burst into predominance in the last century, it is rooted in patterns of thought and organization and personality that have been present in various forms for centuries, but which have until recently been subdominant. Our construction of theological or meta-ethical models demands, if it is to be pertinent, a conceptual model that is historically sensitive. It also demands a reconstruction of our perceptions of those patterns; for what was often dormant is now awakened and active.

Now, if we are going to be theological in the Judeo-Christian tradition, which theology should we choose? The whole of contemporary theological scholarship shows that there is not one theology but that there are many. Both worldwide and in the West. There is not even one biblical view, or one New Testament view—there are many. While this is shocking to many, it is not at all surprising to someone who sees the link between theology and the social-political matrix wherein it is articulated and wherein it works out its own logic.

But there are particular motifs in theology that can be isolated as being pertinent to the urban ethos as has already been suggested. They can be isolated because some theological motifs were engendered in an earlier proto-urban ethos and functioned normatively in it to produce the modern urban ethos. This implies, it should be emphasized, considerable selectivity in the theological tradition. Only some motifs will be recovered for construction into newer models.

Further, the motifs can only be expressed and combined in a limited number of ways to be pertinent to the urban ethos. Some ordering of the various fragments and motifs that are available and pertinent to the urban ethos are highly dubious, because they presuppose agrarian or tribal or feudal or other system in the final analysis. Thus, they tend to destroy the urban ethos while it intends to interpret and mold that ethos.

Here too, however, we can take a leaf from the pages of theological history, and we can note those crucial moments when men and societies faced urbanization and rapid social change to see how they dealt with the theological fragments and broken myths that were part of their intellectual tools.

We must make clear here that we are using the theological

tradition both in a material sense, and in a formal sense. That is, we are looking at the *relationship* between the social political setting in which people find themselves and the *way* in which they articulate models to final meaning and purpose in their environment. Although we are not at all surprised that there are similarities of concept and content, we are not looking in the Bible or the theological tradition for the answers, for "the biblical theology," but for guidance in *how* one conceives of social-political situations when one looks at them in depth. Although the processes and developments toward urbanization were subdominant until recently, the urbanization of man and the creation of an urban ethos have been going on in fits and starts from very early on, and we should derive whatever wisdom we can from earlier efforts to see how they were handled and where they succeeded and failed.

One of the most notable things about the theological tradition is that it has had some of its greatest moments of creativity in periods of rapid transition toward a more urban setting. And in each case, it has drawn from secular forms of thought and transformed them into new syntheses in accordance with a theology of history. The Exodus moved a people from slavery to urban conquest and stands as the primary model of biblical promise. The Jahwist redaction of ancient themes made considerable use of pagan epics and noncompatible oral traditions, weaving together a new interpretation of man during the time that David and Solomon were forming new political bureaucracies and urban-centered religion by moving the tabernacle to Jerusalem. The prophetic schools of the eighth century also drew together certain agrarian protests against the city with clearly urban themes and a new cosmopolitan discernment of international relations. Even the later writings, such as Ezra and Nehemiah, which are usually seen as the lowest ebb in cosmopolitan orientation because of their nationalistic overtones, recognized that the creation of new communities is always accomplished between the boundary of violence and normative consensus. The New Testament contains a great number of Hellenistic themes which are adopted and transmuted into new forms in the cities of Corinth, Ephesus, Rome, and the other trade cities of the ancient Near East. The use of Greek philosophical motifs in

Alexandria, and especially throughout the debates of the Mediterranean Christian world during the rise of Constantine, the
Neo-Platonic themes in Augustine, the much later use of
Aristotle by Aquinas, and the influence of a humanist legal
training on Calvin are all well known. And, most recently, the
importance of the impact of secular social science on the American Social Gospel movement has consequences still.

From this brief survey we notice several things. First, that
none of these theologies has spun its theories out of its own
web. Each was deeply dependent, and explicitly so, on the
secular situations and secular philosophical efforts which they
adapted and transformed into new orientations. While many of
these myths and philosophies are themselves products of theologies and religious practices, often in secularized forms, it is
not in their original forms that they influenced the development
of the modern urban ethos. It is only in their new forms that they
have had consequence. We should note, however, that each of
the theological innovations drew upon old myths, secular
thought, and social realism without apparent embarrassment.
The great urban innovators did not assume that theology contained the whole truth within itself, but that it contained certain
discriminating principles and an ability to organize materials
into an interpretation of history—past and present. And they
linked these materials in a way that joined impassioned commitment, rational structure, and institutional organization not present in any of the resources alone.

Yet, all agreed with what we have also found: that it is not
the material forces of nature or history that finally decide either
the way the human condition is or the way it ought to be. The
fundamental forces and values of the ethos, every ethos, are decisively influenced by invisible, spiritual realities. How odd to
use such terms in the contemporary context of a presumably
secular urban ethos; but what could the tradition have meant, if
one rightly discounts cumbersome metaphysics, but that matters
of *credo*, of meta-ethical models, are at the center of even the
most tough-minded analysis of the ethos in which one lives.

Second, we should note that all of these developments attempted to deal with the whole of mankind, not with some part.
There is universality of concern in the urban theological inno-

vators. The redactor of biblical sources pressed his question of the meaning of life in history to the very boundaries of creation. The prophets spoke of foreign rulers who were also under single reign of the same, single God, and were used as a rod of chastisement against those claiming special privilege. The writers of the New Testament in speaking of the Kings paying homage to Jesus, for example, attempted to extend the importance of the event beyond Israel; and Paul, of course, fought for the inclusion of Gentiles as members in good standing in the new humanity. In the philosophical theologies of the fathers, cosmic concerns were introduced, and Augustine writes a theological interpretation of human history. Aquinas' and Calvin's concern for natural law theory in various ways tried to extend the theological concern to the whole of humanity. The Social Gospel from Walter Rauschenbusch to Martin Luther King pressed continually for universal theological motifs in social history.

Third, and closely linked to the question of universality, the question of sovereignty—of ultimate good power—is linked to proper "ecclesiology." Normative concepts of good community order in each of the above figures drew major motifs from concepts of law. The importance of the objective order of good power can be seen in the Elohist inclusion of the Mosaic materials, the prophetic use of covenant renewal ceremonies, the codification of the diverse sayings of Jesus into catechetical form, the struggles over church order in the fathers, Augustine's polemics against the Docetics, Aquinas' sacramentalism, Calvin's controversies with the Anabaptists, and the Social Gospel's demand for a prophetic church and search for an objectively discernible Kingdom of God.

And finally, all accent the motif of transformation. The natural order is to be brought under human control and even the political order is to be subdued to human control as guided by the objective structures of worthy power. The Jahwist spoke of God's gifts to the children of Adam, the tools of agriculture, spinning, and culture (musical instruments). The prophets saw the subduction of wasteland and an end to the natural enmity of lion and lamb. The early church broke the power of family and ethnic claims when it told those burdened by family piety to let the dead bury the dead and identified the members of the new community as the true brothers and sisters; and it established a communism of consumption (although not of production) in the internal economic order of the church. The fathers, Augustine, Aquinas, and Calvin and the Social Gospel movement also spoke in differing ways of the subduing of the flesh and transforming the whole order into a City of God.

In short, the urban theologians in every major case drew on nontheological materials for fundamental insights; pressed the boundaries of concern to an interpretation of the whole of mankind in a very cosmopolitan fashion; saw the great importance of the relationship of the immediate social-political arrangement to the sovereignty of ultimate good power; and accented the motifs of radical transformationism. If contemporary theological ethics is to provide an interpretive model, a *credo,* that allows people to deal with the contemporary ethos in a comparable fashion, surely it must at least learn from its predecessors.

We find it necessary therefore, to attempt a theological model that does openly what has been done surreptitiously in urban theology before us, that is to take account of the secular social theories that inform us. The fundamental presupposition is that ethical concerns have to and do allow us to select among various broken myths and models and to develop alternative ones in reconstructive fashion. Our focus, therefore, in the next three chapters, will be on a reinterpretation of the three fundamental motifs of the Judeo-Christian movement—eschatology, the formation of critical theology, and ecclesiology. While the tough-minded urban pragmatists may view this as an excursion into arcane matters, it is hoped that the case has been sufficiently made that these kinds of concerns are highly pertinent. The proof of the pudding, however, will have to be judged according to the capacity of these matters to give shape, integration, and foundation to the partial *credos* of contemporary urban theory.

Chapter V

ESCHATOLOGY AND SOCIAL POLICY

I n the urban ethos, man acts toward ends. The very fact that he lives, and chooses to live, in a constructed environment indicates that he has subordinated the given determinants of nature and inherited practice to new intentional existence. The mere recapitulation of traditional ritual acts becomes less and less significant in urban existence. Indeed, by diverting attention from the choices actually made in the shift to urban forms of life, traditionalism and ritualism become dangerous to the future of serious theology and of a human community in an urban ethos. Urban man acts with a purpose, with a vision that allows and indeed demands that he act meaningfully. Urban man's action is instrumental. Projects are undertaken to arrive at some desired state, to accomplish some necessary objective, to explore some possibility. His very attempt to analyze the urban ethos, as we have seen, is in order to find a direction for it. Whether those ends—thought of as possibilities, necessities, or desirables, or some combination of these— are powerful enough to save man from destruction and are of ultimate worth is a theological-ethical question. Are our ends in accord with what is ultimately worthy power? And are our means appropriate to those ends?

The pattern of significant action in the urban ethos requires not only ends, but a sense of ending. There must be endings, not only for the massive tasks of coordination but also for the establishment of normative guidelines. There must be deadlines, due dates, final offers. In short, there must be the possibility of having done with things, summarizing, evaluating and grading and deciding. Without endings, ends have no focus and no boundaries. The possibility of perpetual drift is, of course, present; but people do not in fact live that way. And while the hurry and scurry of the city often testify to the unmerciful succession of endings to which modern man is subject, they also

testify to the sense of imminent finality that is necessarily con-
veyed by living with purposes and endings.

The major figures and instrumentalities of the modern megalopolis develop their ends and endings by *projects,* by planned
thrusts into the future with specific purposes and with pro-
grammed endings. The nature and character of these projects are
decisive factors in the fulfillment or dissolution of the urban
ethos. And, the task of theological ethics is to give an interpretive model, to suggest the kinds and qualities of thrusts toward
the future that are of fundamental importance, for the theological tradition is both responsible for and responsive to the
innovations of future orientation represented in the city.

In fact, the creative moments in religious history have been
when the models and symbols were taken from the past and
redefined through legitimate action toward the future. Isaiah's
expectation of the messianic age, Jeremiah's hope for a new
covenant, Hosea's vision of the reconciliation of the estranged,
and Amos' indications of the explicit judgment of imminent
ending, all bear the mark of reinterpretations of the projects
of man in situations of proto-urban crisis. The other decisive
shifts in the development of the modern world were the New
Testament, the Constantinian period, the rise of town culture
with the breakup of feudalism, and the Reformation-Renais-
sance. In each of these periods, secular and sacred theologians
addressed the fundamental questions of how man might shape
his future from a reconstruction of his past and an ecstatic
vision of the possibilities of the future. The symbols that they
constructed are, if taken literally, one of the fundamental
sources for the distortion of human life; but if they are taken
as symbols, as conceptual models of how to deal with fundamental human problems that are multi-dimensional, they can be
ignored to our peril.

The kinds and quality of expectations and future orientations
that people have are, in short, pressed to their limits in the
theological escalation of language. Projects are radicalized to
their ultimate implications. Nowhere in world history has this
phenomena been more thoroughly explored than in the biblical
traditions wherein the foundations of future-oriented existence
are plumbed.

Biblical Foundations

The ultimate patterns of worth and power, in the biblical tradition, are seen as being revealed in historical contingencies. The whole of contemporary biblical scholarship agrees that it is not in fantastic experiences of *historicus interruptus* that the fundamental matters of right, good, and fit are made known to human societies, but in the storm and stress of experiences also accessible to the social sciences. But how men and societies are to interpret and act on such bases depend on which meta-ethical models they are inspired to develop from them. And for all the variety of traditions within biblical material itself, it is nevertheless possible to identify a very deeply rooted, and fundamentally unified drive in the material that is directly pertinent to our efforts.[1]

The biblical peoples not only experienced a succession of events in life, they saw that those events had a kind of inward unity that stood beyond their power to fully grasp. And, from that unity, they saw that they derived their identity, their social cohesion, and their stance toward life. It was a unity that was in the experience of life, but it was a unity that never seemed to be exhausted there. There was always the promise of more to come which would alter and transform, judge and break down, reconstruct and build, but never utterly destroy, meaning and purpose and the context of life.

What man is called to, on the basis of this sensitivity, is to respond to that ultimate unity of power and worth. Human conduct takes on obligations to support and sustain within the experience of life that unity, to wed empirically the power and the worth of that unity that is present but not empirically so. The experience of the Exodus was the primary experience that became a metaphor for all subsequent interpretation. For in that event, the reality which they knew "overthrew dark powers of chaos and evil rulers, . . . raised up the oppressed and decreed justice for those who had no rights, . . . had compassion on the weak and miserable, championed their cause and chose them for freedom."[2] Yet the freedom was not one of license, but of obligation to keep alive in the midst of the people the consciousness of that liberating force. And that obligation implies a rigorous and disciplined understanding of freedom. It was not merely a freedom *from,* but a freedom *for* a new destiny. Thus in the midst of contingent events and patterns, a unity was discerned that moved toward a promised future. The experience of liberation was not seen as final, but promissory. It is the symbols of the Exodus, and the pattern of covenanted obligations erected in its wake, that are taken as metaphors for the whole of experience, That unity which brought them out and made a no-people a people, a community out of a chaos under tyranny, is also the unity which could bring new possibilities and extend the continuity in the experience of events in history. As Jurgen Moltmann has argued, "The promises were not liquidated by the history of Israel" but continually received "new and wider interpretations." All experiences of fulfillment were provisional, "stages on a road that goes further." There was then in Israel no "religious sanctioning of the present, but a breaking away from the present toward the future."[3] The present and the past are not to be forsaken, however, for the very primal act of creation is seen on the model of an exodus event. It too is a giving of order out of chaos, of beginning a series of historical events which were to have cosmic importance, all of which stemmed from the attempt to find a right, good, and fit ordering of interpersonal, social, and cultural life.

Of course, when we turn to the biblical sources for fundamental motifs that are to be pertinent to the modern urban ethos, we must guard against literalistic urges to transfer the biblical images of the city across the centuries in a way that is just not possible. The biblical cities were little more than agricultural villages surrounded by walls.[4] They have little directly to do with the kind of social matrix in which we find ourselves. What we look for in these proto-urban sources is the way in which a meta-ethical model was generated. As Lewis Mumford pointed out, the ancient cities of the Near East were pretty much alike, and very modest; but they had a religious significance that surpassed their physical dimensions. "Without the religious potencies of the city, the wall could not have succeeded in molding the character as well as controlling the activities of the city's inhabitants. . . . Every feature of the early city revealed the belief that man was created for no other purpose than to magnify and serve his gods."[5] The distinctive thing about the Hebrew pattern of interpretation was the kind of God that it saw evident in this pattern of social organization, a God that was not bound nor constrained by the city as it was, but saw it as a promise of things yet to come. It was this promise that the people of God through their prophets, the priests, and the worthy rulers celebrated, accented, and used where necessary to judge the false prophets, the hired priestlings, the unworthy kings, and, indeed, the people who remembered not and did not therefore feel constrained to covenant in the present nor anticipate a significant future. It was the faithful, the hopeful, and the sensitive against the scornful, the cynic, and the calloused. These were the patterns of right, good, and fit that the God of history and hence of the future sustained. And, in subsequent Jewish traditions, these are the motifs that became central to rabbinic lore.

And the end of all this? It is the establishment of *shalom*, the attainment of a just peace that in fact could not be achieved by human effort, but depended upon the further fulfillment and expansion of the promises already known, if only in fragments. It involves quite concrete elements of basic security, equitable responsibility for, equitable access to, and equitable distribution of economic, political, and cultural resources. It involves a polity based on a law that is written on the hearts of men, and a sense of vocation pervading the community. And it involved a joy, an ecstasy in communion with all under the unity of that worth and power that binds together apparently disparate dimensions of reality. But *shalom* of necessity also remained unspecific and identifiable in symbols that can be only partially sorted out.

From these experiences and the symbols generated on their basis derives a basic sense of anticipation, an eager openness toward the future. A seeking in the possibilities of tomorrow that more will be seen that will add to the expanding sense of promise. Men under the influence of this tradition, no matter how attenuated the self-conscious connections with it have become over the centuries, act with hope and purpose. They live in projections toward the future. Urban man is most deeply influenced by these motifs, and he is a congenital scurrier toward the future even if he has forgotten why and whither. He is constitutionally a progressive incrementalist with a sense of urgency to get on with it.[6] Even reactionary activities are in some serious measure future oriented in a way not present in any other stream of world history.

But this sense of living in projects, in living toward ends, can and indeed has gone in a variety of directions. And the several options available from biblical days frame the urban man's sense of options also.

Eschatological Options

The vision of the apocalyptic struggle of the future is one set of perceptions that is present in the contemporary urban ethos and is fundamental to the tradition as well. Apocalypticism is psychologically, cosmically, and institutionally related to the question of rebellion against the principle of creative order by the creature. All that empirically is is seen as contrary to meaning and worthy projects. Only by negation can an end of creative order be found. The "good," who adhere to the ultimate creative order are seen as opposed by the "evil" who rebel against it and threaten it, but who dominate earthly projects and define worldly ends. Life is lived toward an expectation of an inevitable, impending crisis, an ending of present ends by severe conflict in which the good will triumph and the evil will be shattered. We stand at the brink of a new future, the hallmark of which is violence.[7] The nature of this conflict, and of the parties in it, are variously defined—it may be believers against nonbelievers; whites against blacks; rebellious against loyal angels; rich against poor; generation against generation. In every case, it is given order against given order. Every level of meaning and every purpose is exhausted. All is at stake. The most dangerous conflicts are multi-leveled in which the qualities of ideology, role, class, sex, and race are brought to bear on both sides of the conflict. In this context, some white preachers have found it morally acceptable to run guns to the Black ghettos to overcome some of the power disbalance and to prevent total division, and some church denominations have committed their resources to defend explicitly non-Christian revolutionaries, not to aid apocalypticism, but to undercut it;

just as some white businessmen have been risking financial loss to overcome the divisions. The United States, in the same way, has found it morally "right" to send armaments to both India and Pakistan or to both Israeli and Arab forces. In each case the effort is to prevent the total conflict of absolutism that leads to apocalypticism. The contemporary advocates of an absolute preventive detention to prevent any threats to civil order, and the contemporary advocates of Black or Poor rebellions against the establishment are of the same theological stripe. If it becomes morally necessary to make a choice, of course, the only religious option is with the poor and, in today's context, with the Black. The absoluteness of a moral claim by the oppressed is superior to the absoluteness of the claims of the oppressor, as both Jesus and Marx recognized. But moral ambivalence still exists because both, and not just the oppressor, falsely identify the concept of liberation and new creative order exclusively with their own community. Both sides are psychologically threatened and tend to identify their own humanity with the results of the inevitable conflict that is to come, and in which there is, there must be, victory of the forces of good over the forces of evil. Thus, "they," the "out" group, must learn to respect "our" order; or the "establishment" must acknowledge that it has forfeited its right to remain established because its creative order is neither creative nor orderly. Therefore, a new creative order must take its place. The old ends must come to an ending, new projects must arise. Hence, the attempt to construct a vision of the future obtains beyond the conflict, a future in which creative order truly reigns and which can become the operative model of our present projects.

This notion has taken two forms that cut across the ordinary divisions of liberal or conservative and show the kinds of possibilities that apocalypticism may lead to.

The first is the notion of return. This pattern of future orientation is based on the notion that the reason for the fall, the reason for man's present unfortunate condition is that we have departed from the ideal situation of the past. That may be, ideally, the recovery of the innocence of natural harmony or the recovery of the worship of the true God, from which this artificial environment has separated us.

In either case, the theme of Paradise Lost is linked to a critique of the present culture, and there is expectation that the forces of actual good are entering a painful but inevitable conflict with the forces of evil (but apparent good) out of which may come Paradise regained. Religious (often in secular garb) revivalism, naturalism, or racist tribalism may all be derived from this view. Throughout, the recovery of man's primordial innocence appears in the urban designs that accent the "human scale," that protest any tampering with "natural landscape," that try to reestablish structures of community that are organic—on the analogy of the cell or organism—and that try to establish solidarity structures by designing clan or tribe-sized villages for immediate, "natural" human intimacy. The primary vision of the future is the reintegration of man with some moment of the past, the "real" way of living.

The danger of this, of course, is that it may lapse into a form of reactionism. Very widespread in the urban ethos is a kind of secularized Amishness, a tendency to get spiritually rooted in a given era of the past. Therefore, many urban groups and organizations are based on an antiurban, and certainly anti-industrial, society. New projects are notable for their protest against such things as automobiles, draining swamps, and elevators. These destroy the "natural" harmony of things, by which is meant the cultural conventions of the period that has become the romanticized golden age. Of course, the golden age may vary. It may be the villa of the North Italian Renaissance, the organic towns of the peasant village dominated by a (nonsectarian) cathedral (usually a school or a civic center for the civil religion), a return-to-(glassed-in)-nature dwelling in the woods (without bugs) of the transcendentalist Walden or Brook Farm era, the interconnected but highly independent towns of eighteenth-century England and New England, or even the ethnic street culture of nineteenth-century industrialization. All have advocates in urban-planning literature.

The choices are similar to those in biblical debates as to whether the origins of the true community and the right order of things should be traced to the days of Paul, Peter, Jesus, John, Amos, David, Moses, Abraham, or Adam. The choice of a specific model of the past determines the kind of projects one undertakes in the future and the kind of Paradise one wishes to regain. Appropriation of models from the past for utilization in a constructive statement about the present becomes a religious stance of a specifically romantic variety.

The *utopian* variety of apocalypticism is not oriented to return but idealistically progressive. This is not a restitution of the lost glory of the romanticized past. The projects of this variety of apocalypticism see a great tension between what is and what is to come and demand an assault on the future. By freeing ourselves from the burdens of the past we can establish a totally new order. Not by return to "natural order" but by scientific mastery of nature and polities or by the development of new styles which are worshiped for their orderliness (that makes them possible to control), we can create conditions of perfection. Not by reintegration with some allegedly true pattern from which we are alienated, but by more intensive use of the tools and processes that have liberated us from the past; technology, affluence, secularization, total democratization, and management controls. The conflict is inevitable if we do not develop new techniques of mastery and management rapidly enough.

In this view, the bondage of man is to the images and models of the past; religious images must be destroyed in order to free man to imaginative or rational construction *de novo*. The real need is iconoclasm that melts down the sacred cows of the past and drinks the bitter ashes. Man must recognize that God, Plato, Adam Smith, Lenin, and Einstein are dead so that he can be liberated to create a new perfect community. Some revolutionary advocates of community organization using the rhetoric of Mao, some apologists for new towns, and some concerned to build a whole new technology to control pollution in the contemporary urban ethos represent the utopian perceptions as to the tension of the apocalyptic future with the past. They advocate abandoning the older patterns to build *new* ones, with the expectation that those things that are valuable in the old will survive by virtue of some divine logic that keeps all good things unto eternity. But artifacts or parts of artifacts do not survive naturally. There is no inevitable logic of progress or survival. Death is the natural end of things. The "hidden hand of providence" is a theological presupposition that cannot be validated in these terms.

In theological discourse there is a constant attempt not to settle for the functional medium—which is the usual method of government—but to affirm an order that allows for exploration of the extremes, thus keeping open the whole spectrum of possibility and experience. All things, people, and institutions move toward fuller actualization of their inherent or inherited structures and capacities but, at the same time, they move toward the exhaustion and collapse of those structures and capacities. The pattern of the future, of all projection, is both fulfillment and transformation and never merely one or the other. Thus man must engage in the perennial process of new formation.[8] It is necessary to affirm both the continuity of the future with the past and the radical shifts that take place and allow intentional transformation. Such affirmation which denies, finally, the exorbitant claims of both return and revolution in an urban environment also affirms the remembered order of the past and demands the reconstruction of the future. The biblical tradition presses the question in terms of the relation of the doctrine of creation to the doctrine of the eschaton, insisting that an adequate project must be historical and eschatological in its underlying conception rather than nonhistorically romantic or utopian. And the struggle between this theological perspective and the two varieties of apocalyptic faith are decisive.

An adequate theological perspective can, thus, engage in a continual protest against romantic notions of return and utopian revolutionism in the urban ethos by pointing out the parochial and pretentious restrictions of perspectives. It can and must also engage in continual self-reconstruction.

If these two forms of apocalyptic eschatology are wrong, are there positive constructs that can help in determining whether a particular project is legitimate? That is, what would be the marks of a specific urban thrust into the future that does involve a movement toward ultimate fulfillment and transformation? Inevitably advocates of metropolitanization and localization, bussing of school children, and local control of school boards, public housing projects and poor people scatteration, community organization and casework social service, architectural cosmetics and advocacy planning, expressways and mass transit systems, suburban cluster villages and greenbelts, and urban renewal priorities, all claim that these specific projects are part of the march toward redemption of man and the urban environment. What meta-ethical models are to be used to legitimate creative projects?

The entire New Testament is an attempt to discern and identify the marks of particular personal and social projects that lead toward the fulfillment and transformation of man. Throughout the debates of the various texts, two symbols are crucial. These are "resurrection" and "communion of the saints." These eschatological symbols bear numerous patterns of meaning that, demythologized, can provide some sense of direction.

While an enormous amount of Christian piety focuses on Jesus, and thereby summarizes prophetic, priestly, kingly, and rabbinic motifs from the previous tradition and bears parallels to the rabbinic motifs of wise teacher of the law, the core of New Testament faith is centered around the notion of the resurrected Christ. The notion of resurrection, almost an impossible notion for the modern mind to comprehend because the churches have lied about it so often, actually is decisive for the value systems of those involved in the urban ethos. Like all symbols, it has a number of levels which must be sorted out. First, it means that he who by grace personally exemplified the prophet, priest, king, and rabbi in the human community allowed recognition of the fact that personal life is of such ultimate importance that it continues to have meaning beyond the end of any natural finality. The individual may not be wantonly disposed of because there is an ultimacy in personal life that is worthy of reverence. Not only when a person is a member of a group is he to be regarded, but always. And he is to be empowered to assume prophetic, priestly, kingly, and rabbinic roles. Second, the physical and spiritual life of the person are inseparable. The logic of the very human experience that the welfare or impairment of one affects the welfare or impairment of the other is radicalized to its final conclusion. When one dies the other dies, when one is restored the other is restored. Thus, projects in the modern city must keep body and soul together in quite literal senses. Massive attacks on spiritual and physical poverty are both legitimate and morally mandatory. But one without the other is merely fatal. Third, it means that there is a necessary continuity between the present and the future. The future which negates the present must also fulfill, and not only negate, ordinary historical experience.[9] Most important, it means that those crucified for the sake of justice and righteousness are the first fruits and bearers of that kind of creative order that is decisive for the future. Thus, the moral first loyalty is to those cast into Gehenna, the junk heaps of the city, whether geographically outside society's gates or within the boundaries. Those who actually believe in resurrection, and not some zombie magic, are those who descend into the junk heaps of the cities and free the people found in bondage there. The actualized believers in resurrection are often not confessing Christians. Movements like that profoundly symbolized in the apt designation "Resurrection City," and perhaps the establishment of Israel, provide modern man with a graphic expression of what resurrection means. In these, there is the actualization of a new identity and visibility (which doubters deny as valid) beyond crushing events and oppressive and systemic personal destruction by even the "most enlightened" regimes. Such events are truly revelation in that they unveil the depths of the promise and pathos of life.

Such views stand in contrast, on the one hand, to the false spiritualizers of life. They only want some variety of "immortal life," a concept that comes from their expectations of the future and their planning above physical necessity. Urban priority projects, especially theologically interpreted ones, are, to these, desirable so long as they do not disturb the economic structure or power arrangements but only transform the psychic and interpersonal structures into a more pacific spirit. They want no resurrection, merely an other worldly heaven of eternal bliss. Their "concern" must ultimately be judged egocentric. The promise is believed to be fulfilled in present self. The false materialists, on the other hand always establish some very concrete geographically locatable Heavens and Hells, some exclusive location for their kind of soul, which immediately enters into mortal combat with those outside. But ultimately they have to settle for purgatory where the foreseeable future is sure to be for such projections.

The symbol of the "communion of the saints" also suggests many levels of understanding about the future.

First, it is linked with the notion of resurrection in that that personal event is not separate from a community context. The "general resurrection" of which the messianic resurrection is the particular prototype is a way by which both purely individualist and purely collectivist conceptions of the future are ignored as viable possibilities in favor of a person-in-community and community-of-persons possibility. Any morally and theologically authentic project must involve the possibility of personal fulfillment through participation in a community context, and any community must be structured so as to permit and evoke spontaneous and self-sacrificing interaction among persons.

Second, the notion of community of the saints relates the past to the future. Those who struggle for justice, freedom, righteousness, love, and peace become, from the perspective of ultimate possibility, linked to the whole parade of those who have fought similar battles before and those who will later. We live in immediacy, but "now" does not exhaust that immediacy. Participation in a common life makes the immediate problems of life fall into a structure of worth and power that extends beyond the particular memory of a person or nation or church and anticipates the possibilities of those yet to come. The Hebraic notion that this communion is established with the future coming of the messianic age, and the Christian notion of the Second Coming,[10] are indicative of the extensions of human consciousness beyond any specific social foundation. Man's sense of community can and does leap backward in memory and forward in imagination and is not merely a function of experience. Therefore, it makes sense to read, study, and feel an immediate kinship with prophets of the eighth century B.C., and it makes sense to celebrate a common meal as a symbolic anticipation of the commonality of those past and present with those yet to come.

Third, the notion of the community of the saints is not based upon the recovery of an integration with nature. Heaven and earth, says the mythic formulation, are to be transformed; the entire created order is to be humanized—transformed to serve and grace humanity. And natural differences such as race and sex are in no way crucial categories to fundamental humanity. But both the kinds and qualities of intelligence that encounters nature and the kinds and qualities of technical mastery that subdues it are ethically dependent upon the kinds and qualities of human relations which they serve and express.

In short, a *credo* adequate to the whole of the quest for models by which to identify specific projects in the urban ethos that are valid must have elements in it that theologically have been worked out through the symbols of "resurrection" and "community of the saints."

The Kingdom of God

The "Kingdom of God" is the overriding biblical symbol for the future, and it is a necessary conceptual norm to which all the eschatological motifs, including resurrection and community of the saints, point. The notion of the Kingdom of God, at least twenty-five centuries old, contains a series of related levels that are of fundamental significance for any attempt to evaluate projects toward the future.

First it indicates that the fundamental shape of the future is to be defined politically. The word "kingdom" is the fundamental metaphor by which the biblical tradition understands human social destiny.[11] It indicates the priority of political transformation over both existential or spiritual and natural transformation. Fulfillment and transformation of humanity and community take place first within a social-political context and, through them, secondarily, the humanization of the forces of cosmos and creation.

Second, the notion of the Kingdom of God protects God's sovereignty. That is, God is transcendent. No one can know the ultimate. It is in the establishment of social-political relations that God appears, in those structures that point to nonapocalyptic transformation toward the future, that point toward the ultimacy of personal identity, and toward community. But no one and no group have these exhaustively, thus the prospect of perpetual reform is always present.

The vision of perpetual radical reform toward the future is born only proleptically, only in a provisional way that points toward the breaking of the possibilities of the future into the realities of the now. And it is in distinctive social roles that these possibilities are discovered. The prophet, out of his awareness of the guiding unity of history, his compassion for the people, and his discernment of the disjunction between the two speaks forth in compelling symbols that capture the imagination of the people so that they see the disjointedness of the "is" and the "ought." The priest enacts cultically the celebration of the unity of life, as revealed in the promissory fragments of life as revealed in the transitions of birth, maturity, marriage, work, and death. The king attempts to combine in the patterns of law and statecraft the social mechanisms that hint toward the true Kingdom. And the rabbi, to become the theologian in the Christian traditions, engages in critical reinterpretation of the past as a prologue to the present and as a proximate guide to the future. No one finally succeeds, but each contributes to the discernment of the possible end of man and society that is beyond the empirically present. And each, when they play out their roles with integrity, give rise to an urgency in living toward ends that border on revolutionary power.

Thus, there is a revolutionary motif; but it is not that of the apocalypticists. Transformation is always about to break in from the future. There is an impatience in the symbol and an audacity among those who grasp it. There is to be a new construction of social life, a new covenant written on the hearts of men, a new constitution for human relations, the vision of which relativizes all loyalties to present social constructs and encourages the courageous leap toward new ones. But the new is simultaneously partially present in the promises of past and present. Thus we do not attack that which is past and present. Rather we rearrange it in new ways that point toward the future. And that future can be anticipated among those who declare citizenship in God's Kingdom and not in the past or in the passing present.

But the notion of the coming Kingdom of God is not only optimistic. Transformation bears within it the temptation through moral presumption to overextend one's efforts. Thus the symbol demands a principle of exclusion. Not all and everything is to be fulfilled. Only those things which in fact lead to the ultimate reign of God are to be included. In the New Testament period, people thought they knew what these things were. They were represented in the immediate presence of the Messiah and the subsequent message and movement in his name. These were presumed to lead directly to an immediate transformation in the urban ethos. The injunction of the Lord "from on high" to return to the city and form a new community—with a transformed social-economic life after the near dissolution of the movement—and the bearing of the transformed message of the Kingdom of God to the cities of the Hellenistic world was a relatively faithful attempt to articulate and identify those things that can and cannot lead to the ultimate vision of the future, the Kingdom of God.

The fundamental importance of these themes embodied in the term Kingdom of God has been obscured and trivialized to urban man by a crude literalism. The Kingdom motif has led to notions of autocratic rulership and messianic politics and to a confusion between a particular policy or leadership and the will of God.

The expectation of the pending transformation both in the mythological world of the early church and in much church history has been so literal that the failure of a cataclysmic ending to occur has been taken as a failure of the symbol. Numerous antisocial pietists think the Reign of God has pertinence only within the private sphere and have given succor to the development of modern personalism. But perhaps more subtle and most dangerous has been the notion of divine rule which has been assumed under this concept. Unfortunately, the notion of the Kingdom of God was developed under the impact of a political order that presumed a fixed quantity of political power; hence the notion of the Kingdom of God as the political form of the communion of the saints became authoritarian. If one side (God) had all the power, then the other side (man) could have none and the moral norm of passive submission rose to ascendancy. This zero-sum concept of God, technically called "monergism" and celebrated in even some liberal concepts of ultimate and total dependency, has been under attack by the Separatist and Independent traditions for several centuries. Indeed, one can find a "third history" of the Western church, distinct from either Catholicism or Classical Protestantism and written in the cities by heretics, Anabaptists, and radicals. This tradition is now emerging into prominence as a possible interpretation of the relationship of God to man. This modified "synergistic" concept presupposes that the common rule of God is not contrary to the common rule of man. God's infinite power and authority do not restrict the capacity of human power but expand and serve as a base for it precisely as, it has long been argued, God's love serves as a basis for the human capacity to love. The notion that every man shall by grace in the Kingdom be face to face with God means, among other things, that each person shall have direct access to the source of power and value. Indeed, the Kingdom of God as the normative political structure of the communion of the saints means that any project that hopes to establish love and spontaneity and immediacy between persons must at the same time give the participants in that community direct access to the structures and skills of power and to its legitimating value systems. Otherwise the community is not authentic. It will not bear the marks of the ultimate future and it will not endure. The rule of, by, and for all is a mark of the politically necessary structure of the ethically legitimate project. The fact that the political order envisaged is "of God" means that it may not be contrary to the ultimate structures of power and value.

The failure of the church to refine continually the qualities of projects that lead toward the Kingdom of God has been due, in short, to a continual fixation on the spiritual in contrast with the social-political meanings of religious language, thereby systematically divorcing spiritual life from its ground. But even the failure suggests some very important keys that open the way to fuller social theory.

The symbol of the Kingdom of God fails due to calcification; but it also demands prophetic articulation of where, in the social-political order, God's presence may be found. What are the things in ordinary social life that should be decisive, what best represents what is of ultimate power and worth? And that question, in turn, raises two fundamental issues that we have already faced in other terms: what is the relation between the sacred and the secular social theory; how can we deal with the variations of perspective on what the ultimate power and worth are? And how ought that be structured in urban life?

The partial solution to the problem of an adequate *credo* found in eschatology is yet insufficient. We must pursue the problem further, as did the Judeo-Christian traditions as they faced new urban situations, by looking at the formation of doctrine and the development of ecclesiology.

Chapter VI

THEOLOGICAL MODELS AS NORMATIVE
SOCIAL THEORY

There are many biblical motifs that have importance for human consciousness, but we have claimed that the most critical one for the development of urban styles of life is a peculiar kind of future-orientation. Eschatological accents have given unique shape to the Western world in both their valid and pathological forms. And contemporary styles of life, personal and social, governed as they are by a sense of vision and project, are inconceivable without this foundation.

But the biblical sources did not render a very comprehensive meta-ethical model for large-scale social systems. A sense of purpose and direction in terms of the Kingdom of God did not provide a full-blown *credo* pertinent to cosmopolitan life. Nor did this vision commend itself to the cultured despisers who found themselves bound to alternative loyalties. For the biblical definition of the "good" did not answer the decisive problems of "right" and "fit" that must be a part of a *credo* capable of giving shape to a civilization.

It is in the fourth century that the sectarian Jewish movement called Christianity, with a continuing yet fresh understanding of resurrection, the communion of the saints, and the Kingdom of God, but having had its mythological-magical, apocalyptic interpretations of these fail when the final ending of the world did not take place, had to come to terms with the institutions and structures of urban civilization. For with the rise of Constantine, new dimensions of the fundamental problems of an adequate *credo* were forced to the surface. How was the problem of the one and the many to be solved in the midst of a multiplicity of peoples and loyalties? Clearly the hegemonic polytheism of Rome led again and again to the war of all against all to control the hegemony. And how were the problems of coercive power, as evidenced in the emperor, and worth, as evidenced in the Christian vision of the future, to be joined in a *credo* that could give shape to a creaking, confusing proto-cosmopolitan ethos? To be sure the problem of coercion and violence had been joined for individual Christians and Jews when conscription was the practice of the Roman armies. But now the Christian emperor raised the question of socially structured use of the sword by Christianity itself.

The most readily available tools for the construction of an integrated meta-ethical model for the Constantinian period were those of Roman piety, the Greek philosophies drawn from the experience of the ancient *polis,* and Stoic natural-law theory. Each of these had elements that grasped the human situation in its more profound dimensions, and were therefore relatively strong and durable. But each of these also had ingredients that at their root were dysfunctional. They could not provide, as all tried, an adequate *credo* that gave purpose to the new society emerging in their midst. Badly needed was a fundamental reorganization of the underlying ways of conceiving of reality. As R. G. Collingwood stated some time ago:

> Christian writers in the time of the Roman Empire asserted, and no historian today will deny, that in their time the science and civilization of the Greco-Roman world were moribund. . . . The Patristic diagnosis of the decay of Greco-Roman civilization ascribes that event to a metaphysical disease. The Greco-Roman world, we are told, was moribund from internal causes, specifically because it has accepted as an article of faith . . . a metaphysical analysis of its own absolute presuppositions which was at certain points erroneous.[1]

The Judeo-Christian notions of a single center of power and worth made concrete in human existence through historical events that give rise to eschatological expectations supplied corrective ingredients. But they did not do so without difficulty or resistance. The social-political implications of the Kingdom motif were not made explicit. How then was this eschatologically oriented movement that focused primarily on highly personal, interpersonal, and small-group understandings of reality to render a *credo* that was compelling in a world dominated by powers and values foreign to its own heritage? It did so through the development of the doctrine of the Trinity. Through this doctrine as worked out in the debates of the fourth and fifth centuries, the *credo* was further developed that gave descriptive and prescriptive meaning to cosmopolitan life.

We turn to this period, therefore, because it is the first and most extensive effort in the postbiblical West to articulate a new doctrine. We look at this period not only to draw, if possible, from its content, but to see how the formative theorists did what they did. For out of their efforts was developed the most complete symbol set for the interpretation of the urban ethos the world has ever developed. If, as Whitehead once contended, all modern philosophy is a footnote to Plato and Aristotle, the fundamental *credos* of modern social theory can be said to be a footnote to the basic motifs worked out in the development of doctrine in the Trinity—including wrong and pathological ones. In the formation of the doctrine of the Trinity, all fundamental options, ancient and modern, for the interpretation of "right" in large-scale social systems appear.

Our capacity to turn to this period anew derives in part from the present context in which we live. From the theological side, we note that denominational theology is, for the most part, dead. Protestant tendencies to see this age as the fall of the church and Catholic tendencies to read this history through the eyes of literalistic Thomism are declining. This means, as Roger Hazelton has pointed out, that theology finds itself "within a greatly widened perspective, whether it is called 'mainline,' 'classical' or 'consensus' theology. Under the impact of the ecumenical movement, unexpected correspondences and convergences of doctrine have indeed appeared."[2] And in such a context, the search for common roots gains a fresh plausibility. From the sociological side, urbanized men live again under the influence of imperial societies dominated by a proto-cosmopolitan ethos that does not have the conceptual or symbolic tools to grasp, direct, and frame its many possibilities. And viewed historically, as suggested earlier, there are direct lines of continuity between the fragmentary *credos* of the social theorists and the theological traditions that they reflect in secular form. In this early period, these elements were, in principle, woven together, even if they were not so in fact. Hence, by reconstructing and reinterpreting these early models, we may hope to see the emergence, reintegration, and updating of an adequate *credo*. At least we may point to some of the tools required for "depth-sociology."

The ability to turn to this period also depends on a capacity to read the analogies between debates about the nature of the gods and social theory, for as we have seen, every fundamental dispute about social reality and social obligation is rooted in a battle of the conceptions of the gods—a battle of *credo*. And in this matter there are only a limited number of basic options:

Polytheism, for example, is not only a primitive religious phenomenon that was current in the age of Constantine, but a perennial major alternative in the understanding of social reality.[3] It has had advocates at all stages of civilized life. Polytheism is at root a notion that there is not one true center of ultimate good power, but many. It is the belief that there is an innate and holy vitality in all varieties of natural and social forms and that the fundamental structure of reality is so pluralistic that distinctiveness has its own ultimate validity. There cannot, and should not, finally be discrimination among the powers and values; instead each has its due in spontaneous recognition of its uniqueness, so long as it is dealt with sincerely. In our own experience, the rampant personalism of suburbia, radicalized in the self-mysticism of some contemporary youth movements, is one of the chief modern recrudescences of polytheism, and is both rooted in and expressive of antiurban loyalties.

Historically, polytheism has been unable to maintain itself in the urban ethos. It did not survive the basic critiques of the Constantinian era, nor can it survive today as a dominant way of conceiving of reality without great cost to society. In the name of radical freedom, it has always lead to tyranny. Urban life, with its necessarily deep interdependence, requires the maintenance of common structures that allow predictable behavior across the boundaries of the spontaneous genius of particulars in every period of history. Hence, the creation of early cities in the ancient world, and of viable communities in highly diverse melting pots of modern cities is accomplished by the principle of hegemony of interest groups legitimated by the hegemony of their gods. The more powerful centers of worth and power organize themselves around an especially powerful one and conspire to overrule the lesser powers by sheer weight and force. There is little quest for whatever common features might be found, and each is loyal to the conspiracy for his own benefit and as a means of gaining increasing ascendancy. Worship, a fundamental form of symbolic action, is bribery of the gods. The strongest gods get the greatest bribe. Correspondingly, the primary modes of human action are means of ingratiation with the established powers in order to gain personal status in the given structure. The hegemony need not be gained through physical coercion alone but may be derived from moral, ideological, or fideist consensus. Consensus controls the social will and is both less costly and more enduring than sheer coercion. If radical individuality of many of the powers is proclaimed as the fundamental nature of reality, the only thing that can hold together the community, short of violence, is "thought control." It is not the development of doctrine, in this case, but the development of dogma in the more severe meanings of that word. Dogma, then, tends to be enforced by coercion or more efficiently, through a unified secular, usually bureaucratized, clerical ideology that controls access to social participation. There is necessarily unity at the top in either case.[4] This general human experience was dramatically experienced by the peoples of the Mediterranean stage prior to Constantine's entry.

To challenge such an organization or conspiracy one must organize a counterconspiracy, a dualism. The gods in power find themselves confronted by those who may have benefited sufficiently by the organization that they are rapidly on the upgrade, but who have been systematically excluded from decision-making or symbol-bearing. Such a counterforce, or heresy, gains its own power by collecting lower rank deities into counterorganization. It is true that the initial hegemony has always considered any outside the conspiracy as "the enemy," but we now have a dualistic interpretation of the gods from both sides. The powers of light are pitted against the powers of darkness, and each prepares for and attempts to anticipate the apocalyptic confrontation; each claims to be the force of light, the proof of which is enacted on the established side by paternalistic repression; those in the counterposition by puritanical perfectionism.

The Judeo-Christian tradition has ever felt the danger of these possibilities, although it engaged in a counterforce through Constantine and although these possibilities were subsequently woven into the tradition itself at several points. But it always began its interpretation on another note than polytheism. It began with monotheism. The pluralism of vitalities and values are differentiated from a more ultimate unity. There is ultimately one good power in the universe, not many.[5] Truth is one, Goodness is one, Power is one. There is a center of meaning and purpose for all.

The notion of singular sovereignty, however, leads again and again to the identification of present conditions or the immediate social fabric with the will of God. *Immediate* monotheism, that which accents the direct, unmediated connection between human life and the Divine as in the divinization of political authority tends to be conservative and demands a monolithic unity through a convergence of power and value. But in its primordial urban period, the Judeo-Christian tradition did not allow the unadulterated and immediate monotheism to stand. It was suspicious of social-political claims to immediate experience or authority from God. In contrast, the one God has been seen as distinct from, never fully present in, the state of affairs. The God of the Jahwist, the Prophets, and Jesus was understood to be a *mediate*, not an immediate God, although no less alive and significant. The One is found concretely in promissory events, especially those that produce particular patterns of creative and just order, particular "vocations," political movements, and the indirections of metaphor and analogy that provide a promise of power, worth, and truth.

There was, of course, no single model in the Judaism and Christianity of this early period but there are three metaphors or interpretive models that are necessarily related in Christian thought and both nearly universal in their acceptance within the Christian community and integral to the problems at hand. Still further, these models have so pervaded the shape of Western thought and institutional life that their influence is impossible to avoid. The precise character of the models and the relations between their terms remain crucial centers of controversy, not only explicitly in the theological debates, but implicitly in the courts, in political rhetoric, in educational circles, and among urbanologists; for differences in values, accents, and parameters in the interpretation of these models make tremendous differences when the models are used to interpret the whole ebb and flow of human life, as they frequently are without consciously knowing or admitting the sources.

The three fundamental motifs are: the one, sovereign God makes himself concrete first in creative, just order (The Father); he also becomes concrete in transformed personal identity as seen in his Son (Jesus Christ), who was at the same time fully God and fully man; and finally he becomes concrete in the freedom of righteous, spirited movement (The Holy Spirit). The claim that the ultimate One becomes concrete in these three presences demands that we conceive of the one God as becoming operative in human experience in pluralistic ways. These three conflicting, highly formal, theological motifs or models gather into a single doctrine monotheistic, dualistic, and pluralistic ingredients simultaneously. They may well provide the tools for approaching the crucial problems. The first motif suggests that urban life can have meaningful coherence in creative and just order. While we may not know or see the *ultimate* coherence, the model demands that we seek for innovative patterns of worth and power that engender creative, just order. We cannot presume to give normative guidance in the urban ethos if we do not attempt to adjudicate between conflicting opinions and to work out a coherent understanding of power and worth that issues in a principle of order that is creative and equitable for all in the family of man. The second motif points out that in crucial historical events the divine and the human are integrally related without losing their analytical autonomy and distinctiveness. Thus, not only does transformed personal identity become a concern of ultimate significance, but faith and reason, religion and culture, theology and society are not irrelevant to each other, even if they are analytically distinct. And the third motif indicates that constancies such as those involved in the first two models are made alive only when differentiated and linked to charismatic movement. This accents the necessity for dynamic personal and group freedom and innovation. But we must look at the historical origins and influences of these models if we want to show their continued relevance.

The Background of the Model

The debates leading to the fourth century that produced a re-structuring of the interpretive model of man and his place in the world were at first largely centered on the problems of unity and diversity. It took the form of how to have one God among many pieties. Is there *a* right order? The question of unity had been problematic in Greek social thought at least since Aristotle's defense of hegemony by polemical use of a line from the *Iliad:* "The rule of many is not good; one ruler let there be." Alexander, Aristotle's student, had taken this quite seriously and forged a relative unity out of the Mediterranean world. The problem of unity was also indigenous to Jewish, and therefore Christian, thought, but there were many interpretations of that unity. And what was at stake was by no means "purely" theo-logical; all sides informed, were informed by, and were at each point related to, political and cultural issues. The partisans did not, of course, sit down and think "Now we are going to do so-cial theology" in contrast to other kinds. They were trying to work out the fundamental *credos* of life that could not, in this context and by their nature, be other than social and political. Subsequent divisions between theology and social life have al-lowed many historians and theologians to forget the way in which they both were and must be related, if they are to be vital. But such forgetfulness prevents them from understanding why so much politics was involved in the formation of doctrine, and allows them to quietly muse about how curious it is that people felt strongly about such issues.

The conceptions of monotheistic unity took numerous forms but had several common themes. Prior to Constantine, the dis-cussion centered around the term "Logos," a term that bridged divisive intellectual currents because it was common in the phi-losophy of the day and was identified in Christian sources with the "Word Incarnate." Philo, for example, tended to see in the Logos both "God's agent in creation and the medium by which the human mind gets in touch with him," and thus the Logos was equated with "archetypes in God's mind which are expressed by his acts of creation and providence."[6] What was at stake at this point was a monotheism that sees all the world as a "great chain of being," to use again Arthur Lovejoy's phrase, at the apex of which was the one God. Culturally, this vision provided a pattern for comprehending in hierarchical fashion various dimensions of diversity on a vast scale, it claimed for the diversities a common rationality and it integrated the various cultural loyalties by preserving the monotheistic sentiments common to partially Hellenized Judaism, Christianity, and the intellectual world in general. It was a vision developed in the academic centers of the age, and in that setting it provided a set of conceptual tools by which man could rationally approach and arrange all phenomena. Erik Peterson, for example, states quite flatly that the Logos monarchism was developed for its pedagogical and culturally unifying functions. But socially and politically, also, such a view linked all present power with the single cosmic structure as it had been linked in the pagan world, and it thereby accounts for and legitimates hierarchical, corporative administration from the top down. Not only, therefore, could it provide an apologetic against accusations of subversive teaching and activity, but it suggested a proper obedience to authority for all under the Logos. An organically integrated vision is provided in which "the powerful is that which constitutes the efficacy and end of things, and it appear as the *holy*, as that which has power or excellence. . . ."[7]

For many of the period, there was a series of hierarchical and powerful mediators between God and man, and they saw both these mediators and less powerfully that which was most real about man himself as a universal quality that was manifest in the particular. Hence the elaboration of the universal encompassed each particular and provided the principle of cosmopolitan cultural formation.

Yet, throughout this period, a problem confronted the theorists which recurs throughout theological history. If there is agreement in the unity of the one God, or universal principle, as the creator and order of all, how is it that those who most earnestly confess the single sovereignty are persecuted by the one political order that that God must maintain? The theological idea of one center of power and worth has obvious analogies to a politically monolithic structure; but the one denies the other. Perhaps, argued some, all worldly and social-political powers are not of God, but only pretend to be. The true *Logos* may be religious in contrast to social-political.

It was not long before the viability of this possibility was put to the test, for Constantine came to power in the early part of the fourth century. Here the social-political and religious seemed to be joined. Constantine's sympathy for the Christian God as an assurance of victory and his early toleration of and later recognition of the necessity to use Judeo-Christian motifs to bind together a scattered empire offered the possibility of a social order that directly embodies power and worth in a truly cosmopolitan way. It was necessary to ask whether a meta-ethical model to sustain such an ethos could be developed. A more subtle form of theological *credo* was required.

Many hotly resisted any socially and politically informed theological definitions of the one God. On the one hand, there was a clear recognition of the validity of monotheism. It was recognized that there was one ultimate worth and power and not a multiplicity of worths and powers whose validity depended upon where one lived and what race one belonged to. Each particular set of worths and powers could be brought under more universal criticism. On the other hand, several defenders asserted that Christianity was superior to the worth and power of secular thought and political power, and not merely contiguous with them in a hierarchy of validity. The power and worth of Christ defeated the power and worth of the political order when crucifixion and suppression by political authority did not once and for all seal his worth and power in a tomb. Thus the validity of a purely political *credo* was also qualified.

Often, it was those most committed to sustaining eschatological themes who resisted such interpretations. Tertullian in the West and Methodius in the East, for example, accented the eschatological community of saints in the New Jerusalem and resurrection in a millennial Kingdom. They preserved a crucial distinction between what was given in society and what that promises for the future, between creation and salvation, between what present reality is and what life will in fact be after transformation. Thus they claimed a fundamental tension between even the best social arrangement of powers and values and religious ones, because the former are subject to transformation in the future under the impact of the latter.

It was recognized, accordingly, that monotheistic statements based on a primarily rational Logos doctrine allow no tension, but only continuity between present rulers and the divine ruler. Indeed, as George H. Williams has brilliantly shown, many of the fathers of the church under the influence of the "great chain of being" model were at first betrayed into an uncritical acceptance of political monotheism on theological grounds once a sympathetic ruler came to the fore, and nearly a century of debate had to occur before the church had developed the tools to stand against the emperor when necessary even while affirming political power and worth.[8]

But the attempt to deal with cosmopolitan power and worth through Logos monotheism temporarily obscured major strands of the Judeo-Christian biblical heritage that had to be rehabilitated later. The Jewish concept of monotheism was a radical one shared by Christianity. And "radical monotheism," fashioned out of Israel's social, political, and theological conflict with earlier polytheism, drew a sharp distinction between creator and created, between the divine and that which was not. Indeed, the distinction is accented by the concept of the Fall, which makes the breach more radical and serves as the great equalizer of all men. One cannot know reality or claim righteousness merely by reciting the names of the gods, or by being born into class, sex, clan, or race that has an ancient and honorable mythological heritage. Judgments based on each distinction are never intrinsically right. The natural models of personal and social identity are of course present and powerful, but no longer of the same mold as the normatively valid ones. Natural models are unavoidable but they do not grasp deeply enough either the way things are or the way they ought to be. God is set against the given worths and powers of creation, although they are his. They are to be sustained and maintained only through a transformation in accordance with a model that does not derive from them, but from that on which they too depend.

But if, on the grounds of radical monotheism that entails a sense of alienation in the Fall, one rejects a polytheism of the war of all against all, or a polytheism that has developed into a hegemony of the strong dominating the weak, on the one hand, or a hierarchical conception of unified reality that leaves no room for the reality of tension or conflict, on the other, there would appear to be only one option left. One could turn to dualism, a dualism of the higher against the lower or one of the future against the present. Dualism always, of course, bears the danger of apocalyptic conflict. But it does recognize a fundamental distinction between questions of doctrine and those of social reality, between the promise of the future and the realities of the present. Indeed, large segments of both theological and social theory have subsequently chosen this option. Most forcefully it appears subsequently in the "two kingdom" theories of many Protestants on the theological side when they assert, following Martin Luther, that the Gospel has to do with the private reign of God in the hearts of men, and the Law governs the various and exterior orders of creation that are merely of this world, having nothing to do with the salvation of mankind or society. And it appears on the sociological side in the absolute distinction of ethics of personal obligation and the ethics of *realpolitik* among bourgeois sociologists rooted in the thought of Max Weber (probably under Lutheran influence) as well as in the identification of virtue and the proletariat in contrast to the unrighteous ruling classes in socialist theory from Karl Marx.

Under the influence of an eschatologically oriented tradition, however, the early Christian theorists choose another, more profound, option when confronted with the need to create a *credo* pertinent to the first, massive urban ethos. It was an option now nearly lost in the divorce of theology from the foundations of social theory but one which can be recovered by reconstruction of the doctrine of the Trinity as mentioned before. The doctrine of the Trinity means that the ultimate meta-ethical model must be pluralistic, but it must have a coherence that does not allow the parts to fly into fragmented pluralism. It means that there are never in human possibilities but two options; instead, there is always a third possibility that relates, flows from, and preserves the other two so that dualism never becomes final. It means that while there is only one center of ultimate loyalty, it is such that it may be appropriated in at least three decisive and distinct modes that are both independent and interrelated. But to show how this model emerged and what the various ingredients of it are in greater detail, we need to look at some of the crucial arguments that took place during the development of the model. In each case, the key term was Christological, for it focused on how the eschatological motifs fit new historical phenomena, it related personal identity to the formation of community, and it posed the question of the legitimacy of secular power.

(Many Christian thinkers wrongly see the exhaustion of Judaism at this point, for they perceive the undifferentiated, if radical, monotheism of Judaism as leading inevitably to the conflict that confronted early Christianity: a correct recognition of the separation but an inability to accept God's offer of a new relationship. They see Christianity as responding by accenting Christological formulations in a way that Judaism could not do. In fact, however, we can first see that it was the Jewish ingredients which again and again preserved the new theological awareness from their own temptations to Gnosticism on one side and to Christocentric monotheism on the other. We must, secondly, see that the affirmation of the distinction between creator and created was affirmed in both forms of radical monotheism. In Christian thought it led to a provisional dualism, which could be overcome only by a fatherly notion of a creative, just, and merciful order related to the Christian concept of the Son of God. Within the Jewish community it led to an analogous dualism resolved in structurally similar fashion in terms of the two sides of the concept "Chosen People." The difference is that, at this juncture in history when the fundamental motifs for subsequent development were worked out on Gentile grounds, the Christian way of resolving the necessary dualism had more universal implications and at the same time more personal overtones, while the Jewish integration of chosenness and peoplehood found its primary validity on this question within a specific community. This historical observation, however, does not compromise the universality implied in the Jewish concept of radical monotheism. On such grounds as these, theological ethics may well be inclined to affirm that the Jews are the Chosen People of God's Covenant, that the Gentiles become related to them through Jesus Christ, and that dialogue with the Jews is necessary for Christianity to understand and preserve itself. The problem of Jewish "theology" can, for those informed by Christianity, also serve as a metaphor for the possibility that peoples around the world who do not wish to become explicitly Christian can develop radically monotheistic and eschatological ingredients of an urbane *credo* out of their own experience that are fundamentally valid. But here we are concerned primarily with formal theological responses in the fourth century. The theoretical point is that radical monotheism, any singular view of power or worth, leads to duality, because it demands the recognition of that which is not God. Institutionally, the divine and even the positive concretion of creative order in any given state are not the same thing. Yet some affirmation relation between the poles must be worked out. Otherwise, all of ordinary life becomes religiously suspect or religion becomes socially and politically suspect.)

The Options

There were five major options that appeared during the two centuries of debate:[9] the pietist sectarians, the conservative rationalists, the pluralistic catholics, the liberal rationalists, and the radical sectarians. All were clearly in the Judeo-Christian tradition in that they began their understanding with a concept of one God that was distinct from the created world, but present in it in ways that gave rise to eschatological expectation. They saw themselves as part of a movement that had world-historical significance and they understood the rise of Constantine and the formation of a new cosmopolitan ethos as a decisive chapter in that history to which they had to respond. While there are nuances of difference among people within each major option and overlappings between them, it is quite possible to construct a typology of the options according to the positions of prominent groups and spokesmen.

The first option, rooted in the personal and small group experiences of the churches when under persecution by pagan rulers can be seen in the pietist Donatist groups of North Africa. There was another aggressive wing of the Donatists that we shall treat later, but we should look first at this ultraconservative branch.[10]

The withdrawing, pietistic Donatists understood the one eschatologically concerned God through the prism of a particular understanding of Christ. Through the words of scripture, the Word was made present to each believer. When pagan authorities demanded that the holy writings be turned over because they were a threat to the civil deities, the Donatists refused. The personal moral integrity which they had gained through the power of Christ was such that many were brought to martyrdom. In this crisis experience an intensive, personal, moral rigor and a clear criterion for who was in the holy community (and who was out) was established. Simultaneously, the earlier Christian suspicion of all political power was reinforced and the personal, interpersonal, and small group tendencies of the minority Christian tradition were accented. Under the influence of these factors, the Donatists accented a conception of Christ that made Him the source of legitimation for personal righteousness. It led to a highly disciplined personalism that looked with great suspicion on all objective social institutions. In the face of both pagan and, later, Constantinian civil authorities in collaboration with the church, the suspicion remained, and the tactic for dealing with all large-scale social-political forms became noncooperation. Indeed, even the institutional offices and forms of their own church were suspect and seen as having no validity except where made right by the intense personal moral rigor of those who officiated in them. This is not to say that there was no sense of community, for indeed the term "Our Father," which invoked the first person of the Trinity, was understood to apply to those who were in Christ in a peculiarly personal and morally rigorous way. But there was little of any notion that a single god could give shape to an overall social system. The objective social order is always a power structure that must be resisted. And the Spirit, which was seen as coming from the personal experience under Christ was understood in terms of the inward charisma of the "in-group," that would give comfort to the persecuted.

The withdrawing sectarian understanding, while integrating a community under a personalistic Christ and engendering an existential courage in moments of political crisis that puts many to shame, could not fundamentally contribute to what was most needed: aid in the construction of a meta-ethical model that could give shape to a new civilization. It did, in fact, nurture a pluralism by preserving some of the distinctive religious and social practices of North Africa; but it could not account for the legitimacy of this preservation without negating, in principle, all other possibilities. It could not, in short, render an understanding of personality that would take responsibility for the general shape of things, nor a community that could see itself in a common covenant with the communities of man in a cosmopolitan setting. But it does provide a definition of personality that has a sense of intrinsic right and has a will to stand against great odds in times of adversity, even if it stands at the boundary of a social dualism that had finally to be rejected.

The second option, from among the most vigorous groups, was one that can be called "conservative rationalist." Led by a great theorist and historian Eusebius, this group saw both religion and society as governed by a rational principle emanating from the mind of God. This rational principle, the "Logos," served as a cosmological mediator between the supreme God and the created world of the new society. Indeed, the emerging civilization was itself an emanation of the one God's divine potency. The entire cosmos, including the civil order, was to be understood as a grand morphological system of which the Logos was the inner principle. Christ, the symbol of historical innovation and eschatological possibility was seen as a manifestation of the Logos, as were all great powers and principalities. Indeed, great rulers are also such manifestations. It was, therefore, a short jump to comparing Constantine and his work in creating a new cosmopolitan ethos with Christ and his work of promising a new eschatological order. As George Williams shows, the ruling principles of religion and the political ruler were regarded, by this group,

. . . as alike instruments . . . of the one Eternal Logos, the former to preach monotheism, to exorcise demons, and

to proclaim God's Kingdom; the latter to establish monotheism and, by routing the lesser gods around which the
demonic forces of nationalism and dissension centered, to
usher in the long promised forces of the messianic age. In
thus enthusiastically comparing Caesar and Christ it was
indeed hard for Eusebius not to leave the impression that
the work of a Christian Caesar was of more importance
than the work of Christ.[11]

By analogy, the Eusebians understood "God the Father" in a
similar way. As God the Father, to whom the son, Christ, was
related, was the patriarchal authority to be universally obeyed,
so the universalistic imperial drive of Constantine was to be
honored. And those spiritual centers of social reality that were
not subordinate to the "father" were deemed demonic. Although
individual, nonpolitical contemplative spiritual realities were
both permitted and encouraged, social-political spirituality was
to be brought into submission through the legitimizing exorcism
of the sons of mother church or, failing that, the sword of the
fatherly state.

What the Eusebians did see was the cosmological unity of
creation that makes every social ethos, no matter how "artifactual," dependent upon some ecologically integrated relationship.
The sensitivity to organic structure was frequently lost in the
West after the rejection of this option and a more dynamic rationalism was structured into social order. But the rejection was
for good reason. Unmodified, this view made present political
authority the visible, regnant ingredient of cosmic potency and
worth. The result of this, mostly Greek, view was that Constantine, at the time, and patriarchal authority subsequently in
much of Eastern Orthodoxy, for example, where Eusebian motifs are very important, became highly influential in all creedal
matters that pertained to social arrangement because it was
assumed Caesar embodied the supreme Logos.[12] In this view, a
conception of worth and power is engendered that supports and
sustains imperial power without tension. It is a view that nearly
looses the eschatological tension and prematurely identified the
law and order of the present regime with that of the Kingdom
of God. It is the founding principle of second, third, or other

Romes, and it is in this option that sectarian movements East and West find their greatest enemy.

In the first two views, a unity is found. But in the first it is centered in personal, interpersonal, and small-group piety that cannot give shape to large-scale social systems. In the second, a unity is constructed that is cosmic in scope and morphologically holistic in its conception. But it allows for diversity only through hierarchy and individual relationships with the archetypal patterns of the supreme Logos. In both views, a coordinated sense of right is developed but the former sees right only for "us" under Christ and not for society in general; while the latter sees right in terms of right order as dictated by patriarchal authority. Neither could develop a doctrine that related religious insight to social systems without prematurely identifying an existing state of affairs with the eschatological Kingdom. Hence both lost the transforming drive to new religious and social artifacts.

The option to which we next turn is much more pluralistic than either of the previous two. The "rational liberals" of the Constantinian period were the Arians. The Arians saw God the Father as sole and undifferentiated unity that is radically different from creation. The Logos or Christ for them was the rational principle that was to overcome the dualism produced by radical monotheism. But the Logos was not a part of the reality of God, nor of the world in its given state. It was something other, something created by God, but it had no soul. It was primarily structured wisdom. Speaking of the Logos, the watchword became "There was when he was not." Hence the structure that unites the sacred and the divine with the created and the human is also something created. But it was not really human either. It was superhuman. They asserted that this intermediary being was mutable, it could change or be changed in its essential structure and thus a kind of "liberal" dynamic rationalism was involved. The Logos was neither "fully god" nor "fully man." Leaving aside the more esoteric metaphysics involved, we can from a social-theological perspective suggest that such an assertion makes sense only if one perceives that they were really structuring a series of cultural and religious values that stand hierarchically above man, that attempt to relate God to man,

but that are intrinsically independent of God and of human existence. There is a multiplicity of free-floating values and powers
with no rootage. This led to a view of Constantine and other
rulers that made them beings of superior status to man, for they
were unities of the created Logos. Christ and Caesar indeed,
all given authority, are abstractions, finding their common form
in the fact that they were adopted by God through His created
Logos and gained thereby an autonomous state subordinate to
God but superior to men. The next step, as one might suspect,
was the creation of demigods, of saints, angels, and archangels
—a whole series of religiocultural "Goods" that ostensibly bound
society together and that were unassailable from man's side.
Everybody "knew" that these were right and were therefore
subject to them. Since man was inferior to these powers and
values and since there was nothing that had in fact overcome
the duality of creator and created so that man had access to
anything above the demigods to shatter their pretensions, religious, cultural, and political powers were beyond fundamental
criticism. A relativistic, tolerant, liberal rationalism was the appeal of these "realists." They could live cosmopolitan lives, but
they had no roots, no purpose, no transforming vision. In this
view we find a dynamic and differentiated view of the centers
of human loyalty and rationality that theoretically avoids the
self-righteousness of the withdrawing sectarians and the monolithic totalitarian tendencies of the Logos monotheists. But there
is no critical center, no "right," only a variety of levels and
rights, and no way of finding integrity for self or society. The
split between the divine and the human, between doctrine and
social reality, remains in spite of the proliferation of intervening
categories.

This view often emerges into dominance where conflicting
sectarian or patriarchal ideologies allow no stable peace. And
this view engenders an urbane tolerance of differences devoutly
to be wished in numerous settings. But in spite of its latitu-
dinarian utility, it finally cannot provide a constructive vision of
where to move. For it has no central criteria of right and no
vision as to a destiny.

The Arians were opposed, and finally defeated, by the Athanasians and the subsequent "pluralistic catholics," a fact that

must be troubling to those who see all disputes as determined by power relations, since most of the time the Arians and the Eusebians had imperial sympathy on their side. The Athanasians saw that the two sides of the tension between worth and power were always related, always distinct, always pressing for resolution of the tension, and always resisting premature identification and unity in any way except through divine action that pointed toward the eschaton, the chief example of which was Christ.

The Athanasian view of the one God was a radical one, too, in that it made a clear distinction between creator and created. But the one God was viewed in a more differentiated fashion. There are three dimensions of life where God's "Parenthood"[13] was seen. In the patterns of natural creation and in the creation of just and righteous social orders, the structuring of generative and sustaining and nurturing authority was of God. Yet that did not exhaust the modes of divine operation as the Arians thought. There was also the Sonhood, the innovative integration of creative power and created worth to overcome the alienation of that which is fully of God with that which is of man in historical life. It is an integrative event that gives shape to personal identity and authority; a selective affinity between dimensions of divine activity and dimensions of actual experience in social life that both grasps the decisive aspects of present experiences and renders a normative interpretation of how they ought to be. And there was the Spirit, which was to be the subject of debate later in the century.

The Athanasians were, however, most concerned with Christology, where they focused on the relation of the divine and the human. And they articulated what much of the church has thought was the proper doctrinal understanding—namely, that the dualism of creation and creator to which radical monotheism leads can be overcome only by a principle involving both. And from this conjunction derives a decisive definition of human vocation through transformed identity. Hence, following the option laid down by Athanasius, the Council of Chalcedon, meeting long after Athanasius' death, defined Jesus Christ explicitly as fully God and fully man. Thus was a crucial theological principle established, for the Athanasian motifs as clarified by Chalcedon provided a positive meta-ethical ingredient that shapes all subsequent Western history, social, cultural, and theological.

For the Athanasians and the "pluralistic catholics," even if not always for Athanasius himself, the dualism was overcome by the notion of the "Incarnation," which is distinct from creation. All men, under Christ, are called to a vocation of transformed identity and to take upon themselves responsibility for the general shape of things. At certain points in history, new supra-natural developments bring into being new positive centers of loyalty superior to powers and values found in the given structure of creation. Yet, they gather up and transform without destroying natural potencies by relating them integrally to that ultimate center of worth and power that remains transcendent. Such supra-natural unities relate ordinary existence to ultimate frames of reference and thereby provide leverage against established power and worth constructed only from natural insights and vitalities. The new urban ethos was such a potential unity that promised eschatological possibilities, but the particular structure of communities and persons who dominated in the present were still subject to judgment. On these foundations, man is both transformed and made free to transform and reconstruct. Talcott Parsons, from his particular sociological perspective, rightly sees the significance of this moment:

> The theological significance of the Christ figure as the mediator between God and man is central as defining the nature of man's relation to God. . . . It constituted the differentiation of Christianity as a religious system (a cultural system) from the conception of a "people" as a social system. . . . Further, the development of the conception of the Trinity . . . implied, correlative with the differentiation of the church from secular society, a differentiation within the religious system itself. . . . Action decisions in particular cases had to be left to the conscience of believers and could not be prescribed by a comprehensive religious law. . . . This differentiation occurred, however, within a genuine unity.[14]

To be sure, during this period, the leading theologians were more deferential toward the imperial power than the theory suggests, and they thought it a duty to pray for and support the power of even only relatively just rulers. But standing behind their credentials of Christ, they succeeded in declaring a degree of separation of identity from given created systems, while maintaining the relationship of their vocation to cosmopolitan society.

The doctrine of the two natures of Christ provisionally solved the problem of the relation of the divine and the human, although it took more than a century of sometimes vicious debate to establish a stable agreement as to the meaning of the formula. At least it focused the issues in such a way that some answers were clearly excluded on theological and practical grounds. It further suggested the terms by which subsequent battles could be fought. But it had not solved two other questions with which the fourth century dealt. What is the relation of the one and the many in cosmopolitan society, and what are the specific ethical implications of such a doctrine for urban man?

The terms for solving the first of these, the one and the many, were, however, already at hand. Throughout the Christological debates, the Holy Spirit is treated as subtle counterpoint. If the pietistic Donatists spoke of the pure body of Christ, so also of the pure Spirit. If the Eusebians treated Christ as an emanation of the Logos that fitted into the hierarchical chain of being, so also the Spirit. If the Arians saw the Logos as a rational, dynamic, middle-level "good," so also the Spirit. If the Athanasians saw Jesus Christ as of two natures, so also the Spirit had two aspects. At least, there was the theoretical parallel. In fact they did not work it out.

Very soon, however, three slight shifts of accent altered the victorious Athanasian model considerably. The Spirit was identified with, or placed within, the church. It was stated that the Spirit comes from the Father through the Son. But as the doctrine of the two natures of Christ became organizationally specified in terms of the identity of the "true apostolate," it became a personal symbol of ecclesiastical authority. The priesthood became the true representatives of Christ, deriving that authority from the Father. And the Spirit was seen as flowing through these channels to the collective church. The collective structure, however, only partially engaged the more static material and political powers of the day, and a genuine pneumatology that could give legitimacy to free-wheeling, innovative groups in cosmopolitan society never was established. The divine-human split that had been overcome in Christology was reestablished as a secular-sacred split on the institutional basis. One set of institutions was seen as based on reason and another on belief. A two-level social universe ensues, a natural and spiritual morality, a *Civitas Mundi* and a *Civitas Dei* as we see in St. Augustine's classic, even though it was highly significant that "city" is chosen as the critical word for the decisive area of both divine and worldly activity. Such a development meant, since the spiritual was deemed superior to the material, that the major structures of authority and the major expressions of culture were under the tutelage of the church and the *Civitas Dei* no longer was seen as the eschatological Kingdom, but as the established church. Through the back door, a crypto-Eusebian model actually developed. We have, it is true, come to see that the Middle Ages were not nearly so dark as our grandfathers thought, and that the church did, in large measure, keep alive and nourish cultural and civilizational dynamics. But the church also feared independent spiritual movements and prevented these from developing outside of the authority of Christ, partly because the "Christian civilization" was only precariously covering a deeply rooted paganism. The chief protectorate and bearer of that civilization could not let doctrine develop that would legitimate any movements, that would break its tenuous grip and unleash either the polytheisms of tribal and national loyalties that it had only so recently subdued, the rationalisms that nourished ungrounded relativism and passive tolerance, or the schismatic effects of fresh outbreaks of dualistic religious enthusiasm. Modern industrialization and urbanization that find rootage in the interstices of this system, however, accented Athanasian motifs and finally broke the bondage of these creedal distortions. These are precisely the forces that make it now possible and necessary to recover and reconstruct the more primal motifs in the development of doctrine.

Independence of the Spirit from the Son was not a part of

the major options of the fourth century. But that is not because it was not present, it is because it was suppressed. The fifth option, that of the aggressive sectarian Donatists accented precisely this option. This was the view that an oppressed and persecuted community, especially ethnic minorities, may develop a holy *esprit de corps* for the sake of justice and righteousness and engage in revolutionary action for the sake of a transformed society. All the dangers of apocalyptic, even fanatic, utopianism are present in this view, but when the fundamental rights of groups are suppressed by a social-political system claiming complete theological legitimacy, the restrained and tactical use of violence may be a necessity as an act of judgment against those who deny the pluralism they profess. The notion that the concept of intrinsic right, derived in principle from the need for a creative, just order that stands both in and beyond every given ethos, but pointing toward the ultimate good and power of that ethos, can engender a spiritual potency outside the consciousness of Christ. Such a contribution is suggested but never worked out by the early aggressive sectarians of North Africa. Indeed, the possibility did not gain any clear articulation until the Joachite movement several centuries later. Joachim of Floris is now seen by Marxist and some Christian scholars as a chief forerunner of the Reformation, even where Marxists and Reformers as well as Catholics suppressed the implications of this motif. And in current history, these are the motifs often accented in revolutionary, anticolonial socialism. As we shall see in the next chapter, it is this motif, when brought into conjunction with other motifs, that has in some measure already allowed fresh appropriation of the entire tradition in a way that influences our understanding of contemporary urban militance.

In the fourth century, however, the pluralistic catholics, by their treatment of Christ, had already set the stage for coping at the highest level of doctrine with major dimensions of the cosmopolitan ethos. God himself was differentiated into, and became concrete in human affairs, in three ways without compromising the ultimate unity. And these three ways each bore ethical norms for the urban ethos. In the parenthood principle of creative and just order is the ethical demand for generating and maintaining a nurturing pattern of authority in a non-patriarchal or authoritarian fashion; in the Sonhood principle is the demand for transformed personal identity that can respond with moral fiber in the face of crisis, but which can also take responsibility for the general shape of things; and in contrast with a merely pietistic sectarian position there is the Holy Spirit which bears a demand for the formation of an *esprit de corps* to defend intrinsic rights. Singular power and worth, at the ultimate level, can have, indeed demand, complexities of expression that enrich the common life, but that do not drive it into unmitigated conflict nor apathetic tolerance. This use of the model of the Trinity permitted the fundamental possibility of diversity within unity and unity within diversity that the urban ethos cries for. And it provides it in a way that polytheism, monarchistic unity, anomic pluralism, sectarian radicality, or dualism in sacred or secular form alone cannot. The doctrinal dimensions of a *credo* were established that, in principle, could give a normative definition of "right," compatible with eschatological "good" for the ethos of urban society. Such a notion as the Trinity both affirmed dimensions of the ethos and provided the ground for its reconstruction.

A further word about the Spirit is necessary, however. There was another movement, not yet touched upon, that was relevant to a more fully reconstructed understanding of this doctrine.

A second problem of theories about the Spirit is its two-aspect nature on the analogy of the two natures of Christ and the double character of creator-created implied in the parenthood principle. The two-aspect structure was implied as much in some of the church institutional and historical developments as it was in the articulated model itself, indicating that at some points the theological-ethical link between the dramatic events of history and the interpretive model may not have been sufficiently maintained. Athanasius himself was responsible for the introduction of monasticism in the West following the lead of Pachomius in Egypt—Pachomius was the founder of institutionalized monasticism that involved a "rule," economic production, and literacy as admissions requirements. In the subsequent rise of monasticism many orthodox theologians who belonged in the Athanasian camp insisted that what the church and the culture at large recognized as spiritually legitimate had to take on some organizational embodiment. The proto-monastic movement had attempted to accent radical and pure spirituality by encouraging a hermetic, ascetic life in the wilderness, eschewing all contacts with and dependence upon creations of the human spirit such as culture and civilization. The heirs of Athanasius were much concerned to bring that spirituality into an organized institution, under a group discipline, and into a responsible relationship with the surrounding community by performing certain services to the community, by engaging in economic production, by advancing scholarship, or at least by providing an institutional haven for the spiritually elite outcasts of conventional culture. The concern of these theologians can be seen partially as an attempt to affirm a two-aspect understanding of the Spirit—although it was still a "modified dualism" that was never really built into the doctrine.

From the perspective of the contemporary urban ethos, we can see that the Reformation was the time when the Spirit was unleashed from the encumbrances of its modified dualism and began to relate the spirit to the most mundane enterprises that occupy the human beings in a vitally creative way. The effects of the "Protestant spirit" on economic, political, and legal structures has been the focus of much, much research. But the Protestant movement, we now see, often misunderstood its own insight. It preserved the flow of the Spirit from the Father through the Son, but it frequently privatized the whole process. The relation with the Father was an intensely personal one, Christ became the way in which the internal separation of God and man was overcome within the deepest recesses of the self, and the Spirit became the way by which only the most intimate and expressive interpretations of life were theologically legitimated. It also preserved the thoroughly masculine conception of the Father as the source of all, collapsing the transcendent unity of God into the Father principle. Thus, religious imagery reinforcing male chauvinism and related the psychological dimensions of religion to paternal authority.

The perennial Catholic criticism that the Reformation led to a dissolution of a unified civilization, thus, may well be judged an accurate appraisal of the effects of Protestantism, because the Catholics (and some "Christendom" Protestants) tend to see all Spirit as continuously proceeding "through the Son." All true piety in this mold focuses on a rather "male" individualism. But the contemporary urban theorist, who asserts the necessity of partial independence of and a "two aspects" interpretation of the Spirit, regards such developments as having theological legitimacy only so long as it produces pluralistic civilizational forces. When that is accomplished, as at present, the problem of diversity *in unity* becomes the need of an urbane and cosmopolitan ethos. The *credo* must thus be reappropriated for a larger task.

The Model's Value

What is important, for our purposes, about these traditional formulations is their connection with contemporary issues in which apparently sacred and secular polarities are involved. Most obviously, there is an analogy between the problems of the Constantinian period and those of the present which even the historical distance cannot obscure. The sectarian, Eusebian, Arian, and Athanasian points of view have present-day correlates on similar theological grounds. Then, and now, we see a series of divergent groups moving toward urban and cosmopolitan consolidation and working to find common ground for power and value at the levels of ideological formulation, institutional form, and cultural-political responsibility. And in these historic periods, as now, we see attempts to confine the interpretation of life to collective, channeled means, or to privatize the whole process. And, in the past, as well as the present, we see the tenuous relations of power and worth toying with monolithic structures on one side and anomic chaos on the other.

But there is not only analogy, there is continuity. Not only does Christian periodization of history see the time between the coming of Christ and the eschaton as one time span with common elements, but in fact theologians and social analysts who deal with questions of the one and the many and the divine and the human, use consciously or implicitly the terms from this period, even if they put accents in different places or argue against the traditional formulations. Religions and secular "holiness sects" with deeply rooted histories, for example, are very suspicious of rationalized forms of social life and are usually disengaged from institutional problems that call for specification of the relationship of religion and culture or ethics and social responsibility. Aggressive political and religious sects plan revolutionary tactics for "the right" while withdrawing sects also dualistically accent laws of spiritual purity against the laws of the world and attempt to establish interior purity on the Donatist model often without knowing that their ideas could be traced back over the centuries. A rational and conservative national civic religion of an organic monotheistic variety of enormously complex and deep roots is a part of American urban political life, as can be seen in the Military-Industrial Complex. Rational liberals in the university research a multiplicity of cultural goods, defend the principle of tolerance, and mitigate the pretensions of authoritarians of the Eusebian or sectarian sorts. But they give no vision.

The historical and theological underpinnings of the Athanasian option can be seen recurrently in history where new social philosophies are worked out in the face of urban problems. It can be found in the conciliar Catholics of medieval times (as well as currently), in the Calvinist branches of the Reformation, especially as worked out in theories of the "Covenant," and in the aggressive free church tradition that gave fresh impetus to political democracy. The failure to develop a two-aspect understanding of the Spirit, however, led most of Catholicism and Protestantism to a split between "spiritual" and "material," "gospel" and "law," "revelation" and "reason" that was overcome only in the sacramental forms of the church, for the Catholics, and only in the hearts of individuals through the work of Christ, for example, among the Lutherans. Thus they could not see dynamic political or economic transformation for the right as really spiritual and did not consider it the task of the "spiritual" church. Hence the reaction against religion for the understanding of social and cultural reality by Feuerbach, Nietzsche, Marx, and Freud was an inevitable reaction to a false view of life and history presented by their theological model.

The conciliar Catholics, the Calvinist part of the Reformation, and the sectarian movement that followed on its heels, however, give promise of modern concepts of the relation of worth and power, religion and culture that cannot be neglected. These traditions accepted the basic Athanasian formula, and pressed vigorously for a pluralistic communitarianism not directly dependent upon priestly authority, as well as a more "incarnated" understanding of the Spirit in a variety of ways. It saw participation in freewheeling political action for the right as a legitimate part of man's spiritual calling in society. Social reconstruction is part of cosmopolitan man's vocation. Most clearly laid out in a study of the English revolution, these traditions saw reason as a corollary to revelation, it defined the saint as the citizen establishing a righteous new order in the civil community, and it saw new community formation on a voluntary associational basis as a function of the spiritual vocation of the company of true believers.[15]

Further, the trinitarian motifs as they particularly shaped the development of modern industrial, democratic society through Calvinist theology, accent a concept of the radical sovereignty of a patriarchal God, so acute as to demand an impracticable theocracy in Geneva, the Cromwellian revolution, and Puritan New England. Nevertheless this tradition refocused concepts of the unity of worth and power which allowed a partial synthesis with the rationalistic universalism of the Enlightenment, a well-known development which shaped the destiny of American political and cultural development in a direct way. Yet this radical sovereignty, controlled by a theological legitimation of diversity and differentiation of pluralism, through a continued trinitarian insistence, never succumbed to the drive toward a monolithic structure that was the result of the French Revolution. Instead, it has developed its own pathologies as can be seen in America, South Africa, and England where cosmopolitan and pluralistic concepts have legitimated second-rate citizenship for those members of the community who "by nature" are defined as different. Thus Calvinism has become the occasion for both unifying cosmopolitanism that can easily become cultural imperialism, and liberty through pluralism that can degenerate to racism or sexism. Nevertheless, through these historical connections, the earlier possibilities of trinitarian thought are made available to us in an urban ethos.

Of course, we are omitting a whole series of influences that separate us from our predecessors: conflicting definitions of law, conflicting lusts for power by heirs of Caesar and Christ alike, cultural crosscurrents and population migrations, the rise of science and technology, to mention a few. But these are in part rooted in ultimate meta-ethical models themselves, and, where not, only present civilization with new facts, not with the normative guidelines as to how the facts ought to be treated. Indeed, our reticence to look explicitly at the level of doctrine to find analytical tools for an urban *credo* obscures the continuities; but there are continuities of thought, analogous problems, and direct historical influences that shape our contemporary civilizational artifact, the urban ethos.

We see, then, that motifs deriving not only from the biblical period but also from the age of Constantine have echoes in the underlying problems facing the urban ethos today. Whether we fully agree with this influence or not, we can now begin to specify, looking to the present and future rather than the past, what the implications of these views might well be. Indeed, future efforts to devise viable institutional arrangements will only be satisfactory if certain ingredients of these creedal roots are included.

First, worthy power appears in creative patterns of just order, the *parenthood principle*, that functions to restrain chaos and death, to remind man of his proclivity to falsehood and evil, and to provide positive guidelines by which he can shape his environment. Law, pattern, organization, convention are not *necessarily* oppressive false forms that need to be dispensed with, nor are they eternally fixed, especially when understood as involving nurture, sustained and loving support. Instead they are potential structures that are more or less appropriate to sustaining human projects. It is true that these can become systematized oppression and violence when patriarchally structured or when divorced from the vision of the Kingdom; but then the difficulty is not to dispense with all signs of order, but rather to establish those patterns that do perform the critical functions that lead to creative patterns.

Second, one must look at the question of personal identity and demand conditions whereby the self can experience the promise and possibility of continual renewal. Here the material conditions of physical existence must be conjoined to modes of normative ego identity so as to allow both flexibility and a relatively integrated identity within the context of ordered structures and genuine community participation. Personal identity is confirmed by *vocation* to others and to the society at large. This new personal identity is never the mere victim of whatever conventional patterns obtain; rather this kind of identity is freed from passive obedience and becomes co-creator, engaged in the reconstruction of natural, positive, and traditional principle.

Third, there must be dynamic, creative movement that provides immediacy of contact with the cutting edge of historical development for the sake of justice and righteousness. In its strongest moments, this element is ever linked with the processes of participatory community formation and artistic creativity in the broadest sense. It occurs in the formation of reformist or revolutionary *esprit de corps* and inspired genius which may be related primarily either to the reconstruction of creative, just order or with the processes of finding, creating, or shaping new identity.

The trinitarian theological tradition as here reinterpreted claims that the interrelation of these three factors are primary desiderata for the discernment of ultimately worthy power and for the patterning of projects. It is in creative order, renewed and related identity and spontaneity of community formation toward the Kingdom that God is mediate.

Finally, such a *credo* has specific normative content. Each of the aspects implies alternative emphasis in social-ethical thought, and while these are related both to each other and to the fundamental good power and worth of which they are concretions, the shifting character of theology and society allows the successive dominance and subdominance of the various factors. When the primary emphasis is upon the parental motif, the emphasis tends to be on order and law. Such emphasis may have intellectual overtones in the demand for scientific worth and education; or it may have emotive roots in patterns of duty. The former emphasis appears among intellectuals, the latter among the masses, and they frequently coalesce in efforts to find stability and clear pattern in both the universal structures of nature and the particular structures of the social order. The quest for predictable patterns is linked, inevitably, with technological and bureaucratic means of control by which a new order, usually under the guise of restoring the primal created order, is imposed upon an old one. The periods when the accent has been on the Parenthood motif have inevitably been those times of purification and simplification of worth and power. In these periods, every individual is linked directly to a central single power and worth, either by his natural reason, if it is conceived in rationalistic terms, or by his spiritual affinity, if it is conceived in emotive terms. Normatively and frequently the two are linked, as one can see by the rational mysticism that has continually recurred in the history of man. This simple pattern of the participation of each subunit in the dominant single authority with a unity of worth and power—scientific or emotive— becomes codified and systematized. The question of creative or generative power is a crucial ingredient because the single center is seen as sparking off all kinds of diversity which nevertheless finds its unity in the original, final, structured authority. Man is called upon both to be a radical conservative in the sense that he is to respect the fundamental patterns of creative order, and also to be a co-creative participant in extending the artifactual creative order into those arenas where chaos reigns.

When the "Son" motif is accented, the new identity that one finds as necessary is supra-natural identity. The historic ecclesiastical practice of giving new names and titles when an individual enters a new life, such as in baptism, induction to the religious orders, or marriage, is indicative of the derivation of identity from the community and the transformation of innate personhood. New identity is not primordially present. The identity into which one is called bears a new context of relationship and a new definition of tasks. Further, identity involves effective integration. First, of body and mind, nature and supernature. When one's patterns of conception become separated from actual material conditions, with only natural expression, man is a beast. These can be and ought to be, implies the *credo,* connected in a supra-natural historical reality. Second, it becomes integration into a unique pattern, a unique selection of multiple possibilities in which the self can participate. The self is, in fact, constructed out of the relation between the objective possibilities and the relative integration of subjective conceptual and material factors. Those things are deemed right which extend the range of objective choice without destroying the integration of the mental and material aspect of the self. Man, thus, changes his identity continually when called into working with multiple possibilities that do not destroy his integrity. Identity in the urban ethos is not discovered, but constructed.

When the "spirit" motif is accented, we find a focus on that which is required by the formation of new community and cultural innovation. Right community formation evokes creativity and spontaneity among the people while providing desiderata so that participants do not lose a sense of purpose and direction. It is characterized by a *com-passion,* an emotive withness, a solidarity, a social spirituality that generates new invention and imagination for the right. To attain this it is necessary to presuppose a quality of active, freewheeling participation which allows the expression and transforming refinement of human emotions. When hope becomes a part of a bureaucratic order, when organized forms of change are realized, when community is sufficiently established so that collective spirit can be expressed through design or architecture, literature or music, the total city as a secular basilica can celebrate, and the stages and airwaves will be filled with true joy and the comedy, tears, and tragedy of reality.

In short, if we are to seek a *credo* that sustains a vision of the future for transformed urban existence, we are well advised to draw upon the model of the Trinity, hammered out in a proto-cosmopolitan, but imperial, ethos. Reconstructed in view of subsequent experience, it provides the normative marks of an authentic project in urban society. It demands a pluralism that recognizes a transcendent unity. It demands attending to the concrete powers and values of creative order, the new supranatural forms of identity that overcomes alienation, and the quest for a holy *esprit de corps* that engenders cultural innovation.

The modern city is not these things. The secular city is not and perhaps never shall be all of these; but in the midst of the terribly mundane, anonymous, pragmatic features of urban life, there are embedded the tracks of the Divine, and the decisive patterns of experience that reveal a sacred "rightness" about the city. These patterns are capable of being identified through a reconstructed *credo*. We cannot see the eschatological possibilities for which we hope; nor do we know what God, the ultimate center of power and worth, might be. All we know is that the most significant hints at these become present to man in the several ways grasped by eschatology and trinitarian doctrine, and that the formulation of that *credo* and its modifications are profoundly related to cosmopolitan developments.

Chapter VII

ECCLESIOLOGY AND COSMOPOLITAN POLITY

We have seen, so far, that all major theories of urban society are rooted in *credos*. We have also seen that each is inadequate for it did not touch the depths of the urban ethos either historically or systematically. To do so more adequately requires the development of analytical ethical tools for a depth sociology. We found that, if urban man is to live, it will be as a part of projects, in movements toward a transformed future that is neither apocalyptic nor utopian. Thus the urban ethos is dependent upon eschatology, a peculiar concept of the "good" future. But no finality and certainty is possible for a vision of the future. All that is possible to know is that it must involve a number of ingredients that have been symbolically captured in terms such as "resurrection," "communion of the saints," and "Kingdom of God." To sustain movement toward such a transformed future, and to discern where in a cosmopolitan environment those good features of life are proleptically in evidence, it is necessary to develop a non-dogmatic doctrine, a formal model that identifies where, through the combination of worth and power, those possibilities are alive and where "right" gives normative order to human experience. In the face of cosmopolitan developments, the clash of cultures, and a quest for a new metaphysical hypothesis upon which to base civilization, a highly significant doctrine centering on the doctrine of the Trinity developed. It was, in its ancient form, inadequate in that, especially, its concept of the "Spirit" was wrong. But it was superior to any other fundamental doctrines and represented in telescoped form the critical ideas that shaped the direction of civilization for hundreds of years. Indeed "eschatology" and "Trinity" provide fundamental tools that are themselves capable of reconstruction as we face new civilizational forms in the contemporary urban ethos.

But no vision of the future, and no doctrine, crucial as they are, can sustain themselves or constitute a complete *credo*. They cannot survive without a structured constituency. Projects or doctrines are not decisive for the shape of civilization without organized advocates. Expectations and ideas do not affect the life of man until and unless there is a substructure that attempts to build them into the fabric of social institutions. While they may point to or state the values that man should actualize, and while they identify powers that sustain those values in some degree, it is only when the values are more fully empowered through being made "fit" and operational in social life that the visions and doctrines become operative in transformation. When people catch a vision and develop a definition of the decisive arenas of existence in which it is capable of being actualized, they both feel a new sense of power and organize to sustain and extend that new awareness. They become "people called out"; no longer do the "natural necessities" and social conventions that are given previously rule. They are driven to gather with like-minded people and construct a covenant of purpose. Social-political life focuses upon the empowerment and celebration of the vision and doctrines various groups endorse. And much of all public life is spent in the building of institutions to maintain and extend these, to mediate with, or defend against, or recruit from competing groups with their own projects and doctrines. The result is an *ecclesia,* a body of people called out and arranged in a system of organized authority and roles. Once formed, the body takes on a life of its own. People come and go, power is exercised or dissipated, authority is utilized or abandoned, usurped or transferred, but the institution continues to work toward a particular interpretation of the project and doctrines that gave it life. People who enter it are socialized into its project and doctrines in varying degrees of success. Other institutions accommodate to it or struggle against it on the basis of their own projects and doctrines. And the study of these groups that are called out is called ecclesiology.

Especially important in ecclesiology is the question of polity, of how such groups structure themselves, for how they organize themselves and pattern their distribution of power and author-ity gives evidence both of what they conceive the shape of the future to be, and how they think it *ought* to be under the vision of the future. It also indicates concretely what forms of creative order, transformed identity, and enspirited community are operationally seen as the marks of that which is ultimately worthy and powerful. In short, one learns a good deal about both the project and the doctrine of a group by the polity that is developed. The question of urban power is a question of which *ecclesiae* operate by what power to actualize their own projects and doctrines.

Unfortunately, systematic ecclesiological study has been carried out primarily by theologians, who, because of the realistic emphasis that they put on the intrinsic meaning of projections and doctrines without attending to their social ramifications, obscure the equally realistic emphasis that needs to be placed on institutional and structural questions. Thus, eschatology and Trinity have often been sole tests of faith, the criteria of *credo*. An attempt to define the crucial levels of urban experience from the standpoint of analytical theological ethics demands, however, that the structural or polity dimensions be given equal accent. It also suggests that if one is to accurately take the pulse of urban existence, attention to the variety, shape, and relative empowerment of various *ecclesia* will be highly significant. A fully developed *credo* will have at least three ingredients: eschatology, doctrine, and ecclesiology.

In the history of the West, the organized constituency that has most consistently and powerfully, even if sometimes pathologically, borne the project and attempted to institutionalize the doctrine has been the church. Indeed, *"ecclesia"* is most simply understood as "synagogue" or "church." Thus, we are led to the scandalous assertion that "church" and "synagogue" are decisive categories by which urban power and organized constituencies are to be understood. Such an assertion is scandalous in terms of the ordinary presuppositions of most urban theorists. Yet it is precisely those networks of trust built up around purposes and consciously operating in terms of doctrine to transform the shape of human existence that are determinative for the future of the urban ethos. Further, if the project toward the future is related to biblical eschatology both systematically and historically, and if the decisive normative doctrine was formed in theological terms, as has been previously argued, then the institutional constituencies with the greatest consciousness of these are especially sensitive pressure points by which to take the pulse of the urban ethos. But such notions are so far removed from current presuppositions that a fuller explanation is necessary.

The Church in a Cosmopolitan Ethos

Several decades ago, neo-Reformation authors gave rise to a surge of ecclesiological concern, raising the fundamentals of the immediate implications of eschatology and traditional theology for the company of those called out. Diverse interpretations of the sacraments, the ministry, and the peculiar *kerygma* of the church as they derived from the Bible, the early church and the Reformation forced numerous examinations of the theory and practice of the church. Focal points for the debate were decidedly on those dimensions of the church which set it off from any other social institution. The "true gospel" was often couched in anti-philosophical, anti-social-scientific, and anti-"religious" categories in an attempt to identify what was uniquely Christian. There was, I think, an awareness that the world was beginning to undergo a fundamental theological and cultural shift. But, far too often, this awareness was inhibited from full development because attention to the human and empirical functions of the church were muted or opposed. The positivist theology did not allow discernment in history. The existential emphasis of the movement also carried anti-institutional overtones, and the attempt to find a pure dogmatic basis on which the faith could stand obscured the doctrinal problems that were rooted in social history. And attention to regularities and patterns in religious social organization was frequently declared theologically irrelevant and, sometimes, sinful because it refused to acknowledge God's radical freedom. One can understand such a reaction in a world shattered by wars, depression, revolution, oppression, and rampant racist nationalism. One can also see a powerful corrective to naive liberal interpretations of the nineteenth century. And one can understand the relevance of these quasi-Reformation concepts to the kind of crisis that Europe experienced under Hitler, since strands from the Reformation contributed to that crisis. But an increasing historical perspective on the neo-Reformation period may lead us to conclude that the questions of ecclesiology were not answered by it, that some hard questions from both the tradition and contemporary urban experience were shouted down or not heard, and, indeed, that the neo-Reformation movement was only partially the beginning of a new era of ecclesiological theory. In the main, it represents the closing brackets on the Reformation or Protestant period of Western history.[1] Historical breaks are not sharp or even necessarily clear; but in ecclesiological terms, at least, the church has already begun to enter a new period, anticipated in several nineteenth century motifs, deeply influenced by both the insights of social science, and open to a number of contemporary influences, not the least of which is the fresh perspective on the conciliar Catholic tradition since Vatican II.

In this post-Protestant period, fresh reflection on ecclesiology is also occasioned by the dramatic social forces presently changing man's environment—and hence the church's environment—to a more urban one. The incapacity of ordinary Catholic or Protestant ecclesiology to deal creatively with these developments is manifest. It is not yet clear, for example, what the rapid ecumenical development entails. It may be the noble but futile last efforts of Christendom to consolidate and preserve its fading strength in the face of religiously disintegrating pressures. It may also be a consortium of like-minded and well-intentioned, but basically irrelevant, religious people who are merely following the pattern of internationalization and diversification that presently is occurring in all large-scale organizations. Or it may be, as I believe it to be, a highly significant and prophetic development that represents on the one hand the churches' relative success in both responding to the modern world and transcending the parochial loyalties of nation, race, special tradition, and ideologized polity to which Christians no less than others are often bound, and on the other hand redefining *ecclesia* in such a way that it is no longer confined to "churchiness." In any event, it is clear that the church is shaped by, as well as shapes, the ethos in which it lives. And it is doubtful that either the shaping or the being shaped is more a concretion of ultimate worth and power than the other. Sociological as well as theological perspectives must therefore be brought to the understanding of the church, in contrast to the theological tunnel version of the neo-Reformation study of ecclesiology.

But if we attempt to develop an ecclesiology pertinent to the urban ethos, we must expand our horizons several steps further. We need to ask on the one hand what normative insights are to be gained for an appropriate *credo* for the urban ethos by the study of ecclesiology. And on the other hand, we need to show sociologically that the study of ecclesiology is pertinent to the new social forms aborning in our urban ethos. The contemporary study of ecclesiology, thus, may turn much of the study of the church on its head. While drawing on the wealth of material developed during the past century under the auspices of sociology of religion and theology of the church, it may also suggest how ecclesiological analysis, criticism, and reconstruction are fruitful for the shaping of sociological and theological reflection, and necessary to the ethical definition of the urban ethos.

Ecclesiology in this frame of reference is intended to refer to the critical analysis and reconstruction of the operative patterns of creative order, identity formation, and enspirited community among those who are called out of ordinary existence to actualize a vision of life as transformed under the conscious influence of the ultimate and most worthy power or powers of existence. The organizational support system for those on the way to fulfill the human vision of a transformed future under a doctrine of right is the focus. Such a definition is intended to distinguish ecclesiology from ecclesiasticism. Ecclesiological literature is widely muddied by ecclesiasticism, both as it connotes parochial and often bureaucratic loyalties to clericalism, and as it means sectarian or denominational apologetics. The vast body of literature on ecclesiology is a rather pretentious tractarianism by exegetes trying to prove that their own polity derives directly from the pages of the Bible while all other polities represent a corrupt accommodation to nefarious social forces. Such myopia focuses on doctrinal or confessional formulations and attempts to infer relevant social organization by deduction from revealed truths, thereby failing to see the critical point of affinity between ideas and social forces that selectively influence the development of both. One dimension of these ecclesiastical apologetics is basic, however. The underlying motivation of their research has been their conviction that fundamental theological visions and doctrines are to be understood in part as an organized movement; these are not limited to subjective faith, or a singular relationship of one man and his God, or a set of beliefs, or moral attitudes. Negatively, they have rejected the dominant Lutheran, cultic, and spiritualistic notions that ecclesiology is neutral—that it is primarily a question of pragmatic adjustment and worldly wisdom and not a matter of critical theological and ethical import. Positively, they have affirmed what Catholic, Calvinist, and Radical Sectarian traditions have held to be the case: good social organization of "those called out" in decisive intentional communities is a question of fundamental importance and an integral part of any *credo* pertinent to man and society.

The more analytical and reflective use of the term "ecclesiology," however, includes in its purview a wider range of social groups than either theological tradition. Those groups who participate in the process of transforming life in nonapocalyptic and nonutopian ways and who accent creative order, transformed identity and enspirited community are faithful to the project and the doctrine whether or not the members of such a group confess a particular religious tradition or use the terms "God" or "Christ." In short, this broadened definition does not limit ecclesiology to Christians. Humanistic discussion and action cadres, research and development bureaucracies, planning agencies, artistic and revolutionary groups engaged in the reconstruction of operating patterns under the aspect of a fundamental definition of the ultimately good and powerful are all part of the subject of analysis. It is one of the marks of the necessary new style of ecclesiology that it reaches across usual limitations, defining the ecclesiological boundaries, with their eschatological and theological dimensions structurally and functionally in the first instance, and only confessionally in a secondary sense.

Such a definition of ecclesiology, of course, raises several problems. It shatters the illusion of membership in a particular religious tradition or in any of the churches as a necessary mark of belonging to the covenant of those called out. The experience of those within the tradition who are existentially engaged in the new styles of urban ministry, church life, theological reflection, and social action, indeed, have found such illusions ludicrous and even destructive to efforts to make a genuinely urban project and doctrine operative. In contrast to the widespread antinomianism and anti-institutionalism of those who criticize the church on structural or functional grounds, however, this definition finally does not depart from the implications of the traditional formula *"extra ecclesiam nulla salus est."*[2] It assumes the necessity for organized group activity as a mark of those called out. But it allows broadening and refinement in the definition of ecclesiological groups. The church has always held that those in "the Kingdom of God," those to be "resurrected," the "communion of the saints" are not necessarily coincidental with the membership of the confessional church, but it has far too often acted as if they were. Nor has it held that everyone had to consciously understand or agree with the details of Trinitarianism; but again it has hounded those who did not, even if they worked unconsciously within its frame.

The definition of ecclesiology presented here presupposes finally, that the group life of those called out is an historical reality susceptible to analysis. Any *ecclesia*, any organized movement, that is subject to serious analysis has a symbol system or language system, a polity, an economy, a pattern of mores, and constituent members—all of which interact whenever the *ecclesia* functions. It is, in short, a meta-system, a parallel organization to the whole society. The *ecclesia*, however, intentionally reorganizes the priorities of the various levels of the social system. It has economic, legal, political, and social systems as does the host society. And the relationship of the host society to the *ecclesia* is always close. But it attempts to integrate the various levels of its internal structure (and sometimes those of the whole social system) in a way that is consistent with its vision of the future and its understanding of ultimate patterns of worth and power.

As was suggested earlier, we need not only a definition, but some evidence that ecclesiology is an important place to look for new styles of human relationships especially as they pertain to theology and sociological concerns which are so important to the contemporary scene. There are two converging types of evidence which suggest that we can proceed in this fashion.

First, it is a sociological "law" that new insights, charismatic breakthroughs, fresh accents must be institutionalized if they are to have any long-range effect. Some see such a "law" as evidence for the doctrine of the inevitability of the "Fall," for they want projects and doctrines to remain unsullied by worldly contact. But those who see human institutions and patterned necessities as part of the realm of grace as much as spontaneous spirituality of imagination and image will acknowledge the capacity for institutionalization as one of the marks of an authentic spirit. Ideas, emotions, fresh perspectives which lack an organized constituency fade and are blown away by the first shifts of the winds. Although they may have great private significance for someone, they are historically irrelevant. Great ideas, powerful emotions, and genuine new insights that become genuine projects and doctrines tend to become incarnate in specific groups. There must be structures to appropriate and propagate them. And the way in which fresh perspectives become operative is through the formation of ecclesia. The formation of a committee, an association, a league, a club, a front, a party, or a caucus is the first indication of the vitality of a project and a doctrine. The capacity to evoke positive response, gain adherents, and provide meaning and coherence for life, personal and social, determines whether the worth will be empowered. The process of "institutionalization of charisma," as Max Weber called it, has been one determinative factor of innovation throughout history. However, the range of social forms available in an environment deeply influences the selection of innovations that are to endure and, indeed, encourages or discourages innovation of project and doctrines in the first place. There is a mutual selection process that takes place among vision, doctrine, and institution. Thus, in a context where there is a conscious quest for innovative interpretations of the new style of life in an urban ethos the study of ecclesiology is required.

Second, ecclesiology has been, historically, a crucial means by which to discern the decisive structures of a society and its conflicting definitions of power and authority in a way that links the structures of that society with its major cultural allegiances. No sociological or anthropological study today is considered complete until the fundamental structures of the society are related to the organization and practice of religion. As myth and, more recently, theology may be seen as systematic and reconstructive reflection on the fundamental clusters of symbols that are the self-transcending precipitate of a *culture,* so ecclesiology may be seen as critical reflection on, and reconstruction of the prototypical and self-transcending precipitates of a *society.* And all the subtle interactions of culture and society are involved. This can be illustrated in the West negatively if we look at the traditional definitions of heresies; they were seen as much a threat to the social order as they were a problem of truth and cultural deviance.

But not only is there interaction between culture and society. From ancient biblical times to the present there has been interaction between patterns of organized religion and the fundamental structures and movements of the host society.[3] The interaction of the social order and ecclesiology is a two-way traffic, just, as we saw earlier, as is the interaction of theology and culture. The ecclesiologists have, usually without explicitly acknowledging it, selected among the multiple tendencies in a society, adopted some of them as part of the general operating procedure, and baptized them by including those ingredients in the statements of normative ecclesiology. Such adoption has strengthened certain tendencies against others and shifted the sociological and political patterns of legitimized "good order." Roman Canon Law, Calvinist Institutes, the Methodist Discipline, and the constitution of the United Church of Christ, for example, all contain ingredients adopted from the host societies, while Roman Law, the English Parliament, the American Constitution, and the United Nations Charter are overflowing with only partially secularized theological and ecclesiological presuppositions. Or one could point to the slogans from battles past that reveal the interaction: "No bishop, no king." "Presbyterians for a Strong Parliament." "Baptists for separation of church and state." Nor is it possible to argue that such religious developments are merely the ideological product of social-economic forces. Too much evidence supports the "bourgeois" contention that religion is a *relatively* independent variable—contrary to the claims of the Marxist social theorists. Nor can we argue that these patterns are the result of a Machiavellian exercise of power. Overt coercion or force, the inevitable, necessary, and tragic ally of order, can only sustain itself without producing counterforce when it claims and gets legitimacy, a certification of worth that rests ultimately in the capacity of a movement to evoke confidence. It must be seen as relatively compatible with the contemporary understandings of what is appropriate to the final project and doctrine. Power and its exercise depend, in the long run, upon legitimacy, and a political system without ethics or theology is finally inconceivable. (As is theology or ethics without politics.) The history of ecclesiology and of the schisms and divisions in the church is the history of competing selection and endorsement of those structural dimensions of society that are deemed conducive to man's confrontation with that which is ultimately worthy and powerful. And the shifting structures of government are due to the successive institutionalization of projects and doctrines adapted from competing ecclesiological groups. The fact that personal and group self-interest enters at every point is only evidence of the existence of egocentric theologies and tribal polytheism.

At the same time the churches and synagogues tried to spin off organizations that mediate those powers and values to the individual or create conditions wherein such confrontation is possible. In some cases (such as parochial schools, hospitals, missions, and charities) and in some areas (such as religious political parties and unions), the church or synagogue has been reluctant to release the child after it has long since reached maturity. Nevertheless, the history of civilizational forms cannot be written without reference to competing attempts to select or to provide frameworks wherein the human enterprise of discerning and appropriately responding to the ultimately powerful and worthy is possible. And these movements could be shown to correspond organizationally with the eschatological projections and the theological interpretations of the relationship of identity, community, and order that dominate a given ethos. Many of these efforts in education, welfare, politics, and science were later secularized and became a function of the society in general. The fact that the church has made some horrendous errors both in terms of what it has selected and what it has "spun off," and the fact that some of the creative innovation occurred in groups that were explicitly antiecclesiastical and antireligious does not compromise the significance of the attempt or of ecclesiological theory. The broadened definition of ecclesiology is, historically, a very critical point at which to take the pulse of significant movements in society.

One may, of course, ask whether such is the case today and whether our urbanized, technologized, and "secularized" society does not differ from previous human communities precisely at this point. Are there not secular movements and activities that actually displace the church or synagogue today? In many cases, the answer is an obvious "yes." But a broadened definition of ecclesiology makes such an answer suspect. It ignores the highly symbolic march from the churches to the courthouse in the civil rights drives. It ignores the multiplicity of groups, from the Boy Scouts to the Kiwanis, to the Blackstone Rangers and Women's Liberation, to draft counseling and low-income housing corporations to experimental drama and sensitivity training sessions who meet, find legitimacy and cohesion in church basements.

At different levels, the role of the National Council of Churches in the intensive lobbying for the 1965 Civil Rights Bill, the struggle of the denominations over "reparations" demanded by the "Black Manifesto," and the legitimizing of revolutionary efforts in the "Third World" under certain conditions by the World Council of Churches are further evidence and confirm the suggestion that there is a relationship of ecclesiology and cultural-political innovation. Other examples can be found in the Peace Corps, that secularized Christian mission program, in the program of the Clergy and Laymen Concerned about Vietnam which anticipated and shaped the moral consensus of the nation very early in the war, in the "Urban Priority Budgets" that are apparently developing in the churches of every metropolitan area known to this observer, in the imperative to attack white racism "by any means necessary" voted by the Y.W.C.A., and Christian-Marxist dialogue under the auspices of the World Council of Churches and the Vatican. In fact, the list is too long to exhaust here. But these are the issues that occupy the main debates about budget allocations in the churches and synagogues. These are the issues that create the most vigorous debate about the kind of vision of the future that "ought" to be supported and that do or do not show the relationship of God to right and just order, transformed personal identity, and the presence of the Spirit. The reciprocal processes of discerning among the multiple secular movements, "baptizing" some and not others and the "spinning off" of new groups to deal with new cultural and social issues are ecclesiological movements today that do not, in fact, separate the contemporary situation from previous epochs. Rather, they provide us with a wider range of comparative tools. Nor should one allow the parochialism of local churches and synagogues to deter one from seeing the larger pattern. It is possible to state the general import and impact of public education without being confined to the inadequacies of a particular teacher or neighborhood school. It is possible to speak of legal processes without forensics on the superficiality and incompetence of a particular lawyer or local court. And it is possible to speak of trends and developments in medicine without concentrating on a specific doctor or clinic.

One can also point to developments in the twentieth century where competing ecclesiologists came into direct conflict. In the name of ultimate definitions of what is worthy and powerful, Stalin in Russia, Hitler in Germany, Mao in China, and both Giap and Thieu in Vietnam have engaged in massive efforts to control and destroy any ecclesia but their own. When the synagogues and churches, political ecclesia and social ecclesia have been destroyed, people can be disposed of one by one and the definition of heresy and schism is at the hands of singular authority. Systematically, alternative ecclesiologies have been subverted, and any buffer between the macro-structures of the state and the micro-structures of intra- and interpersonal relations have been wiped out. The prominence of the contemporary journalistic term "infrastructure" and all that it connotes as the critical locus of social and ideological formation is evidence of the importance of ecclesiology today.

In short, projects and doctrines must have an organized constituency to have any effect; ecclesiology is a crucial means by which to take the pulse of a society; and ecclesiology understood in a broadened sense is the decisive level of societal development, because it is in ecclesia that the ultimate definitions of worth and power as developed in projects and doctrine are made concrete. And the synagogues and churches play a particularly strategic role because of their access to and cultivation of the normative symbols, because of their historic role as bearers of the decisive values in most societies in the West wherein the urban ethos developed, and because they reflect the subtlety of the interaction of *credo* and culture in their own midst. With these factors in mind, we need to look at fundamental patterns of ecclesiology to see what possibilities lie open to the future. We need to know what kinds of structures have been, are being, and can be built, and we need to know what the possible effects of such building might be.

The Possible Polities

Only a limited number of underlying patterns of ecclesiology exist in the urban ethos—each bearing fundamental conceptions of the social order that best represents ultimate worth and power. And these patterns can best be grasped by a set of comparative models, a typology.

The most usual way of dealing with these fundamental patterns is one that was first developed by Max Weber and Ernst Troeltsch.[4] The "church-sect typology," as it is usually called, has come under increasing criticism on several fronts in the last decade or so. The criticism comes primarily from sociologists of religion who claim that it does not provide clear criteria for sociological prediction of religious group formation or development.[5] The typology is ultimately based on the contrast of priestly and prophetic functions of religion, a fact that contributes to its continued use by social ethicists and ecclesiological reformers. But before we proceed, it is necessary to sort out some of the issues in the use of ecclesiological typologies.

The criticisms indicate at some points the contemporary inappropriateness of the widely used categories and at other points a misapplication of the categories where they may be appropriate. Usually, the church and sect typology is seen as a sociologically descriptive law that gathers into itself such wide ranging factors as socioeconomic class, the coincidence or noncoincidence of church organization with political boundaries, mediatorial or charismatic roles of leadership, diffuse or intensive discipline, implicit or explicit understanding of faith, generational or voluntary membership, and accommodating or resistant attitudes toward the dominant culture. The typology has sometimes been used to imply that the identification of one or several of the above factors in an ecclesia would allow one to infer the other characteristics. It is well to abandon such over-simplifications as some scholars have demanded, because the typology does not describe necessary sociological laws. Moreover, as the typology stands in its classical formulation, it fails to take account of denominational, cultic, and spiritualist developments. Primarily because the typology was fitting and appropriate to the European scene, the choices open to ecclesiological development were, for the most part: cooperation with the establishment which had accommodated itself to the recalcitrant elements of human society; formation of a select group of disciplined spiritual elites who opposed the establishment; or development of a personal, usually mystical, philosophy. But on the present urban scene, other postures are possible, and new fitting models have been and are being developed. Thus, the typology does not meet the test of inclusion required of sociological categories for the urban ethos. The failure to deal with denominationalism is especially critical, because denominationalism has become the major pattern of ecclesiological organization in modern urban-technological society.

Denomination is neither "church" nor "sect," although it may derive from either—the former if it is forced into a position where it is not protected by, or part of, the government, and the latter when it intends to extend its organization and influence into larger groups and beyond a first generation of converts. A denomination is primarily a nonestablished religious organization that (a) may be coterminous with political boundaries but includes only some of the population in its voluntary membership, (b) admits that it does not have a corner on the truth by encouraging, or at least not undercutting, pluralism, and (c) develops an independent economic structure by which it attempts to mobilize sentiment and material resources to serve mankind. It is reformist rather than revolutionary or acquiescing. It rejects some aspects of society while accepting other aspects. A high ethnic or class bias appears in a denomination both as a pathological possibility and as a means by which some ethnic groups (such as immigrants) have been able to sustain their identity and maintain a form of enspirited community during times of difficult transition. Conceptions of leadership and authority and mission in the world are variable in the denomination—some being quite churchlike and some sectlike.

The problem is that the relations between the various dimensions of the church-sect factors are contingent and not necessary. Thus, factors which are ordinarily "church" may appear in any number of given "sects" in a way that is clearly contrary to the logic of typological formulations as often understood. Troeltsch and Weber, thus, may well have identified major dimensions of their environment, but their descriptive typology has sometimes been extended beyond its own intents and forced to do work for which it was not designed. When made to function as a universal law, it fails. It only functions in contexts shaped by a peculiar vision of the future and a particular doctrinal history that limits the possible constructions of social organization.

If, however, we accept what Weber and Troeltsch *intended,* and attempt to describe the "inner logic" of characteristic forms of ecclesia that *in fact exist* on the historical scene, typological categories may be useful. So long as the typology is not established as a sociological law, but as an analytical portrait of the patterns of meaning that are woven together in competing ecclesia in the social fabric of life in the modern world, rooted as it is in the motifs of biblical eschatology and Constantinian doctrinal controversy, the articulation of that logic is one of the legitimate and necessary tasks for the analysis of the urban ethos. Our purpose, then, is to set forth the inner logic of the major contemporary ecclesiological trends.

There have been three traditions that on the American continent and in several of the developing countries have woven together a series of theological and sociological structures claiming the relevance of one to the other. Deriving historically from those three traditions that have attempted to establish an ecclesiology as fundamental to the question of the destiny of man and society, the Catholic, the Calvinist, and the Sectarian traditions, three prototypical forms of denominational social organization make up the constitutive patterns converging into a fourth, synthetic possibility in the urban ethos. From the three forms of denomination is emerging a "conciliar" denomination-alism that is structurally very significant for both theology and sociology.

The Catholic denomination is fundamentally marked by a corporate structure governed by a hierarchical pattern of authority. Matters of ultimate power and worth for the health of the corporate body are mediated through the corporate body by the hierarchical structure. This form of ecclesia is undergirded by a metaphysical world-view or a theological conception of organic relationship between the patterns of good order, the transformed identity of official personnel, and the enspirited community. The corporative type includes today not only Roman, Anglican, and American Methodist religious traditions, but has very strong analogies with corporative centers of power in the modern metropolis such as machine politics, business corporations, welfare organizations, and school systems. The structure need not be, and usually is not, monolithic. It is frequently quite differentiated in the functions it performs, the skills it demands, and the services it provides. And its overall visions or doctrines that govern both policy and polity are worked out by votes of elders meeting in council. But its differentiation is dependent upon its overall unified pattern of order and authority. Its differentiation, thus, is for application or implementation, not for definition, of what is ultimately worthy and powerful.

There may be, and usually are, responsive appeal mechanisms among the levels of mediation, and the mediation includes two-way communication and feedback. However, decision-making and fiduciary responsibility, in points of conflict at a particular level, reside with the next-highest level of authority. Change occurs by organic growth and increasing differentiation, which must be ratified or initiated by the higher levels of authority. Such differentiation frequently forces division of roles or role conflict. This introduces stress, but new divisions of labor reduce the tension. The participation of lower-level persons in such a structure occurs primarily because each person is both a recipient of services and authoritative directives and a reservoir of physical and psychic resources. The structures of mediation facilitate and regulate the flow of authority and services from the higher echelons of the hierarchy to the community and the persons in it and also the flow of resources of persons and local communities up to the hierarchy.

Corporate structures assume several ingredients as central to ecclesiological principle. First, the vision of the future is predominantly fulfillment. Apocalyptic and utopian pathologies are carefully avoided while the natural patterns of creation are seen as organically striving for fuller and richer development as they move into higher and higher stages of existence.[6] There is the perennial temptation to prematurely identify the eschatological symbols of communion of the saints and Kingdom of God with present institutional structures and to thereby claim a nearly total loyalty.[7]

Second, there is a drive to wholeness or catholicity that obtains both in the effort to incorporate wider and wider ranges of experience and in the attempt to provide and demand relatively complete services to the person within the corporate structure. Further, the principle of hierarchy is rooted in both a functional and metaphysical conception of the Trinity that took on both Eusebian and Arian ingredients. Built into all life is a necessity for structural authority and obedience to higher principle to prevent chaos and separation. The Father, through His vicar, the Son, establishes a father-figure and the priesthood, the sons of the vicar. These are understood as the source of divine management, superior to and set apart from primary physical or psychic resources. Presupposed is a bank of disorganized "natural" resources which are brought into a "supernatural" relationship according to rightly understood "natural law" through divinely ordained management. Properly managed, a relatively organic order, tolerant and rational except when threatened by what it perceives to be sectarianism, results. The "Parenthood" principle of divine order reigns supreme, and the questions of personal identity and enspirited community are subordinated.

While such patterns border on totalitarianism they also preserve the sense of organic involvement of every person in a total natural, social, and spiritual system. Such a full-blown system builds barriers against, even if it does not always prevent, antinomian self-gratification and egoism. It also preserves a sense of order and patterned authority which is necessary to society and creates an atmosphere of security. An ecclesiology thus constructed, however, does not easily tolerate explicit rejection of the system or its parts and sees all such radical efforts at reform as rebellion, self-gratification, and antinomian. Thus the system's response in the face of criticism is either new differentiation to reincorporate or reassertion of order and authority.

It is this pattern which critics of the power elite see as operative in the present urban social system. Indeed, the presuppositions that inform their research are, more often than not, shaped by the social thought of Europe where protest against precisely such patterns of authority helped bring about the shift from a feudal to an urban society. At the depths of their social analysis is the continuing division of Church-type and sect-type of social organization, although the theological origins of the interpretations have been lost. Instead, a modified class or racial analysis has been substituted, with the poor or the Blacks or the students or women becoming the focus of a new sectarian organization that is to depose the feudal arrangements.

And it is this model that was theologically argued for by the Eusebians, defeated in principle by the Athanasians, and readopted by the medieval church in modified form. From there it has become a part of our cultural history and has endured in both projects and doctrines as embodied in a multiplicity of structures, especially in the interior organization of economic life.[8]

Another type of sanctified social organization is derived from the Calvinist or covenantal type, the product of the second form of religious social philosophy. This prototype of sanctioned sociological pattern exists in secular form in the university, the research corporation, professional associations, publishing houses, and other media of communication, the plethora of "authorities" developing in metropolitan and regional government, and most trade unions, all deeply influenced by Calvinism, often in non-theological garb. The fundamental characteristics of this mode of organization are oligarchical appointment or election to authority, based on competent definition of and obedient behavior to that which is of ultimate power and worth as recognized by certified peers. The structure is marked by pluralistic centers of power based on specific variations in definition of role and performance. The centers are not, however, created by differentiation of previous centers and subordinate to a dominant authority pattern; they are created through the contracting of like-minded persons who coordinate their interests and bind themselves to a discipline and a given aim. The creation of a functioning group is frequently planned to be intentionally independent of the socially dominant authority structure, but to adhere to a unique normative concept of personal authority, law, or duty for those elected to that group. Unity is gained through intergroup alliances and federations and by the designation of representatives to interpret or specify the rules for the interaction or to consolidate coalition action on specific issues. Governing federal bodies are important in that the rules of the game are there agreed upon. There the advantages and disadvantages of the particular groups are determined. But in contrast to corporative arrangements where unity is presupposed and differentiation is derivative, governing bodies are structurally derivative in the covenantal model.

The dominant patterns of group relations are seen in terms of conflict and tension. The perennial struggle is to find points of voluntary consensus within which dissensus may take place. Decision-making is thus based upon a combination of technical competence, consensus formation, and codes of discipline. Change occurs usually by shifting the specifications of competence, consensus, or discipline. It may also be brought about by the creation of new centers of competence and consensus. Group formation forces a new recognition of the right to participate in consensus and dissensus processes within a structured society.[9] Individuals do not usually relate to others directly, but through participation in one or more covenantal centers. Such centers provide a structured means for man to express his concerns and they demand from him certain competences and commitments. Theologically and socially the covenantal group is the chief center for making concrete a holy *esprit de corps* by which the ultimately powerful and worthy are identified. The person's loyalty to one group is limited and explicitly so, however, and his participation in a number of covenantal centers demands the juxtaposition of numerous commitments and claims, producing both anxiety and a highly differentiated, selectively skilled personality living under tension.[10]

Federal-covenantal structures affirm democracy among the elite, the competent, those within the fold; but rather rigidly preserves the prerogatives of those who have the capacity to form new consensus, perform technical roles, and abide by specified codes. The federal claim to universality lies in the necessary universal principles to judge behavior, the quest for truth, and the vision of someday obtaining universal, voluntary, and explicit consensus on fundamental rules to control dissensus (especially, the terms of tolerance). Conflict, brokerage, and the organization of countervailing powers are the necessary structure of social relations until the goal is attained. It both preserves the possibilities of a pluralistic, open society, and makes such a society necessary. Relative and provisional integration, nevertheless, is found at two levels: (a) that of federal conventions to regulate the interaction of participating persons and groups, and (b) that of personal uniqueness wherein each one participates in a variety of covenants and arranges his own logic of participation subjectively. But the decisive level for influencing both levels of integration is the covenanted community.[11]

The chief pathology of this form of organization is that the standards of excellence that ostensibly define membership are betrayed by identification of the covenant with divisions of class, race, or interest group. Calvinistically influenced urban civilization often exercises a hegemony over others to resist the formation of new covenantal groups that make similar exclusive claim. When this occurs one is presented with the illusion about the pluralistic character of society.[12] But such patterns preserve the ideal, even where not actualized, of a pluralistic, open, competent society that is of long-range importance. The number, strength, and character of the covenantal groups and their accessibility for all persons are determinative for the shape of society.[13]

It is this model that provides the fundamental conceptual framework for the pluralist theories of urban power. They do not expect much from centralized leadership except brokerage of conflicting interests between competing groups. Centralized leadership is indeed derivative leadership in the first place. They recognize that there are relatively stable leaders in the various covenantal groups, but do not take this as a sign of a "power elite." Rather it is seen as a sign of competence. The dangers to this view are twofold: one would be the merger into a solidified, organic, monolithic structure; and the other would be the decay into fractionalized charismatic groups that cannot actually perform competently, that will not undertake the discipline of a covenantal group, and refuse to negotiate federal agreements.[14]

It is this model also that found its theological ground in the Dutch and English "Federal Theologians" who legitimated the nation-state, but saw it bound into a web of international obligation, as in Grotius and Althusius, as a mark of the sovereignty of God. It most directly, however, put its stress on the transformed identity of the elect, binding them into a disciplined, inspirited community that would include all social and political institutions.[15]

The third type, the sectarian or "movement" variety of Christian social philosophy, has always been the minority report of the theological tradition throughout the Catholic and Protestant denominational perspectives. In its traditional and withdrawing forms, it has led to an intensive personal and small group pietism; but it has also, especially since the Cromwellian revolution, renewed aggressive and social reformist motifs as a mark of true spirituality. It appears in Unitarian-Universalist, Quaker, and some Baptist traditions, in evangelical and populist movements, in the revolutionary cadres of the third world, in the civil rights movement, and as the dominant orientation in much of the current American countercultural movements.

Since the early church's debates over its relationship to the Zealots, and the Constantinian question of the relationship to the radical dualists of either the aggressive or withdrawing sects, and the rise of the Joachite movement (as treated in Chapter V), this sectarian view has tried to define the fundamental line of division between good and evil in the world. Though the tactics differ—some try to avoid the evils of civilization while others try to confront and transform them—sectarian movements have perennially claimed that every individual has the innate capacity to, and must take on the responsibility of, deciding whether he is in or out, and must organize his life around that decision. That is, essentially, what decides one's authenticity. The decision may be emotional or rational, mystical or moral, but it must be personal and involve the voluntary assumption of a new style of life that is ethically (variously defined) transformed. In any case, it is suspicious of corporative and covenantal forms of social organization.

This view has recently become more dominant. The increased differentiation of the corporate type of existence, and the competition for loyalties produced by the federal covenantal type has intensified the focus on the individual and his direct, nonmediated relation to that which is ultimately worthy and powerful. Many contemporary spokesmen have identified this as a modern privatization of religion. But it is more deeply rooted. The phenomenon has emerged from the limbo to which Catholic and Protestant scholars have relegated it to become a critical feature of the contemporary scene. It bears the highly ambiguous marks of utopian messianism of personal fulfillment in a mass society and the vision of participatory democracy, and is frequently linked with social-political movements and artistic or aesthetic innovation. It is the "Third History" written by alienated Jews, heretics, Anabaptists, and humanists; and it can only recently be seen as a major thread in relationship to theological and social development and not only a threat to Christianity as the Catholics and Calvinists have taught. The movement is based upon the identification of a manifest center of loyalty to which all individuals may become personally and directly related. Thomas Münzer and other Anabaptists saw this as an implication of Luther's early teaching, but Luther ultimately turned against them. The center of loyalty may be a radical sovereign directly concerned with each individual in an unmediated fashion to which each must respond, or the capacity of each individual to know directly and existentially what is ultimately worthy and powerful (traditionally spoken of as "individual soul-competency"). The nature of that center of loyalty and of the human capacities which appropriate it may vary widely; but organizationally the results are identical.[16]

The notions of pure democracy that may be found in this type vary in form from charismatic leadership by spontaneous acclamation to a radical liberalism that emphasizes the universal rights of man (depending upon whether the accent falls on the importance of the unity or the importance of the diversity of individuals that may become related to that unity). In this type, organizational mediation and structural centers of loyalty are considered negligible or negative in importance. They are useful only if they provide universal possibilities of membership and participation in what is ultimately worthy and powerful and provide for the total involvement of the individual. Yet the aggressive forms of the sectarian type resist the built-in temptations to anarchism or antinomianism. More dangerous is the temptation to produce messianic figures of demagogic leadership who demand a total commitment—a temptation inhibited only by the affirmation on the part of both Christians and Jews that the proper center of ultimate loyalty is transcendent and the consequent exposure of any immediate claimants to such loyalty as frauds. Such an aggressive sectarian type of ecclesiology bears a pair of accents on the ultimacy of the person and the transformed legal-political structures that must be accessible to him in a direct way that has had considerable impact on democratic life and formal political structure. Structural authority in this view may not unduly impinge on the individual. Some aspects of a man's life may not be socially regulated. Both corporative and covenantal forms of polity are seen as destructive to the immediate spontaneities of the spirit. Liberation from the dominance of these is primarily negation of overarching establishments and prescriptions. Such assumptions have been of fundamental importance in ecclesiological theory on the American scene since at least Roger Williams. At times, they have threatened to displace the previous ecclesiologies entirely, but they have not been able to mobilize resources effectively due to the suspicion of hierarchy and expertise.

Each type of ecclesiology has had its distinctive form of eschatology and its distinctive theology. The corporative has for the most part been decidedly antiurban and antiprojective. Theologically it has subverted eschatology and trinitarianism by making them vertical and hierarchical. It has had built in a recovery of the primordial total harmony by reliance on a theology that is quite Eusebian.[17] The covenantal variety, too, has its characteristic progressive-utopian form of eschatology and tends to lead to a bourgeois concept of God that is frequently "Arianized" into a liberal, rational pluralism without genuine coherence. The sectarian type has often become, as we have noted, quite apocalyptic and dualistic in its basic conceptions.

But this is not the end of the story, for several things have happened structurally in the twentieth century that have laid the groundwork for the emergent new style of ecclesiology.[18]

Corporative structures have had their authority threatened by both covenantal and movement types of organization. Both lay expertise, organized in elite groups outside the ordinary structures of authority, and democratic ideals have compromised the unique status of those mediating grace. And the resistance to that compromise in the twentieth century has encouraged complicity in reactionary politics by corporative groups. Thus the claims of exclusive authority have been discredited. Labor in corporations, consumers in marketing, the poor in welfare, the elderly in medicine, revolutionists in Asia and Latin America, parties in government, and lay assertiveness in ecclesiastical circles, students in universities, are all part of the same movement to fulfill the promise of Protestantism against corporative social organization.

Covenantal groupings, however, have allowed and sometimes promoted the proliferation of racial and class centers of loyalty and have de facto supported oligarchic rule in industry, labor, and politics as well as religion (even though it has often been only the religious elite, a minority of religious leaders who have challenged openly the theological pretensions of race and class). Only under the pressure of countervailing covenantal groups have structures been realigned and new personality structures produced—thus institutionalizing conflict and group egocentrism. To deal with this, it is necessary to construct alternative complexes that strengthen the consensus at the top. An urban-industrial complex, a poverty-education complex, a foreign aid–development complex are necessary cosmopolitan counterstructures to such stunning organizational achievements of the covenanting period as the Military-Industrial Complex.

Aggressive sectarians have proven incapable of resisting the twin temptations of messianic politics and the dissipation of energy in passing causes with little institutional impact. Yet they continuously appear, indicating a power and worth in them that we have not fully learned how to sustain. We do not have a conceptual framework that awards them a significant place.

In response to all of its major forms, therefore, the church consciously and unconsciously has been engaging in a theological and ecclesiological "casting about," trying to find new structures by which it can actualize the valid dimensions of each and avoid the pathologies of the various options.

What is emerging is a "conciliar denominational" pattern. Vatican II; The World, National, and local Councils of Churches; the Council of Christians and Jews; the United Churches of Canada, India, etc., are developing structures that suggest the possibility of a new form of social organization and may well become the basis for a new Christian social philosophy, and a new way of sustaining urban projects and making the normative *credo* operational in an urban ethos.

Contemporary conciliar denominationalism has drawn from the several traditions and roots and is recombining these selected patterns in new ways according to a dynamic inspirited movement internal to its own genius. At each point in this prototypical development fundamental conceptions about the future, and about God, man, and society are at stake. But the shape of this conciliar denominationalism is up for debate. It is clear that elements from previous structures must be included; they are operative in life. But which of them should be predominant, and how are the pathologies of previous eras to be minimized?

Two Shifts

There are two primary accents. The first derives from a modification of the covenantal type of organization toward the corporative and the corporative toward the covenantal. The conciliar structures that were necessary to adjudicate disputes, consolidate coalition, take action on specific issues, and promote fellowship in the Calvinist-covenantal tradition are now moving toward priority over the covenanted structures themselves as the center of loyalty and action. The denominations that developed councils are now becoming subsidiary in prestige and moral persuasion and in their capacity to attract talent to their efforts. And, the conciliar structures are being theologically legitimated even though economic and organizational weight still remains in the covenantal centers. The increased activity at the conciliar level has demanded sustained bureaucracy and patterns of authority which are similar in many ways to those of the corporative type, even if traditional Protestant hostility to organizational theology has prevented clarification of good order. However, there is a fundamental difference. In cases of dispute, the appeal is to the next lowest level of organization, the covenanting body, which may choose to comply or not. The authority of all levels is a derivative authority subject to the voluntary compliance and consensus of a constituency. Unity is theologically seen as transcendent goal and norm, while concretely found in provisional cooperation. The unity is secured practically through active affirmation of the "rights of error" and the acceptance of "loyal oppositions." And it is secured theoretically by the affirmation of the mystery of the pluralistic character of unity. The motifs of Vatican II that speak of the collegiality of the bishops, suggest the benefits of a diocesan senate, and hint of the possibility of electing the bishops are, in fact, indicative of the movement of the corporative type of organization toward this model as well.[19]

The second shift is toward formalizing the sectarian impulse and legitimizing its tendency to radicalize, thus partially domesticating and stabilizing it and partially providing it with institutional support. On the one hand, these groups press for the recognition of individual and group liberties, unique communal styles, personal or intentional community freedom to let the spirit blow where it will. More dramatically, this shift is accomplished by the formation of new congregations or ecclesiola, "task forces," "caucuses," "research teams," "action groups," and "emphasis commissions," that mobilize around specific issues. They either dissipate once their objectives are accomplished and the situation passes or they may become a covenantal group related to the conciliar center as does an already established group. More enduring needs of the church are also closely related to these "ecclesiolae." They bring innovation and charismatic urgencies that break through the structural crusts. These groups intentionally foment dissensus on dubious, but accepted, policy within a generalized consensus at a rather high level of abstraction.

The shift of accent to the ecclesiola on the part of conciliar denominationalism is accomplished by corporative or covenantal types into confrontation with decisive radical movements. Personnel in positions of authority are called out of the ordinary securities and conventions to encounter social and cultural innovations (such as idiosyncratic developments in the arts, technology, morality, or revolutionary group formation). The ecclesiolae either create their own synthesis or legitimate secular innovation. The two sides of the attempt to formalize and legitimate the sectarian elements involve both the selective "baptism" and the "spinning off" of secular social organization. The shift toward ecclesiolae provides a counterbalance to the more structured shift mentioned above and becomes a way of institutionalizing self-criticism, legitimating change, and addressing ad hoc problems without overly investing the general structures in a specific situation. If a specific situation changes, the general structure does not collapse with it. The shift toward ecclesiolae also provides a center of loyalty that involves personal commitment and involvement on a direct level. Thus, the massive organizations of modern life are given a structural connection to persons and small groups, and not a structural barrier against them.

But the emerging conciliar denominational structure is not primarily a countercomplex to either the world in general or any specific ecclesiological body, although it may promote counterstructures in the face of institutionalized evil. Rather it is a cosmopolitan meta-society or para-structure struggling partially within and partially without the present organizations, secular and sacred, to reach in a symbolic and normative integration in the modern ethos. It demands an altered theological focus on several points.

First, that which is of ultimate worth and power to man does not become concrete in any one way. There are many levels and dimensions in life manifesting themselves in different ways at different times. The church as the prototypical meta-society has the primary function of discerning within and without itself which levels and dimensions of life are pointing toward creative order, transformed identity, and inspirited community that sustain the vision of the future. Its form is a quite modified covenantalism with a dual accent on councils—institutionalized forms of conversation and deliberation and negotiation—and on congregations or ecclesiolae—the task forces at a local level that concentrate on expression of concerns, action, and response (within, without, or even against the parish structure).

Second, the conciliar denomination recognizes that it does not contain all the various dimensions of power and value. It is only an approximation to these, and it must therefore be in constant process of discerning, joining where possible and opposing where necessary, those other worldwide denominations such as communism, Islam, various nationalisms, and with a sense of special affinity, Judaism, according to their capacity to bear, even partially, the vision in their cultural contexts and give forth creative order, transformed identity, and inspirited communities to the end of worthy and powerful projects.

Third, the special centrality and importance of the covenantal type of ecclesiology in the history of the development of conciliar denominationalism may well require theological acknowledgment. Coupled with the importance of biblical conceptions in any renewal of the church, the term "covenant" may well remain as a central category in theology and ethics. The contributions of the Calvinist tradition to the urban ethos are unavoidable. But the boundaries of the covenant will be redrawn as suggested and the marks of the covenant respecified in new project and creedal terms by the conciliar denominationalism of a post-Protestant period.

Fourth, conciliar denominationalism must come to some clarity about the division of labor between the several levels of its constituency. As Paul Ramsey has suggested, conciliar denominationalism must not be turned into a "social action curia."[20] But we should not overstate the case against this danger, as Ramsey does. Conciliar denominationalism must not be concerned only with stating and exemplifying the normative of principles of good order but must encourage study and action on questions of policy at other levels of organization.

Further, conciliar denominationalism provides a focus which

both spins off movements and legitimates "secular" movements of a nontheological or even antireligious bent what are discerned to provide possibilities of legitimate project and *credo*. There is the possibility, then, of constructing a polity around a studied and intentional flexibility that recognizes the ability of man to confront God in at least three ways: through the structures of authority that are concretized approximations of good order, through the formation of a new liberated identity finding citizenship in the kingdom and at work in the world, and through direct encounter with artistic, emotional, or sociopolitical movements that are now seen as legitimate ecclesiological movements outside the church. In short, a Catholicized Protestantism and Protestantized Catholicism are converging in a new denominationalism centered in a council. It will surely have executive leadership, but that authority is dependent on ratification, approval, and consent of the council which, in turn, will appeal to subsidiary covenantal groups. Were that all, however, the ecumenical movement might legitimately be seen as the last energy-conserving gasp of dying Christendom. The other dimension, the intentional formation and support of "congregations," of freewheeling action and study groups, is the critical new feature which, in combination with the conciliar ecumenical movement, provides the new structures with both stability and change, consensus and dissensus, order and freedom, theory and action.

The implications of the development of conciliar denominationalism as a legitimate new ecclesiology can be seen in both theological and sociological terms. Theologically, the relations between God and man are not considered to be exclusively direct nor to be mediated by an institution of objective grace. Both radical sectarian and covenantal forms of Protestant as well as Catholic and Marxist forms of corporate exclusivism are challenged. The relation of God to man is considered to be for the most part mediate, not immediate; but the ecclesiastical institution *does not mediate within itself* so much as *seek* ultimate worth and power as *mediated in the world* by maintaining structural principles which allow discernment of where in the world those called out are forming community and transforming life under the aspect of the divine. Those groups engaged in urban change and those engaged in foreign development, bringing new constituencies into cosmopolitan consciousness, and promoting the construction of organizational complexes to sustain urbane existence, for example, would be seen as decisive.

Sociologically, the ecclesiology of conciliar denominationalism suggests that the fundamental assumption of innovation through the increased division of labor and differentiation is now in question. Innovation occurs also at another level, a conciliar level, and by a process that presupposes differentiation and that demands a move toward reintegration, but not at the price of specific innovation. It is a constructed (artifactual), intentional, and provisional order that builds in self-critical devices and recognizes the fact that it may only approximate that which is ultimately worthy and powerful. Concepts of membership and citizenship must be directed toward an ultimate cosmopolitan unity, but this is accomplished by building operating, differentiated infra-structures brought into coalitions to judge and fulfill parochial loyalties. The sustaining body that represents coalitions and nevertheless spins off ever new centers of creativity that may compromise the stability of that same sustaining body is the critical structure for seeing the shape of history in this epoch. Thus, the contemporary ecclesiological developments suggest that both bourgeois sociology from Max Weber and Emile Durkheim to Talcott Parsons and proletarian sociology from Marx and Engels to Mao needs correction. The former tradition is rooted in the underlying concept of the transition from organic to differentiated society. Couched in the distinctions of *Gemeinschaft/Gesellschaft,* Mechanical Solidarity/Organic Solidarity, Rural-folk/Urban-industrial society, the various sociological concepts by which we deal with much data are rooted finally in the transition theologically and socially from Catholic-feudal to Calvinist-enlightenment ecclesiology. As deeply dependent as we must remain on the work of these theorists, it may well be that some of the trends captured by these concepts are being reversed and our incapacity to conceptually grasp the shift due to fixed conceptual loyalties compounds the crisis of contemporary social thought. In regard to Marxist sociology, the concepts of inevitable historical logic of conflict and singularity of material causation blind researchers to the partial ways in which alienation can be overcome symbolically, voluntarily, and structurally in a way that affects, and is not only affected by, material factors. If this is the case, the consciousness of these possibilities and radical action on these premises would bring the revolutionary changes demanded by the times but without the terrible human cost that is now seen as necessary in this tradition—a tradition basically irrelevant to an already urbanized-industrialized society.

The churches and the new style of ecclesiology developing in their midst, by attempting to integrate the various modes of organization, may well be anticipating a polity that provides both stability and freedom and radical shifts toward good order that does not yet obtain in the secular political order. The high-level muddling-through that attends the most self-conscious *ecclesia* of Western history, however, is a critical point at which to understand the new directions of polity in the urban ethos. What happens in this arena will necessarily be paralleled by and influenced by what happens in the institutions of modern life in the urban ethos. Should conciliar denominationalism fail, it will indicate the failure to find a theologically significant social-political order that can make structural sense of the urban ethos in terms that relate to the decisive projects and doctrines of Western culture. There is, at present, little evidence that universities, courts, corporations, parties, or any other major institutional body has yet begun to come to grips with these issues in comparable ways.

But we have come to a point where we can identify what is required for an adequate *credo:* eschatological visions of the good, trinitarian concepts of right, and conciliar denominational organization of the fit become the three decisive ingredients of a meta-ethical model for the urban ethos. These render the ethical criteria for project, norm, and polity that are required for the artifact of the urban ethos. It remains, still, to work out the implications for the stances taken by the secular theologians, the urban theorists.

Chapter VIII

ETHICS IN THE URBAN ETHOS

From an analysis of the presuppositions of urban theorists we have seen that all fundamental views were rooted in *credo*. Both ordinary observers and trained theorists rely upon basic meta-ethical models of what this structure of human existence really is and ought to be to interpret their experience of the city. The various theorists accented *credos* that do indeed grasp basic dimensions of man's existence in the urban ethos, but that are both incomplete due to their dependence on broken symbols and often distorted because of their reliance on natural models to deal with a supra-natural artifact. To deal more adequately with the very dimensions of the urban ethos that they see and accent, it was argued, it is necessary to develop a depth sociology by use of an analytical ethic. Such an ethic self-consciously turns to decisive elements of *credo* that have given rise to the urban ethos. These elements are the visions, doctrines, and polities that give shape to good projects, right meaning, and fitting organization of cosmopolitan urban existence by reflecting the joining of worth and power.

There is both continuity and change in those visions, doctrines, and polities. They exist over great expanses of time and condition, yet need continual, and sometimes rather basic, revision and redefinition. The most important ingredients of decisive *credo* raise fundamental perennial issues and have an expansive quality that allows contextual application in particular situations over the centuries. Minor ones crumble and fade, like plots with no end, linguistic fads, and *ad hoc* committees in the subcultures of modern society. Without a rooted *credo* that has a vision of an end, a doctrine and an organized constituency that tries to preserve the wisdom of the past by intentional transformation, man is left to drift. He gets caught in programs with no purpose, symbolic trifles, and an inconsequential plethora of meetings for he finds himself bound unknowingly to secularized creeds against which he has no critical stance. He becomes chained to the rehearsal of cliché. The urban ethos requires, by virtue of its continuity and discontinuity with the past, a critical appropriation of tradition, a selective modification of the models of the past in a way that does not do violence to the past while it gives guidance toward the future.

In spelling out these ingredients, we have seen that the three related motifs are rooted in the Judeo-Christian traditions. Eschatology was treated as necessary to any project toward the future, the source of radical motifs of transformation, and the symbolic statement of worthy ends for all serious human projects. A trinitarian concept of God was treated as the symbolic identification of pluralistic structures of good power as it is present in cosmopolitan life and as the specification of those arenas of human experience where ultimately worthy projects may be most significantly expected. And a broadened understanding of conciliar denominational ecclesiology was suggested as a contemporary and normative model for urban community life, organized under the aspects of a pluralistic understanding of ultimately worthy power and straining toward the ultimate ends of life. These constitute the decisive *credo* of and for a cosmopolitan urban ethos.

No detailed attempt has been made to show the import of this *credo* or the urban ethos for cultures beyond the direct influence of the Judeo-Christian tradition. That must await further study. But, it has been implied throughout the argument that the contemporary artifact of the urban ethos is a recapitulation of, a product of, and an occasion for transformation of the Judeo-Christian self-understanding of social life beyond the idiosyncrasies of contemporary Western cities. From the freedom from the innocent tyranny of nature worship and the formation of a people, under one God, who attempt to define ethical, social, and political reality, to the formation of radical expectations of the future with the further extension of freedom from nature (in the denial of ethnic ties and sexual roles as decisive for entrance in the future Kingdom), to the specification of what may and what may not be ethically expected in human projects, to the growing awareness of the necessity of a doctrine of worthy power pluralistically operating toward such ends (and the articulation of its structure and locus), to the development of institutions that are genuinely instrumental in accomplishing those ends—that is the argument in an historical nutshell. But a very difficult set of problems remains: how, more precisely, does this *credo* give shape, wholeness, and normative guidance to the fragmented *credos* of secular theologians? How, in short, does such a *credo* render an ethic for existence in the urban ethos?

An ethic rooted in *credo* does not render, in the first instance, rules. Rather, an "analytic ethic," as we have called it, brings contemporary life into a particular focus wherein specific laws, priorities, and sensitivities can be seen as normative. It provides a perspective, a way of looking at the various dimensions of the urban ethos that allows us to see the traces of divine promise in it and that calls us to a lived response.

Credo and Urban Power

An ethic for urban power derives from, and is given legitimacy by, this *credo*. Such an ethic both grasps the structure of power in the urban ethos and gives direction to its ordering, allocation, and usage. The two predominant theories of power, that which accents the power of the wealthy and that which accents the power of formal decision-processes by leadership, have not looked deeply enough into the nature of power. To be sure, they have seen that money and authority bear concrete potential in the urban ethos, but they have not seen that these very concrete forms of power are themselves dependent upon a more pervasive, and finally more decisive, form of power. For people gain the wealth and authority which they exercise by the assent of the community. People gain, maintain, and increase their wealth and their authority by the apparent or actual fulfillment of what the community expects to be good, believes to be right, or considered fit organization. In their most concrete form, these expectations, beliefs, and senses of appropriateness are woven into an explicit legal structure. Thus, the power behind wealth and authority is law, and the power behind law is *credo*.

When ostensible power structures are confronted by dissidents or exposed by urban theorists, the protesters are patted on the head by those with wealth and those in authority, and nothing happens. Those with wealth and those in authority shrug their shoulders and say, "We did nothing illegal." And when particular programs are, in more characteristically urban and therefore pluralistic settings, jockeyed through a multiplicity of decision centers with the allocation of vast sums of money, it goes into effect whether or not those affected like it. Because it is legal. In either case, groups may modestly modify the structure or program by persuasion, so long as they accept the presuppositions and legal constraints of those in authority. That is, so long as they secure assent by relating technical requirements to values, beliefs or truths that transcend the particular judgments involved, as already established by law.[1] But nothing much is modified.

Wealth and authority, in the formal institutional environment of the urban ethos, are rationalized by law. And the law serves as the overt and public form of any urban ethic of power. It is through law that formal influence is structured and legitimated, permitted, or forbidden, so that it becomes operative. Indeed, it is through law that violence is seen as legitimate in the form of necessary coercion, structured to override dissent, or deemed criminal. If dissent or the attempt to influence escalates beyond the boundaries of law, to violence, it is by the influence of wealth and authority that coercion is used to crush dissent. Similarly, attempts to gain wealth or exercise authority without law or to engage in projects without the proper legal certifications can be authoritatively stopped by law, and by legitimatized coercion if necessary. Power in the urban ethos is expressed in money and authority, but any attempt to analyze the urban power structure will have first to look to the law that legitimates that wealth and authority.[2]

Law, in large-scale social systems, is positive law. It is rules and regulations that govern vast ranges of human conduct and institutional arrangement. Urban law is not mere custom or folkway, but explicitly stated public norms worked out into systems of role expectation, responsibility, permissibility. These define the boundaries of wealth and authority. Such law is capable of modification and has, historically, undergone considerable change. It is subject to revision and criticism. Every specific law is temporal even if the need for law is eternal in human society.

The problem of power in the urban ethos, then, is who or what controls the law. And this not only means who knows the police chief but who has access to the expectations, beliefs, and sense of fittingness that are seen as embodied in the law. And at this point, the power structure, elitist or pluralistic, does not reign supreme. For the law is the institutionalized form of what the society conceives to be right, good, and fit. In urban society, more strikingly than in any society known to man, access to these exists among people and institutions that are not the power structure as well as the power structure. It is the relative agreement by the citizens individually and the institutions collectively on the right, good, and fit that provides the decisive threads out of which the whole fabric of law becomes woven. Wherever, therefore, people and institutions can be organized, there arises a capacity to change the law. The decisive level of urban power is at hand. Indeed, the urban ethos invites such intentional organization, for the fetters of nature and custom are broken and insofar as nonchaotic conditions exist at all, they exist by intentional ethical decision.

Of course, law can become rigidified and highly preferential to particular groups who manipulate it and coercively enforce it for their own ends in contrast to the ethological requirements of urban existence. But because the law does not sustain itself, it is always possible to disobey it by either taking upon oneself or a group the consequences of coercion in a visible act of civil disobedience to raise the sense of right, good, and fit in the public consciousness. Or, persons and groups may declare an alternative law right, good, and fit, developing alternative institutions which will authorize countercoercion of violence. Such alternatives, however, require new specifications of the right, good, and fit, and a *credo* to legitimate them. In either case, since the old or new law cannot sustain itself, it must be sustained by violence or *credo*. When a relatively coherent and unified *credo* is not present or clear in the society, violence increases. Where it does reign, violence decreases. In the final analysis, however, *credo* is more important and powerful than violence, for *credo* can displace violence more easily than violence can displace *credo*.

The analyses of power structures, and the interpretation of

them as covert or systematic violence at the hands of wealth, as the power-elite theorists suggest, or as legitimating processes of decision-making, through democratic means, as pluralists suggest, are in fact debates about the terms and implications of the *credo* that dominate the society and legitimate the distribution of wealth and authority. The *credo,* as it gives shape to law and through it to the allocation of wealth and authority, and not merely the cliques benefiting from it, must in a subtle analysis of power, therefore be the first target of analysis. For the departure of these people, if the *credo* remains unchallenged and the law therefore remains unrevised, would only mean a new set of wealthy, authorized tyrants.

The hope, therefore, for the fulfillment of the promise of pluralistic power in the urban ethos resides in the custodians of *credo.* And in the urban ethos, this means that all men are called to be rabbis and theologians. Each man is to meditate on the law day and night to work out the implications of fundamental commandments for the right, good, and fit made necessary by a perennial new ordering of life beyond the exodus from control by tyrants. It means also that every urban man is to be a theologian by self-consciously raising up the ultimate issues of *credo* that legitimate and shape the structures of authority. Further, following Athanasius against the Arians, it is recognized by a proper *credo* that all men are capable of engaging in such a task when they take upon themselves a transformed identity, for they then have access to the divine life that stands beyond and can criticize the mere liberal-rational creation of autonomous nodes of power.

Such people, however, are not merely to meditate or reflect in the privacy of their own hearts. They are called into organized constituencies. Voluntary associations, committees, unions, fronts, coalitions, parties, and "machines" generate and sustain visions, doctrines, and polities in such a way that they become embodied in the law. These are the tissue of urban association behind the law that constitute the decisive visible power under the power of *credo.* For these are the groups that wield the influence to change the law, and hence the structure of wealth and authority, by bringing about a fresh institutionalization of the legitimating *credo.* These are the groups in an urban environment that shape the perception of public images, that debate the acceptability or incredibility of slogans which symbolize the values and interests of constituencies, that create the arenas wherein leadership skills are developed, that engender competence in the complexity of urban issues, and that create buffers between the arrogance of official wealth or authorities and individuals.

These groups may be dominated by oligarchs, and a limited number of such groups may temporarily dominate. But in the urban ethos the number and extent of such groups are not limited. Power of this sort is not a fixed quantity, but may be socially created in geometric ratios. It is difficult, painful, and slow; but possible. Whenever created, such groups can demand the rearrangement of influence under law. Certain kinds of such power are limited, however, by the principles of its *credo*. *Credos* based on "natural" distinctions of race, sex, or class cannot survive forever in the urban ethos even if they have enormous residual potency in the short run, because urban identity is finally not dependent upon "givens" and because some account of the factual and normative obligations of pluralism have to be taken into account. The kinds and qualities of human relationships are not naturally given and have to be decided upon ethically. Thus, such distinctions in the urban ethos must be judged decisively unethical. They cannot, in the final analysis, link power and worth in a normative vision, doctrine, or polity.

Of course, in some settings not fully urban, the law mitigates against the formation of organized constituencies that want to develop visions, doctrines, and polities. But in such circumstances, the first step is and must be the development of a more complete *credo*. As life is worked out in these terms, it brings a change in the law. Laws restricting the formation of ecclesiological groups are by every canon of the *credo* illegitimate. They do not allow the emergence of new projects toward the future, they do not accent the necessary and ordered pluralism wherein man encounters the divine, and they do not permit a fitting polity for an urban society. Where coercive powers under this pre-urban law therefore predominate, the radical, aggressive sectarian option of revolution for the sake of righteousness becomes a possibility. Once the repressive regime is deposed, however, all of the requirements of pluralism and relative stability come back into play, and a new law, rooted in the fuller dimensions of the *credo,* would have to be articulated.

Decisive among all these groupings that determine the critical form of visible power are those feeble reeds, churches and synagogues. The churches and synagogues serve as the prototype of these freewheeling ecclesias of influence. Not only do they most self-consciously remember, refine, redefine, and promulgate among the "little people" the *credo* most pertinent to the very foundation of the urban ethos, but they do so in a fashion least plagued by overt coercion and violence. Further, out of the synagogues, and out of the conciliar Catholic, Calvinist covenantal, and aggressive sectarian churches have again and again come the quite concrete forms of leadership training, organizational skills, and political sensitivity, with an ethical drive, that has engendered social movement after social movement. By no means have these custodians of the *credo* been universally progressive in their influence, and by no means have the social movements engendered by them been always urbane. That is due in part to the fact that much of what they did socially was done unintentionally, in part to the egocentrism that they, no less than other groups, are heir to, and in part to the failure to understand the social responsibilities of their own groups in terms of their own *credos.* But it is clear negatively that when these groups falter and fail, or are suppressed, the prospects for a genuinely urbane and cosmopolitan ethos fade also. There are other groups—business corporations, more hierarchically organized than most corporative churches, and dedicated to profit; universities, necessarily and properly operating on rational-liberal presuppositions for the intellectually elite; governmental bureaucracies, proceeding on preprogrammed legal directives; or mass media, creating by their flood of information a global village, and the like—that will attempt to dictate the *credos* of urban society. But they cannot bring the depths of the human condition, symbolized in the *credo,* to organizational fruition for they are not in the final analysis theologically competent.

The urban ethos is not, cannot, and ought not be formed according to such patterns. As Max Weber has shown with regard to capitalism, the impulse to acquisition has in itself nothing to do with the formation of a culture: "This impulse exists and has existed among waiters, physicians, coachmen, artists, prostitutes, dishonest officials, soldiers, nobles, crusaders, gamblers, and beggars. One may say that it has been common to all sorts and conditions of men at all times and in all countries of the earth."[3] To paraphrase him further, one might add that it ought to be taught in the kindergarten of cultural history that this naive idea of business as being able to generate or sustain an ethos must be given up once and for all. Nor, after Germany's experience of the early twentieth century can we say that the influence of rational-liberal education guarantees the survival of cosmopolitan perspectives. In the face of the Vietnam War, it is difficult to see how present dominant governmental bureaucracies, such as the Department of Defense, can promote an urbane existence. Nor is it clear, given present programming techniques, that the mass media can generate the values to structure the flood of facts it makes available. And so on one could go. These significant institutions for modern society are necessary, but not finally sufficient institutional models for civilization. No urban society can exist without business, higher education, bureaucracy, and communications. Significant new patterns emerge in their midst as from all institutions. But the criteria for deciding their rightness, goodness, and fitness for the whole culture, rest beyond them. They reside in the churches, often semisecular ones. The vibrant ideas of and for business presently derive from sensitivity groups, ecology action groups, Black Power groups, and consumers' advocacy groups. The transformation of university institutions is taking place at the hands of student organizations, faculty associations, and women's liberation groups. The most striking remodeling of governmental bureaucracies is being demanded by peace groups, welfare rights organizations, and civil servant unions. And the mass media draw their news from the activity and impact of such groups. In each case, quietly and undramatically, it has been the churches and synagogues that provided space for, helped organize, gave legitimacy to, or debated the merits of such groups in the face of the people by trying to make rabbis and theologians of every man and woman according to basic criteria of right, good, and fit. And even where specific efforts have failed, the churches and synagogues, through sustaining hope, proclamation, and liturgy, have preserved the *credo* beyond the boundaries of dominant social operations so that even if a civilization crumbles, the *credo* does not finally fail but can shape society anew. And the church makes such a *credo* operative not only among the rich, the bright, the organized, and the informed, but among the poor, the dull, the incompetent, and the uninformed. The people are truly empowered. They, through the churches and synagogues, become capable of both judging the dominant society and becoming a part of the mainstream of history. This, and not merely formal decision-processes of a pluralistic sort is genuine democracy. Of course, under the influence of Protestant individualism, many pseudo-churches accent only individual salvation and passive acceptance of national civil religion—as today exemplified in Billy Graham rallies. But such trivial phenomena only contribute to the understanding of mass psychology, nothing more, for they bear, finally, no vision, no doctrine, and no ecclesiology.

If, therefore, the urban ethos is to be sustained by the society at large, it would be well to adopt so far as possible the models being worked out in the pluralism of conciliar denominationalism. For here is a coordinated pattern of order, a structure that is specifically designed to aid, support, and evoke the highest responsibility from individuals, and a pattern of stabilized group formation that stands at the cutting edge of social and cultural problems. It is this institutional matrix that accents the possibilities of power among, for, and to the people and can, therefore, normatively shape law, wealth, and authority. This focuses man's moral energy on the formation of an urban complex oriented to the promotion of urbane, civilized, cosmopolitan life demanding the legitimation of democratic allocation of both wealth and authority. And this means that the churches themselves must as a whole come to a fresh appreciation of the implications of their own polity decisions for the long-range shape of civilization.

Vocation and Identity in the Urban Artifact

The *credo,* however, not only directs us to social and institutional reconstruction. Every social ethos also requires and produces a characteristic and normative definition of personhood. It was just suggested that the rabbi and theologian would be prototypical in an institutional setting required by the institutional matrix of the normative *credo.* What, more precisely, does this entail and how does it give shape to the problem of identity discovered in the personalist fragment of a *credo* and to that of vocation discovered in the partial *credo* of the morphologists?

It is seen, in the normative *credo,* that natural identity is not sufficient. Only a concept of transformed identity captures the way personality is in the city and the way it ought to be. Man does not find himself by more and more intensive plumbing the depths within his psyche but discovers and continually finds the depths of the self transformed when he pours the self out for the sake of others and the general shape of things. It is in such transforming "dying to the self" that genuine fulfillment of the self is discovered, for the self also discovers judgment against the self and its egocentricity when it encounters the other and the ethos. Self focused on the self within the self is too small to find fulfillment.

Such an outpouring of the self is made viable whenever there is developed an individual self-consciousness with regard to the possibility and obligation of the self to develop a *credo* in concert with others that links the most profound visions, doctrines, and polities of humankind with the purposes of the self by becoming aware of a sense of vocation. Here vocation is not to be understood as a job or a business alone, but as an awareness that one is called by the structure of ultimate worth and power to exercise concrete worth and power in the social arena in specific ways. It is in such sensibilities that the genuine assumptions for the understanding of personhood are to be found. For in the urban ethos, the question "Who am I?" most often masks a hidden agenda, "What am I to become?" And the answer is only to be found when a connection between personal capacities and socially structured options leads people into commitments that enable them to preserve or reconstruct some part of the fabric of the community under a sense of power and worth. Then, people are able to engage in projects, to attend to the right, or to fit into a worthy polity.

The development of such self-consciousness, found in a matrix that invites the outpouring, transformation, and continual rediscovery of continually re-created self, has several dangers. It breaks the more simple harmonies of organic relationships between people. Ties of kith and kin, male and female role expectations, and grouping by clan or ethnic ties are reduced. Wherever the institutions of the city come in contact with pre-urban peoples (one of the chief institutional functions of the modern university, by the way), there is the discovery of a new transformation of self, a self freed from natural and traditional necessity by mastery and concious reflection on the mystery of both. And this brings new possibilities of a selfishness of competence. The egocentric use of the fruits of this competence by one or some in turn becomes built into the social fabric of the artifactual environment. Original sin, that primordial and inevitable tragedy of man born of liberation from pre-given structures, becomes institutionally transmitted to succeeding generations. And when organized into institutions it corrupts creative order, destroys persons, and represses inspirited communities. Counterinstitutions, institutions to promote and sustain creative order, institutions with a vision of a radical future, and a profound doctrine that relates to the vocations of individuals are required to compromise the powers of death that are in the egoisms of man merely liberated.

The constructs of urban existence provide the possibilities, and a normative *credo* points to the moral necessity, of bringing man out of his egocentrism to a point where he can or must acknowledge the interests and concerns of others. Wider interdependencies are implicit in urban existence and these bend and limit him. Also, in the urban ethos, it is possible to construct more complex structures of technology. Thus, man can free himself from certain drudgeries of repetitive necessity. Freedom to explore the frontiers of the human mind and spirit is available. Indeed, such is a primary hope of man. But these possibilities need support structures and have eventually to find normative personal direction, else his transformed identity becomes oppressive or empty.

We found, in the analysis of the eschatological dimensions of the *credo,* that the biblical tradition identifies three decisive personal roles: prophet, priest, and king. Man finds his identity in urban existence, in three analogous ways: as liberator of man, woman, and child from merely naturalistic worship and from the tyranny of pre-given structures; as a professional, gaining technical mastery of bodies of wisdom and relating these to the practical service of others in a way that recognizes the wider interdependence of man; and as a statesman, participating in the formation of communities that bring a cosmopolitan and just peace into existence. Each of these ordinarily operate at the boundaries of conventional vocational consciousness, yet the *credo* sees them as crucial and links them with other motifs. The early Christian movement broadened normative concepts of prophetic, priestly, and kingly identity to include resurrection, membership in the communion of saints, and citizenship in the Kingdom. The Constantinian period of Western history established the patterns of religious vocation by showing how the priestly individual at least had access to resources of power and worth beyond mere cultural principalities and values and how he could therefore be critical of social-political forms. The Reformation extended the priesthood to all believers. Today, under impact of the same *credo* as modified by the urban ethos, we must extend the concept of man's identity still further: modern man's more differentiated vocation is not to a job nor merely to be a priest to himself and his neighbor, but to find transformed identity by pouring himself out as all three: liberator, professional, and statesman. The kind of rabbi and the kind of theologian that all are called to be is the kind that accents and works for the prophecy, priesthood, and kingship of all citizens.

To be prophetic, to be a liberator, means that man must find, define, and act for or against those dimensions of social-political life that either contribute to or inhibit transforming projects toward the future. It means that all are called to an articulate pluralistic doctrine that takes issue with the worship of race, sex, class, or other natural patterns of worship by man. And these it does in full view of ultimate worth and power that demand social empowerment of worth. All men are capable of this who can squeak when their wheel needs grease and, more importantly, who can speak forth on behalf of people who cannot squeak, or who can organize the people who will demand a constructive reshaping of the future. By "forthtelling" that discloses the gaps of meaning and coherence in a society with the pending disaster that such gaps portend, they foretell the necessary reshaping of that society. Under the focus of the ultimate center of power and worth, they stand at the "edges of the community's experience and tradition. . . . [They view] man's life from a piercing perspective and [bring] an imperative sense of the perennial and inescapable struggle of good against evil, of justice against injustice."[4]

To be professional, a secular priest in the urban ethos, means to profess, to articulate, define, and apply on the basis of a normative *credo* and in a technically competent way, the values upon which an area of human life depend. The proliferation of so-called professional associations and "new professions" in the modern urban ethos hints at this possibility. But far too often, such groups center on egocentric protection of privileges and the purely rational quest for the technological "fix" for civilization, or the accrediting of personnel who passively accept the presuppositions of a craft, then sell themselves to the highest bidder. But such behavior is not truly professional; it is a new form of a hired priestcraft. Such accents merely produce "experts" who pretentiously claim and capitalize by a corner on the market of "salvific technique." True professionals *profess* something. They are governed by a *credo,* and an accompanying ethic specified to the technical requirements of a particular and necessary social function. A professional maintains, extends, and demands empowerment of worth in the transformation of nature and society. He does so, ultimately, out of a sense of calling to service and self-sacrifice. All men can become professional in an urban ethos, for all are called to participate in voluntary associations as well as in jobs requiring technical skills. They can assume a transformed identity that is at once highly personal and socially structured. Those involved in religious bodies have already sensed this possibility ritualistically upon ordination or commissioning, as have political appointees when they are "sworn in," doctors and lawyers when they repeat their oaths, or firemen when they assume the responsibility of community protection. In the urban ethos all "jobs" could be so structured through the actions of professional associations.[5]

To be a statesman is to adjudicate between competing claims and to serve as a broker of interests in a way that both mitigates disputes in favor of a just peace, and finds or creates those polities upon which community can be built. He imaginatively negotiates worthy projects through a multiplicity of power centers, constructs new symbols or modes of expression to evoke inspirited response, and builds a constituency into a good order that sustains and extends personal identity and group intimacy. Further, the statesman recognizes the painful, occasional necessity of coercive violence and the regular need for formal legal authority to bring the common potentialities to fruition; but he does not worship the possession of formal legitimacy or the exercise of force.[6]

The whole urban man is a rabbi and a theologian who, in all public actions, is a liberating and professing statesman.[7] But more, he *means* it. To be a liberator, a professional, a statesman requires not only the performance of these functions but a profound differentiated inwardness—an internalization of the ethos of future possibility—found ironically by the outpouring of the self for the sake of the general shape of things. Such an inwardness makes these patterns of behavior authentic expressions of one's essential human condition. Individuals can phenomenologically drop out of inadequate or corrupt society through private emphasis on merely personal identity, but they cannot by any action separate themselves from society. Thus, definitions of personhood that accent normative social role under vision, doctrine, and polity are the decisive ones. The moral or responsible self in the urban ethos takes on the reality of the social condition as the primary arena in which to work out normative identity. The possibilities of a genuinely cosmopolitan ethos, thus, are partially dependent on the kinds and quality of prophetic, professional, and political commitments of men and women. The character of society is built not only into the project, doctrines, and polities of cultures, but also into the hearts of people. An "objective" analysis is inseparable from the "subjective" analysis of the morally significant aspects of person-hood, for the ways in which these are joined allow or prevent the possibilities of personal vocation. And it is only by the assumption of normative, objective roles that the subjective possibilities of personal authenticity and significant interpersonal intimacy become pervasive in the urban ethos.

The responsible urban person, then, is one who is "called out," but at the same time, he maintains his presence in the present patterns of society and tries to discern where in the present there are good projects, doctrines, and patterns of worthy power. If he organizes or participates in a group that tries to anticipate those patterns within itself for the sake of all, he is forming an ecclesia. He is in the covenant of those called to the new formation.

This means, for the full time leadership of the various *ecclesia,* those we call Rabbis and Theologians proper, that they become enablers. It is they who must assume the excruciating task of enabling the people, group by group, community by community, to find, articulate and actualize a sense of vision, right order, and organizational appropriateness that can give shape to our amorphous, yet highly complex civilization. Such a painful and exhausting task can only be assumed under the impact of a sense of divine vocation.

The Urban Ethos as Ethical Revelation

Our accents in the ethics of the urban ethos, so far, fall on institutional form and vocational identity. These, for an ethic of the most elaborate artifact ever created, are basic points of departure, for the urban matrix of life is a peculiarly human one. The right, good, and fit and the linkages of power and worth must therefore focus primarily on those supra-natural phenomena of self and society that constitute the peculiarly human.

As a peculiarly human phenomenon, the urban ethos has more purely all the pathologies and potentials that are inherent in human beings and human artifacts. It is the potentialities that have been accented in this study, for the pathologies are well known, often experienced, and part of the substratum of consciousness by which modern man conceives of the city. Indeed, the pathologies are frequently more visible and dominant than they need be, for the fragmented *credos* by which conventional wisdom operate fail to grasp the promise, and thereby compound the pathologies. Yet the urban ethos is needful of both defense and direction. What we are attempting to deal with is of such significance that if the nation-state fails, if particular institutions die, and if new civilizations rise from the ashes of today's social arrangements, the urban ethos will endure as the goal of future societies to attain and surpass. And this is because the urban ethos has brought a new revelation of ethical possibility more visibly into the arena of history than ever before.

But if this is so, three final questions remain: first, what should be the morphological shape of the urban ethos? What physical form should the urban revelation take in time and space? Second, what relationship to nature is normative for an urban ethos? If it is to be sustained in time and space, what should be its relation to the "given" patterns of these? And, third, what is the relation of the urban ethos to the divine life? If it is claimed to be a form of revelation, what is its connection to the ultimate center of worth and power which transcends time and space?

There are, already, in the urban ethos, liberators, professionals, and statesmen struggling to articulate and implement the more profound dimensions of normative *credo*—often working at the boundaries of the conventional rabbinic and theological constraints of their secular disciplines. E. Bacon[8] and Paolo Soleri,[9] for example, are among those who in quite distinct ways attempt to bring the questions of ultimate ends, right understandings, and institutional polity to bear on urban design and architecture. In these efforts, the desired morphology attempts to provide all citizens with an aesthetic arrangement of space that touches on the mystery of urban, technological existence, quick accessibility of distance, an opportunity for interaction, intimacy, and institutional creativity that reminds all of roots in the past, evokes imaginative plunges into the future, and makes the necessary routines of sustaining the urban ethos available, transparent, and nonalienating. The way in which the environment is structured, and the processes by which it is reconstructed either restricts the vision of the future or invites participation in it. Normatively, the physical structures should communicate to people an invitation to engage in viable projects, to participate in articulating the governing doctrine, and to organize into ecclesias.

Under these conditions, the urban environment can become a vast and new kind of human cathedral, a sacred and emotive structure that is simultaneously efficient and rational, standing as an inducement to continuous new formation. As such, it not only invites to the future, it communicates the qualities of the past that provide man with the spiritual and conceptual resources for reconstruction. The ways in which the past can and does contribute to the possibilities of the future are accented. Thus, for example, even such parochial matters as the recycling of disposable waste become an occasion for community awareness of concrete dependence on the past and the possibilities of reconstructing toward the future. Or, the celebrations of triumph over tragic suffering by oppressed groups in the past become the occasions for plumbing new dimensions of the spirit, communicated through interethnic and interclass contact intentionally designed into community patterns. Or, preservation of historical styles of architecture by functionally including such structures in new building becomes a way of sustaining the concrete spiritual insights and creations of the past. The peculiarly historical character of human existence dictates the design and use of space.

Further, urban morphology can be so designed that there is a celebration of that kind of ultimate unity that does not obscure pluralism, corrupt creative order, destroy possibilities of transformed identity, or inhibit inspired community. The uniqueness of particular locations and movements must communicate relationships to larger patterns and the interdependences of particular centers of identity, in ways that evoke recognition and empowerment of overarching values. Power and worth are thus mediated in ways that are transparent and accessible. The morphology is well planned if it invites people to participate in its control and transformation through decision-making in the name of purposes beyond themselves. The decisive criterion of a well-shaped collective life is its capacity to engage people in constructive social action for the future through pluralistic polities. Authorities which deny that capacity must be exposed and made accountable to public scrutiny and, if necessary, to protest or reformation.

The precise definition of good morphology, of course, varies from situation to situation. Models may be drawn from several desirable levels of experience, perceived or imagined. It makes a difference, to be sure, whether one is building on a tribal or village, township or county, commercial, industrial, or residential base. Projects that are good for Brasilia may not be good for Columbus or Providence. Further, these projects are not good forever. They are relative to a particular time. Urban renewal in the broadest sense is a constant pattern of transformation and retransformation which in a genuinely urban ethos living under a full-orbed *credo* is done not out of desperate need or as a once-for-all project, as it often is now; but in such a way that each transformation of the environment may mean transformed routinization and spatialization of projects, creeds, and social patterns that bring normative power and worth to the fore, and thus the possibility of richer perceptions of values, powers, and possible projects. Reprogramming, reformation, and reutilization of resources are necessary normative patterns of the urban ethos—not because change is indigenously good but because the sustaining of the urban ethos brings continual expansion of human horizons. Each new horizon requires new transformation, and each transformation requires further adjustment as its implications are extended throughout human patterns of behavior. One enters thereby more fully into the process of humanization through confronting new ranges of ethical decision-making. Thus, the calculation of particular situations requires the explicit development of a new theological-ethical seriousness that is already informally present among some professional urban planners and designers. But, at present, it is more frequently devoid of systematic reflection on the fundamental presuppositions which inform their actions and values.

Such a theological-ethical seriousness is also necessitated by the presence of many variations in patterns of accountability and capacities to sustain the urban ethos, technologically and organizationally. But the process itself is the critical theological-ethical ingredient.

Therefore, priority in planning the collective morphology must be given to those projects which invite transforming activity in the formation of inspirited community. And these are to be tested by their capacity to support creative order and to shape personal identity.

Such efforts to make the potential of the urban ethos concrete in time and space take place, of course, within the constraints of natural possibility. But the entire argument here presented accents the insufficiency of naturalism as a normative source of meta-ethical models. It is an argument, instead, that focuses on the supra-natural possibilities and necessities of the urban ethos.

Human projects under the symbols of the Kingdom and the Trinity and by those called out take precedence over projects that draw their models from nature. Greenbelts under certain conditions may be sacrificed to those projects that create new community for all men. Rivers may be diverted, swamps drained and hills leveled or built to transform the given toward the constructed if it contributes to a pluralistic experience of creative order, transformed identity, and inspirited community Nature, itself, is understood as a created "Rorschach" with no right and no wrong; and it may be constructively reordered according to the imaginative powers of man under the power of God. In urban ethos the pattern of presumed "natural" relationship of tribe with tribe, parent and child, male and female, stages on life's way, are culturally and not naturally defined. "Fatherly" authority may be redefined in broader parental terms. And sonhood becomes a metaphor of human vocation. The selection of concepts or dimensions of nature as normative is itself now understood as a function of supra-natural perceptions. And under the impact of these there is nothing about nature that may not be transformed and made serviceable to the project of a transformed future. The debate then is about the kind and quality of supra-natural power deemed valuable.

Are there, then, no limits which human projects, theology, and polity may not overcome? The city makes man free, but it does not necessitate licentiousness. There are limits; but they are not limits in nature. They are limits in artifacts and constructs and in capacity of artifact to deal with nature. That is, the limits are built into the ethos, and are expressed in religion. From religion the patterns derive that shape society and its tool, technology. Religion is thus a more decisive guide than nature. The possibilities of society and technology are dependent upon the shape of the religious ethos. The decisive powers and the decisive limits are, in short, supra-natural. As John F. A. Taylor recently wrote: "The first question of philosophy is a question of civilization not of nature, a question of obligation not of fact."[10]

In principle, then, there are no transformations of nature that may be judged a priori and intrinsically immoral because they are "unnatural." There is no "natural" definition of personhood, morphology, or political power that has normative authority. But there are limitations on what can be done. Supra-natural artifacts, if they are to survive, must gather the unfulfilled and unhistorical potentialities and values of nature into themselves if it disturbs them as given. If the natural eco-systems are disturbed or destroyed, new, transformed, and comprehensive eco-systems must be designed in a way that sustains and not merely exploits the future. The harmonies and vitalities of the cosmos may be disrupted and humanized by the intentional transformation of nature so long as new harmonies and vitalities are constructed. The intention, here, may be seen by understanding the two interpretations of the concept "spaceship earth" as used by current ecology buffs. The first accents the "earth" part of the symbol and sees the earth as a closed eco-system given by nature into which humankind must adjust by integrating himself into natural foodchain and recycling systems. The call is for a new "earth ethics." The second accents the "spaceship" side of the symbol and calls for the artifactual creation of new eco-systems that can sustain life for the humanization of the cosmos even in the midst of a potentially barren environment. The call here is for a uniquely "human ethics." The necessities of the urban ethos, both material and creedal, support the latter option out of conviction, calculation of probability, and in view of the consequences of not moving in such a direction. For if such a relation with nature is not constructed, Calcutta is the city of the future.

This means that there are constraints laid upon man: first, man must not transform in such a way that the normative patterns of institutional arrangement will corrupt the possibilities of survival. That is, if the artifactual means of humanizing the cosmos are not sufficiently built up, but the natural harmonies are fundamentally disturbed so that the only way of saving man from self-destruction is tyrannically imposed technocratic rule, the ethos is fundamentally unethical and must be opposed. If the ethos is so structured that only an elect few can attain personal fulfillment and transformation in liberating, professional, and statesmanlike roles the promise of a humane and universal cosmopolitan ethos is betrayed.

Second, a proportionality must exist between the disruption of the natural environment and the capacity to construct new, more comprehensive eco-systems. Man's capacity to construct artifacts out of the stuff of nature must not outrun his capacity to sustain civilization for the future. Fragmented control of production, distribution, and consumption at the hands of corporations insensitive to public projects, doctrines, and polities, it is widely claimed today, often exploit the natural eco-systems without constructing new ones. If so, they undercut the possibility of an urban future while using many of the tools of urban civilizations. Hence, those organizations invite the false responses of monolithic or dualistic organization or lead to the dissolution of the urban ethos. The ecological struggle, in the face of the urban environment, is not against *all* supra-natural artifacts, but with those who have not yet been made urban and are therefore irresponsible.

In sum, then, a morphology for the urban ethos must take form in space and time, in the context of nature, but not on its models. And this involves the legitimate re-creation of intentional eco-systems, the gathering up, preservation, and humanization of natural "givens" through reordering their relationships in an artifactual environment. But the decisive models and obligations with regard to these artifactual eco-systems are drawn from the supra-natural *credo* and its human, ethical implications.

The final question, then, has to do with the relationship of the urban ethos to the divine life. And it is here argued that the urban ethos is the context of ethical revelation. "Revelation" is a loaded word, and it could be asked whether or not these same conclusions could also be arrived at by "secular man." And indeed they could—by urbanized, cosmopolitan man already influenced by a *credo* now forgotten. But how are such men to account for their validity? How are they to structure such conclusions into a *credo* so that they will elucidate the roots of human ethical reflection and sustain them into the future? And how are such notions to gain legitimacy except by coercive power if there is not consent to their validity on symbolic grounds? If, as Sir Ernest Barker reminds us, "we believe that ethics is the study *par excellence* of the purposive activities of man and the ends by which they are guided, and if we accordingly hold that ethics has an 'architectonic' quality, we shall say that the political theorist must . . . find the touchstone of social life and political activity in some ultimate ethical principle."[11] And for urban man, divorced from nature by the matrix of his life, experiencing the transformation of personal identity, and unwilling to be merely the victim of social engineering or power struggles, this leads to theology or nowhere. It is therefore here suggested that only by explicitly treating the urban ethos in the context of *credo* can the concrete values and powers that are joined in it be judged where found corrupt or trivial, adopted without cultural imperialism where found valid, and altered radically—at the roots—where found deficient. The urban ethos is, then, revelational, demanding theological, ethical, and social recovery and reconstruction.

In the most important efforts dealing with theology and urbanization in the last decade four fundamental motifs have been accented. Gibson Winter of Chicago argued that the church must appraise its new setting, metropolis, afresh in order to know how to convey the "Christian Message."[12] Harvey Cox of Boston argued that the casting off of doctrinal and "religious" trappings in favor of a secular city was a cause for theological celebration.[13] Herbert Richardson, now of Canada, argued that Christianity must affirm a "sociotechnical intellectus" implied in the city out of recognition of its inevitability. As theology has decisively shaped Platonism, Aristotelianism, and a bourgeois individualism, so also it can now shape a "Christian sociotechnicism."[14] And in France, Jacques Ellul culls through the

Scriptures to show that, from a biblical perspective, every city is the "whore Babylon," seducing man into sins of pride, arrogance, and destruction.[15] The present effort could have been written without these efforts and is indebted to them throughout. But in an attempt to move the ongoing discussion one step further,[16] it is argued here that not only the setting of the church has changed, involving new responsibilities, but indeed the terms for understanding both the city and the Christian message itself have to be reconstructed. It is also argued that the future does not demand secularization so much as it does a new sacredness through a necessary theological reinterpretation of an urban *credo* and its ethical implications. It further argues that the "sociotechnical intellectus" of the urban ethos has indeed normative implications for theology and that it is, further, an occasion for theology to clarify its social-ethical implications and make manifest its latest social-cultural functions. And, it is here suggested that while the present city often crucifies people, the urban ethos it engenders is nevertheless a sign of the promise of redemption and human possibility. The city is in principle a twice-born social context. It thereby represents a greater vision of society's heightened possibilities and its wretched actual condition. The urban ethos is, in short, a form of ethical revelation.

To make such assertions requires that the contemporary urban ethos be understood in two ways: as a distinct level of that which fundamentally unveils the human condition, and as a sign of grace.

Revelation, in traditional theology, has been understood as of two kinds: it is either common revelation, consisting in what all know by reason and common experience to be worthy and powerful. Or it is special revelation, consisting in the unique moments in sacred history where the foundations of faith are laid. The urban ethos, it is here claimed, provides a matrix where the two are related in principle, but in a way that is not reducible to either of these possibilities. The urban ethos, connected at each point to both common and special theological realities, uniquely unveils the peculiarly ethical level of existence. It produces an "ethological" matrix that has a distinctive character, into which flood all the ethical and moral dilemmas of human existence in a way that cannot be answered by reciting the names of the gods or turning to nature. Indeed it creates new complex ethical problems and demands altered ethical methods for confronting them. From this condition there is no retreat, but from it also derives certain universalizable requirements of large-scale social systems that will be part of the human future as far as we can see into it.

The unveiling of such possibilities is a gift of grace. Grace is an unmerited concretion of power and worth that captures human will. Grace reconstructs human institutions and allows a faithful response. Grace is not discovered or found as are, for example, the vitalities and "laws" of nature, but it comes to man. Grace is a kind of "given" that is distinct from the "givens" malleable to human technological control, for it requires existential, social, and ethical response. When present it is recognized as a new kind of "given" and becomes the material upon which and from which the human powers of creativity work. Man shaped by this new quality of "givenness" is enabled to participate in the reconstruction of both life and views of life. Man so shaped becomes co-creator with the source of the gift; he synergistically participates in the visionary construction of an environment, in developing a conceptual apparatus, and in an organizational basis to sustain the gift.

But most important for our purposes, the urban ethos challenges the formulations of "eternal truths" that are part of every cultural or religious heritage. The question is no longer the reaffirmation of "*the* message" in new context, nor abandonment of sacred beliefs in terms of pragmatic adjustment, nor the temporary retooling of ideas for a new temporal understanding of life, nor the use of classical formulations to condemn the present. Instead, the urban ethos can be understood as grace in that it brings new unveiling of fresh patterns of meaning which liberate us from the mere rehearsal of past formulas. We are freed to participate in conscious reconstruction, reinterpretation, and redefinition. We do not merely search the Scriptures or the traditions to find the truth which we then apply to the new situation. Rather, we are given the audacity by the urban ethos to begin to do what the authors of Scripture and tradition did; we use the wisdom of the present and the mytho-poetic materials of the past to rationally and symbolically reconstruct projects, the doctrines, and the ecclesia for today and for tomorrow.

But the audacity by which we live in the urban ethos is bounded at several points. The visionary dimensions of our audacity must necessarily be controlled by a realism. The prospects of final transformation continually recede into the future. The weight of tragedy that accompanies even the best of expectations, orders, and communities does and will prevent immediate fulfillment of the promise of the city. But, mitigation of evil, renewed vocations, and improved structures are possible even if they are enormously demanding. Thus, we stand in the midst of a tension of vision and reality. The grace of the urban ethos allows us to possess and live by the vision so that our realism does not lapse into cynicism; and the urban ethos demands that we encounter realism so that we do not leap into visionary apocalypticism or utopianism.

We have no guarantees that the new definitions of personhood, the new patterns of creative order, and the new inspired communities will take substantive shape. We live by faith, but we have no guarantees. On the one hand, the possibilities of new definitions of personhood are opened up, but they may move in directions quite contrary to creative order and inspired community. When new patterns of creative order are designed, they may be unable to evoke new personality formation and may clash with inspired communities moving in quite different directions. And when the option of inspired community formation is at hand, the new spirits may tyrannize over persons and subvert emerging and therefore insecure patterns of creative order. And, on the other hand, the uncertainties of transition may cause reaffirmation of old certainties. Present national policies concerning the cities seem very much to be the recrudescence of corporative consolidation in economics and frontier-protestant federalism in polities, while protest groups dissipate their energies in sectarian isolation. The notion that attention to the urban ethos is a matter of ultimate concern has not been institutionalized in national policy or polity. The vision of new cosmopolitan possibilities and a *credo* that seeks to reflect cosmopolitan structures is left to the pseudo-*ecclesia* of the

Military-Industrial Complex. Nor is this attributable merely to conspiratorial elites; it reflects the dominant, if not fully conscious, piety and theological ethical loyalties of the nation. But the urban ethos requires and bears a more profound *credo* and more genuinely humane complex that is valid even if it is not empirically dominant or guaranteed.

Hence, two tasks attend the recognition of the urban ethos as a sign of grace. The patterns of novelty that arise must be tested in terms of their cohesion with other centers of worth and power. The new definitions of personhood that are developed must be judged by the possibility of their contribution to creative order in inspirited community. Fresh patterns of creative order are to be evaluated by their capacity to protect and evoke new understandings of the person and communities with an innovative *esprit de corps*. And the formation of imaginative communities is deemed normative only when they assist in the development of creative order and new personality.

And the whole must become actualized in the minds and hearts of people and through them institutionalized in local, national, and international affairs. A new urban piety rooted in eschatological vision, doctrinal substance, and an organized constituency is required; for piety determines polity, and polity determines policy. If, indeed, the urban ethos is a new sign of grace, to betray it becomes a betrayal of all that is holy. But to see the ultimate questions that are at stake in it, and to organize one's projects, thought, and group formation around this realization, with all that this entails in terms of reordering human priorities, is an act of obedience to that which alone is of ultimate power and worth—God.

NOTES

CHAPTER I

1. Consult particularly Gibson Winter, *The New Creation as Metropolis* (New York: Macmillan, 1963); Harvey Cox, *The Secular City* (New York: Macmillan, 1965); and Gabriel Fackre, *Humiliation and Celebration* (New York: Sheed and Ward, 1969).

2. For surveys of the antiurban strain in intellectual history, see Morton and Lucia White, *The Intellectual Versus the City* (Cambridge, Massachusetts: Harvard U. Press and M.I.T. Press, 1962); H. J. Dyon, "Some Historical Reflections" in *The Quality of Urban Life, Urban Affairs Annual Review*, Vol. 3 (Beverly Hills, California: Sage Publications, 1969), pp. 31–60; and H. Cox, *The Secular City* (New York, Macmillan, 1965), pp. 39 ff.

3. Theodore Roszak's *The Making of a Counter Culture* (Garden City, New York: Anchor Books, 1969) and Charles A. Reich's *The Greening of America* (New York, Random House, 1970) best represent the popularization of these motifs, while the raft of sensitivity training groups represents their bourgeois institutionalization.

4. I have attempted to explore these issues in *The Ethics of Necropolis* (Boston: Beacon Press, 1971).

5. Barrington Moore, Jr., *Political Power and Social Theory* (New York, Harper & Row, 1965), p. 102. More recently, Alvin W. Gouldner has made a more self-conscious attempt to make this case, but finds it necessary to become explicitly confessional in social theory and to assert that such a stance is epistemologically more true and metaphysically more real. *The Coming Crisis of Western Sociology* (New York: Basic Books, 1970).

6. This is Alvin Toffler's term (*Future Shock* [New York: Random House, 1970]), by which he means the rapid succession of changes and novelty that has a disjoining effect on persons and society. In fact, however, there are highly significant forms of continuity, and some of this "rapidation" may be more apparent than real. See especially, Victor Ferkiss, *Technological Man* (New York: Braziller, 1969).

7. Robert Nisbet, *Community and Power* (New York: Oxford U. Press, 1953), p. 53.

8. *Ibid.*

9. Cf. Ernest Becker, *The Structure of Evil* (New York: Braziller, 1968), esp. Appendix.

10. See, for example, the striking publication *Counterbudget*, pub-

lished by the National Urban Coalition, ed. R. Benson and Harold Wolman (New York: Praeger, 1971).

11. This view is in direct contradiction to that of the present head of President Nixon's Task Force on Model Cities. Edward Banfield argues, in *The Unheavenly City* (Boston: Little, Brown & Co., 1970), that the racial problem in the country is primarily due to the fact that Blacks are "low-class," having all the pathologies attending the psychology of other lower economic strata. Racism, particularly institutionalized racism, is implicitly denied as a decisive social factor. That classism is indeed a macro-ethical problem can hardly be denied. And the relationship between racism and classism is indeed complex, but I am not convinced that racial matters can be reduced to class analysis. Cf. my "Reparations," *The Lutheran Quarterly,* XXI, 4 (Nov. 1969), pp. 358–380, and "Whatever Happened to Reparations?" *Andover Newton Quarterly* (Winter, 1970), pp. 61–70.

12. The vast literature now appearing on this topic cannot be recounted here. But especially pertinent to this effort are those sensibilities best represented by the writings of Mary Daly, *The Church and the Second Sex* (New York: Harper & Row, 1968), and Janice Raymond, "Ethics and Patriarchy," *Andover Newton Quarterly* (Jan. 19, 1972).

13. The two best collections of essays that move substantially in this direction are, in my judgment, R. M. Fisher, ed., *The Metropolis in Modern Life* (New York, Russell & Russell, 1956), and the several-volumed *Urban Affairs Annual Review* (Beverly Hills, California: Sage Pub., 1968–). Irving Howe also pursues similar lines in his critical survey of novelists' and poets' views of the city. "The City in Literature," *Commentary* (May 1971), pp. 61 ff.

CHAPTER II

1. Cf. Norman O. Brown, *Love's Body* (New York: Random House, 1966), and Robert M. Bellah, *Beyond Belief* (New York: Harper & Row, 1970), ch. 14.

2. Even Sartre, who was the spokesman for this perspective for nearly a generation, has modified his view. He now points out that "after the war came the true experience, that of *society*." Cf. "An Interview with Jean Paul Sartre," *New York Review of Books* (March 23, 1970), p. 22. In this country, the antidraft movement both gained its vitality from and suffered enormous

frustrations because of the personalist element. See Michael Ferber and Staughton Lynd, *The Resistance* (Boston: Beacon Press, 1971).

3. These views often have greatest currency among university students whose social situation is primarily one that extracts the self from the social matrix.

4. See the far too neglected treatment of this in Leon Bramson, *The Political Context of Sociology* (Princeton, New Jersey: Princeton University Press, 1961), especially Part II.

5. For example, Gabriel Almond and Sidney Verba, *The Civic Culture* (Boston: Little, Brown & Co., 1965), and George Rosen, *Madness in Society: Chapters in the Historical Sociology of Mental Health* (Chicago: University of Chicago Press, 1968); E. Thornton, ed., *Planning and Action for Mental Health* (London: World Federation of Mental Health, 1961).

6. *Man Makes Himself* (New York: The New American Library, 1951).

7. *The Urban Process: Cities in Industrial Societies.* (New York: The Free Press, 1964), p. 98.

8. Cf. Ernest W. Burgess and Donald Bogue, *Contributions to Urban Sociology* (Chicago: University of Chicago Press, 1964), especially Part I; and Louis Worth, *On Cities and Social Life,* ed. A. J. Reiss, Jr. (Chicago: University of Chicago Press, 1964), especially chapter 12 for a critique.

9. Cf. Regional Plan Association, *Urban Design Manhattan* (New York: The Viking Press, 1969).

10. Cf. Hans Blumenfeld, *The Modern Metropolis: Its Origins, Growth Characteristics and Planning* (Cambridge, Massachusetts: The M.I.T. Press, 1967), especially Sections II and III.

11. Thomas Reiner, *The Place of the Ideal in Urban Planning.* (Philadelphia: University of Pennsylvania Press, 1963).

12. Eliel Saarinen, *The City: Its Growth, Its Decay, Its Future.* (Cambridge, Massachusetts: The M.I.T. Press, 1965).

13. John B. Calhoun, "Population Density and Social Pathology," in *The Urban Condition,* ed. by Leonard Duke. (New York: Basic Books, Inc., 1963), pp. 33 ff.

14. Burgess and Bogue, *op. cit.*

15. *Op. cit.*

16. See Norman Faramelli, *Technethics* (New York: Friendship Press, 1971).

17. January 27, 1970.

18. "The Historical Roots of Our Ecological Crisis," *Science*, Vol. 155, No. 3767, March 10, 1967, pp. 1203 ff.
19. *Ibid.*, p. 1204.
20. *Ibid.*, p. 1204.
21. *Ibid.*, p. 1205.
22. *Ibid.*, p. 1206.
23. *Ibid.*, p. 1207.
24. *Ibid.*, p. 1206.
25. *Ibid.*, p. 1207.
26. See Robert H. Hamill, *Plenty and Trouble* (Nashville, Tennessee: Abingdon Press, 1971), and Richard A. McCormick, "Notes on Moral Theology," *Theological Studies*, Vol. 32, No. 1, 1971, pp. 97 ff., for excellent bibliographical references.
27. In *The Urban Condition*, ed. Leonard Duhl (*op. cit.*).
28. R. Ardrey, *The Territorial Imperative* (New York: Delta, 1968).
29. *Op. cit.*, p. 1203. One exception is Lewis W. Moncrief, "The Cultural Basis for Our Environmental Crisis," *Science*, Vol. 170, pp. 508–512, who nevertheless criticizes White for being too monocausal in his statements.
30. "The Perspective of Mental Health" in *The Quality of Urban Life, op. cit.* Cf. also Edward T. Hall, *The Hidden Dimension* (Garden City, New Jersey: Doubleday & Co., 1969).

CHAPTER III

1. The "Military-Industrial Complex" for example, can be conceived as a form of urban organization divorced from its geographical roots. Cf. p. 10 above.
2. Cf. Don Martindale, "Prefatory Remarks: The Theory of the City," in *The City* by Max Weber (New York: The Free Press, 1958), pp. 9–67. I have in mind the recent developments of the European common market which establishes controls and patterns beyond the realm of any political sovereignty. This differs significantly from the hegemonic patterns of nation-state dominance.
3. The body of literature on this topic and with these presuppositions to see what has been highly influential or representative is vast, especially W. Lloyd Warner, *Social Class in America* (Chicago Research Associates, 1949); Floyd Hunter, *Community Power Structure* (Garden City, New York: Doubleday & Co., 1953); Floyd Hunter, *Top Leadership, U.S.A.* (Chapel Hill: Univ. of North Carolina Press, 1959); Carol E. Tomety, *The*

Decision Makers (Dallas: Southern Methodist Press, 1963). Parallel to these studies and since their appearance, more than a hundred significant studies in this area have appeared. Perhaps the best recent effort to summarize and analyze this vast body of material is Terry N. Clark, ed. *Community Structure and Decision Making: Comparative Analyses* (San Francisco: Chandler Publishing Co., 1968).

4. *Community Power and Political Theory* (New Haven: Yale University Press, 1963).

5. William Jennings, *Community Influentials* (New York: Free Press of Glencoe, 1964).

6. *Ibid.*, p. 201.

7. Leon Bramson, *The Political Context of Sociology* (Princeton, New Jersey: Princeton University Press, 1961), p. 104.

8. This perspective is acknowledged by both Robert Presthus, *Men at the Top* (New York: Oxford University Press, 1964), and Delbert C. Miller, *International Community Power Structure* (Bloomington, Indiana: I. U. Press, 1970).

9. Daniel Lerner, ed., *The Human Meaning of the Social Sciences* (New York: Meridian Books, Inc., 1959).

10. Cf. William F. Fiore, "Media and Democracy" *Christianity and Crisis,* Vol. XXXI, No. 8 (May 17, 1971), pp. 94 ff. As this goes to press, the publication by the *New York Times* of the secret Pentagon study is causing wide-ranging discussion of the role of the free press and democracy.

11. See Louis J. Knowles and Kenneth Pravitt, eds., *Institutional Racism in America* (Englewood Cliffs, New Jersey: Prentice Hall, 1969), especially pp. 134–176. The implications of this effort are, I believe, devastating to cruder power elite theories.

12. Peter H. Rossi and Robert A. Dentler, *The Politics of Urban Renewal* (New York: Free Press, 1961).

13. Edward C. Banfield and James Q. Wilson, *City Politics* (Cambridge: Harvard University Press, 1963).

14. Wallace Sayre and Herbert Kaufman, *Governing New York City* (New York: Russell Sage Foundation, 1960).

15. Robert A. Dahl, *Who Governs* (New Haven: Yale U. Press, 1963) and Raymond Wolfinger, *The Politics of Progress* (New Haven: Yale U. Press, 1964).

16. Roscoe Martin and Frank Munger, *Decisions in Syracuse* (New York: Doubleday & Co., 1965).

17. William Kolb, "The Social Structure and Functions of Cities," *Economic Development and Cultural Change,* Vol. 3, 1954–1955

(Johnson Reprint Corporation), pp. 39 ff. See, for similar in-
terpretations, Robert E. Dickenson, *The West European City*
(London: Routledge and Kegan Paul, 1951), and Walter Firey,
Land Use in Central Boston (Cambridge: Harvard U. Press,
1947). From quite a different perspective, cf. the significant con-
tribution made by Ritchie Lowry, *Who's Running This Town*
(New York: Harper & Row, 1965 [revised edition]), especially
Part I, and Gideon Sjoberg, "Theory and Research in Urban
Sociology," in *The Study of Urbanization,* eds. Hauser & Schnore
(New York: John Wiley & Sons, 1965), pp. 157–190.

18. Max Weber, *The City, op. cit.*

19. Ernst Troeltsch, *The Social Teachings of the Christian Churches,*
tr. by O. Wyon (New York: Harper & Brothers, 1960), vol. 2,
passim.

20. Gabriel A. Almond and Sidney Verba, *The Civic Culture* (Bos-
ton: Little, Brown & Co., 1963). Also, of prime significance, see
D. B. Robertson, ed., *Voluntary Associations* (Richmond, Vir-
ginia: John Knox Press, 1966), and J. R. Pennock and J. W.
Chapman, eds. *Voluntary Associations, Nomos XI* (New York:
Atherton Press, 1969).

21. I use, of course, Robert Merton's classic and useful distinctions.
See *Social Theory and Social Structures,* revised and enlarged
edition. (Glencoe, Illinois: The Free Press, 1949), especially
Chs. I, VIII, and X. But one could also draw upon certain parts
of Amatai Etzioni, *Complex Organizations* (New York: The Free
Press, 1961), or on Almond and Verba, *op. cit.*

22. Cf. Scott Greer, *op. cit.*

CHAPTER IV

1. Clyde Kluckhohn pointed out, nearly a decade ago, what is now
much more widely recognized: "Ethical conceptions are not only
related to what people *believe* to be the facts about the world in
which they live . . ." but "the activity of science surely carries
value-commitment." Richard Kluckhohn, ed., *Culture and Behavior* (New York: Free Press, 1962), p. 285.

2. Efforts in the direction are beginning to appear from several
perspectives: See especially Gibson Winter, *Elements for a
Social Ethic: Scientific and Ethical Perspectives on Social Process*
(New York: The Macmillan Company, 1966); and James
Sellers, *Public Ethics* (New York: Harper & Row, 1970).

3. This entire discussion is an alternative formulation to the prevail-

ing discussions of "the naturalistic fallacy" in British analytical ethics. Cf. Mary Warnock, *Ethics Since 1900* (London: Oxford U. Press, 1960). Cf. also my earlier reflections on this problem in "Technical Data and Ethical Norms," *Journal for the Scientific Study of Religion,* Vol. V, No. 2 (1966), pp. 191–203, from which some formulations here are taken.

4. This point is made tellingly by Robert Heilbroner, *The Worldly Philosophers* (New York: Simon & Schuster, 1953), Chapter VI.

5. Cf. for example, Jacques Ellul's use of "Neo-Orthodox" categories to deal with the city in *The Meaning of the City* (Grand Rapids, Michigan: Wm. B. Eerdmans Publishing Co., 1970).

6. Cf. Joseph Fletcher, *Situation Ethics* (Philadelphia, Westminster Press, 1966).

7. The theologian finds long-familiar notions in "systems analysis" now taught and debated in courses of the avant-garde of computer technology. See the striking treatment of alternative systems models in Robert Boguslaw, *The New Utopians* (Englewood Cliffs, New Jersey: Prentice Hall, Inc., 1965). The point at which systems analysis of a cybernetic sort breaks down, however, is in the determination of ends. Cf. Richard Taylor, *Action and Purpose* (Englewood Cliffs, New Jersey: Prentice Hall, Inc., 1966), especially Part II.

8. I use Arthur Lovejoy's phrase, *The Great Chain of Being* (New York: Harper & Brothers, 1936).

9. See William O. Shanahan, *German Protestants Face the Social Questions* (South Bend, Indiana: Notre Dame Press, 1954), for the nineteenth-century issue of this as the Lutheran tradition faced the first surge of modern industrialization and urbanization on a massive scale.

10. David C. McClelland points out the interaction of these motifs with certain developments in the Jewish tradition in "Religious Overtones in Psychoanalysis," *The Ministry and Mental Health,* ed. Hans Hofmann (New York: Association Press, 1960), pp. 48–68.

11. Cf. Raymond S. Duff and August Hollingshead, *Sickness and Society* (New York, Harper & Row, 1968); Leonard J. Duhl, *The Urban Condition* (New York: Basic Books, 1963); Irving Horowitz, ed. *The New Sociology* (New York, Oxford University Press, 1964), especially Ch. 7; and James L. Adams, "Social Ethics and Pastoral Care," in *Pastoral Care in the Liberal Churches* (Nashville, Tennessee: Abingdon Press, 1970).

12. Ray C. Perry, *Christian Eschatology and Social Thought* (Nash-

ville, Tennessee: Abingdon Press, 1956). Cf. Lewis Mumford, *The Story of Utopia* (New York: Viking Press, 1962 ed.), and T. Reiner, *op. cit.* Lawrence Haworth, *The Good City* (Bloomington, Indiana: Indiana University Press, 1963), represents a more philosophical dependence on these roots.

13. George H. Williams, *Wilderness and Paradise in Christian Thought* (Boston: Beacon Press, 1954).

14. A. S. P. Woodhouse, *Puritanism and Liberty* (Chicago: University of Chicago Press, 1965), and Michael Walzer, *The Revolution of the Saints* (New York: Atheneum, 1968).

15. Ernest Tuveson, *Millennium and Utopia* (New York: Harper & Row, 1964), p. 112. Cf. also Robert Nesbit, *Social Change and History* (New York: Oxford U. Press, 1969).

16. Robert M. Adams, "The Origin of Cities," *Metropolis in Crisis*, ed. Jeffrey K. Hadden, et al. (Itasca, Illinois: F. E. Peacock Publishers, 1967), pp. 33 ff.

17. *The Ancient City* (Garden City, New York: Doubleday & Co., Inc., *n.d.*), first published 1864.

18. R. Niebuhr, *Man's Nature and His Communities* (New York: Charles Scribner's Sons, 1965), p. 33.

19. See Sylvia Thrupp, ed., *Millennial Dreams in Action, Comparative Studies in Society and History, Supplement II* (The Hague: Mouton & Co., 1962), and Vittorio Lanternari, *The Religion of the Oppressed* (New York: The New American Library, 1963).

20. See, especially, his *The Religion of China* (Glencoe, Illinois: The Free Press, 1951) and *The Religion of India* (Glencoe, Illinois: The Free Press, 1958) in comparison with his better-known writings on the West. In different forms, similar arguments are made by Edward Banfield, *The Moral Basis of a Backward Society* (Glencoe, Illinois: The Free Press, 1958), and Eisenstadt, *The Protestant Ethic and Modernization* (New York: Basic Books, 1968).

21. See, especially, Robert Bellah, *Tokugawa Religion* (Glencoe, Illinois: The Free Press, 1962), for a close look at the Japanese case. P. D. Devanandan and M. M. Thomas, eds., *Christian Participation in Nation Building*, for the India situation; and A. T. Van Leeuwen, *Christianity in World History* (New York, Chas. Scribner's Sons, 1964), for a broad-gauge interpretation.

22. Cf., on this, Karl H. Kraeling and Karl M. Adams, eds., *The City Invincible* (Chicago: Chicago University Press, 1960); Henri Frankfort, Thorkild Jacobsen, et al., *The Intellectual Adventure of Ancient Man* (Chicago: Chicago U. Press, 1946);

Gideon Sjoberg, *The Pre-Industrial City* (Glencoe, Illinois: The Free Press, 1960); Lewis Mumford, *Technics and Civilization* (New York: Harcourt Brace, 1960); Gerhard Lenski, *The Religious Factor* (Garden City, New York: Doubleday and Co., 1961); Ernest Best, *Christian Faith and Cultural Crisis* (Leiden: E. J. Brill, 1966); Ralph Tanner, *Transition in African Beliefs* (Maryknoll, New York: Maryknoll Publications, 1967); and John S. Mbiti, *African Religions and Philosophy* (New York: Praeger, 1960).

23. Émile Durkheim, *Elementary Forms of Religious Life* (London: George Allen & Unwin, Ltd., 1957). This motif has been accented in fresh ways by Robert Bellah, *Beyond Belief* (New York: Harper and Row, 1970).

24. See Sanford Seltzer and M. Stackhouse, eds., *The Death of Dialogue and Beyond* (New York: Friendship Press, 1969).

25. Non-Christian religions of, for instance, Japan, formed under the impact of exposure to Western religions and the urban environment bear close parallels to these ingredients. Cf. Fujio Ikado, "Trend and Problems of New Religions: Religion in Urban Society," *The Sociology of Japanese Religion*, ed. K. Moraka and W. H. Newell (Leiden: E. J. Brill, 1968), pp. 101–117; and R. P. Dore, *City Life in Japan* (Berkeley, California: University of California Press, 1958), especially Section V.

CHAPTER V

1. I am deeply grateful, in the following paragraphs to Verne Fletcher, whose notable article, "The Shape of Old Testament Ethics," *Scottish Journal of Theology*, Vol. 24, No. 1, 1971, pp. 47–73, not only serves as a useful annotated bibliographical resource on the topic, but contributes constructively to the discussion of biblical ethics as well.

2. *Ibid.*, p. 54.

3. *Theology of Hope* (London: S.C.M. Press, 1967), pp. 100–108, as summarized by Fletcher, *op. cit.*, p. 56. Cf. also Gerald O'Collins, *Man and His New Hopes* (New York: Herder and Herder, 1969).

4. I am indebted on this point to preliminary research on this topic done by a student, David Roones, as reported in a term paper, "The City in Old Testament Theology." Mr. Roones takes strong issue with the treatment of the city in the Bible offered by Jacques Ellul, *The Meaning of the City, op. cit.* For further dis-

cussion of this, see particularly, Harvey Cox, *The Secular City, op. cit.,* Chapter I; James Muilenberg, "Biblical Images of the City," in *The Church and the Exploding Metropolis,* ed. Robert Lee (Richmond, Virginia: John Knox Press, 1965), pp. 45–59; George Peck, "The Secular City and the Bible," in *The Secular City Debate,* ed. Daniel Callahan (New York: The Macmillan Co., 1966), pp. 38–45; and Harvey Cox, "The Ungodly City," *Commonweal,* Vol. XCIV, No. 15, pp. 351–357.

5. *The City in History* (New York: Harcourt, Brace & World, Inc., 1961), p. 74.

6. How distant such an orientation is from those discovered by development experts in other cultural traditions, as reported in private conversations. One particular example, I think, illustrates the point. A group of planners were asked by President Kennedy to develop an extensive water-resources program in one of the developing countries that would provide the agricultural support systems necessary to the burgeoning urban growth. All the technical possibilities were solved and the program was taken to the elders of the region. The elders asked one question, "Why," and gave one answer in rejecting the program: "The gods will not have it." The technical planners were nonplused and took their amazement home where they found it necessary to turn to theologians in order to find the ways of dealing with nontechnical questions that blocked their efforts. And there they had to confront all the problems of "conversion," "cultural imperialism," and the possible development of "indigenous theologies."

7. Cf. Amos Wilder, "Apocalypticism, Ancient and Modern," paper given at the American Academy of Religion Annual Meeting, 1970.

8. Theologians will recognize that I am opting for modified "synergistic" concepts of power. James Gustafson states the case well when he summarizes his reflections: "Confidence in God and in the Gospel, we have, but we are the secondary agency of part of God's work." *The Church as Moral Decision-Maker.* (Philadelphia: Pilgrim Press, 1970), p. 163.

9. This, I believe, is one of the crucial and central insights of Reinhold Niebuhr's monumental *The Nature and Destiny of Man* (New York: Charles Scribner's Sons, 1941, 1943).

10. This is the Christian acknowledgment of the Christian incapacity to hold the view consistently that the messianic age has already fully arrived. This acknowledgment directly links Judaic and Christian (Gentile) expectations with promises from the past.

11. See Paul Lehman, *Ethics in a Christian Context* (New York: Harper & Row, 1963), pp. 81 ff.; Martin Buber, *The Kingship of God* (London: Allen and Unwin, 1967); Walter Rauschenbusch, *The Righteousness of the Kingdom, op. cit.;* and James Cone, *Black Theology and Black Power* (New York: Seabury Press, 1969), Chapter II.

CHAPTER VI

1. R. G. Collingwood, *Essay on Metaphysics* (New York: Oxford U. Press, 1940), pp. 223–224.
2. Roger Hazelton, "Truth in Theology," *The Christian Century,* Vol. 88, No. 25, p. 772.
3. See Max Weber, *Ancient Judaism* (Glencoe, Illinois: The Free Press, 1952), especially pp. 155 ff.; Ernst Troeltsch, *Der Historismus und Seine Problemen, Gesammelte Schriften III* (Tübingen: J. C. B. Mohr, 1922); Fustel De Coulange, *op. cit.;* and John S. Dunne, *The City of the Gods: A Study in Myth and Mortality* (New York: The Macmillan Co., 1965).
4. And this became, indeed, the pattern after the insights of the trinitarian controversy were nearly subverted by later, quasi-monolithic Catholicism.
5. I am indebted throughout this section to: George H. Williams, "Christology and Church-State Relations in the Fourth Century," *Church History,* Vol. XX, No. 3, pp. 3–33 and Vol. XX, No. 4, pp. 3–26; Erik Peterson, *Der Monotheismus als Politische Problem* (C. Jacob Hegner, 1935); Paul Lehman, *Ethics in a Christian Context, op. cit.,* especially Chapter 4; and Charles M. Cocrane, *Christianity and Classical Culture* (New York: Oxford U. Press, rev. ed., 1944).
6. Gerald Slogan, *The Three Persons in One God* (Englewood Cliffs, New Jersey: Prentice Hall, 1964), p. 13.
7. Peterson, *op. cit.,* p. 27.
8. Williams, *op. cit.,* No. 3, pp. 6 ff.
9. H. R. Niebuhr traced out these options in a quite different, but not incompatible, way in his classic study *Christ and Culture* (New York: Harper & Row, 1951). See below, pp. 155 ff., for a discussion of typology.
10. From among the many, many sectarian groups that could be used here, I choose the Donatists for several reasons: they had both a pietistic and an aggressive wing in contrast to several other sectarian groups, and this distinction becomes important in

later history. They became the center of many controversies due to their encounter with one of the greatest political theologians of all time, St. Augustine. In legal history, also, the laws of suppression that were finally passed against them were the laws that were used in late medieval and Reformation periods to suppress groups with similar notions. Finally, the analogies between these groups and numerous fringe groups on the contemporary urban scene are too striking to ignore. See, especially, Herbert Deane, *The Political Ideas of St. Augustine* (New York: Columbia U. Press, 1963), most notably pp. 175 ff.

11. Williams, *op. cit.*, No. 3, pp. 16 ff.

12. See Ernst Benz, *The Eastern Orthodox Church* (New York: Doubleday & Co., 1963), especially Chapters IX, X, and XIV. Cf. Vatro Murvar, "Occidental Versus Oriental Cities," *Social Forces*, Vol. 44, No. 3 (March 1966), pp. 381–389.

13. We should, I think, desist from using the term "Fatherhood" of God in favor of "Parenthood" when we come to the normative model. The social roots of male chauvinism are theologically (and psychologically) reflected and legitimated in the "Fatherhood" term. Urban existence de-differentiates sexual roles except during the active childbearing periods of life. The decline of the influence of naturally determinative categories is appropriate to the environment and proper in terms of the equality before God, the equality of worth and power available to both male and female. The Catholic solution involving the elevation of the status of Mary, and the Protestant solution, extending the concept of Priesthood to all believers, male and female, are not radical enough for fully urban society. I mention this at some length here, for I wish the reader to be aware that I am consciously engaging in reconstruction and not mere historical reporting of the theological tradition although I am obligated by the canons of scholarship to be fair to what I perceive to be the fundamental ways in which these symbols functioned in these early debates.

14. Talcott Parsons, "Christianity and Modern Industrial Society," in *Sociological Theory: Values and Socio-Cultural Change*, ed. Edward A. Tiryakian (Glencoe, Illinois: The Free Press, 1963), pp. 40 ff.

15. Michael Walzer, *The Revolution of the Saints* (New York: Atheneum, 1968). Cf., also, G. P. Gooch, *English Democratic Ideas* (New York: Harper & Bros., 1957, first published 1897); G. R. Cragg, *Puritanism in the Period of the Great Persecution* (Cambridge, England: Cambridge U. Press, 1957); Christopher

Hill, *Society and Puritanism* (New York: Schocken, 1964); and G. H. Williams, *The Radical Reformation* (Philadelphia: Westminster Press, 1962).

CHAPTER VII

1. Cf. Paul Tillich, *The Protestant Era* (Chicago: U. of Chicago Press, 1948).
2. Literally: "outside the church none is saved."
3. The literature on this topic is vast, but to indicate the range of material available see, especially, Otto Gierke, *Political Theories of the Middle Ages* (Boston: Beacon Press, 1958); James H. Nichols, *Democracy and the Churches* (Philadelphia: The Westminster Press, 1951); Guy Swanson, *Religion and Regime* (Ann Arbor, Michigan: The University of Michigan Press, 1967); and Gerald C. Brauer, ed., *The Impact of the Church upon Its Culture* (Chicago: University of Chicago Press, 1968).
4. For the primary formulations of these motifs, see Max Weber, *Economy and Society*, eds. Roth & Wittich (Totowa, New Jersey: Bedminster Press, 1968), pp. 1164–1166, 1207–1210; and Ernst Troeltsch, *op. cit.*, pp. 993 ff. and 997–1002. The "mystical-type" is not pertinent here for, as Troeltsch points out, it has no explicit social or ecclesiological theory.
5. As, for example, in Paul Gustafson, Erich Good, N. J. Demerath, Allen Eister, "Church-Sect Reappraised," *The Journal for the Scientific Study of Religion* (Vol. VI, No. 1, Spring 1967), pp. 64–90.
6. The importance of the thought of Teilhard de Chardin in the contemporary Catholic community is a highly significant illustration of this motif. The higher and higher forms of existence, from muck to mind, vertically organized in the classical Catholic theology, is adopted and adapted to a horizontal, developmental process by this theorist celebrated by Catholic denominationalism. It has numerous points of identity at the level of underlying philosophical presuppositions with the hidden theological convictions of urban bureaucracies. Cf. especially his *The Future of Man* (New York: Harper and Row, 1964).
7. This criticism that has been made through the last several centuries by Protestants about pre–Vatican II Catholics is now made in secular form by protesters against the corporations, against the urban authorities and agencies, and against socialistic and fascistic forms of government.

8. Cf. especially, John P. Davis, *Corporations* (New York: Capricorn Books, rev. ed., 1961); Alvin L. Schorr, *Explorations in Social Policy* (New York: Basic Books, 1968); and Daniel P. Moynihan, *Maximum Feasible Misunderstanding* (New York: The Free Press, 1969).

9. See J. L. Adams, *By Their Groups Ye Shall Know Them* (Hibbert Lectures, forthcoming).

10. Cf. Scott Greer, *op cit.;* and Almond and Verba, *op. cit., passim.*

11. Cf. J. E. A. Taylor, *The Masks of Society: An Inquiry into the Covenants of Civilization* (New York: Appleton, 1966).

12. Contrast, for instance the treatment of Blacks in the Catholic cultures of the new world and in the American setting. Cf. Stanley Elkins, *Slavery* (Chicago: University of Chicago Press, rev. ed. 1968). Cf. also the resistances against equity dealt with theologically in Philip Wogoman, *Guaranteed Annual Income* (Nashville, Tennessee: Abingdon Press, 1968), and Charles Powers, *Social Responsibility and Investments* (Nashville, Tennessee: Abingdon Press, 1971).

13. The case is empirically made in Almond and Verba, *op. cit.* and theoretically made from the perspectives of classical political philosophy in J. Roland Pennock and John W. Chapman, eds., *Voluntary Associations, op. cit.*

14. Such are the criticisms of university "liberals" against campus "radicals." Such also were the criticisms of the Calvinist theologians against the sectarians of the sixteenth and seventeenth centuries.

15. Cf., for the implications of these motifs on the American scene, Perry Miller, *The New England Mind* (Boston: Beacon Press, 1961 ed.), Vol. I, pp. 432 ff.: and Loren Baritz, *City on a Hill: A History of Ideas and Myths in America* (New York: John Wiley & Sons, 1964).

16. See Franklin Littell, *The Church and the Body Politic* (New York: Seabury Press, 1969).

17. Cf. the official letter sent on behalf of Pope Paul VI to the French *Semaines Sociales* as discussed in Daniel Callahan, ed.: *The Secular City Debate, op. cit.,* Chapter 5.

18. See, especially from the Catholic side, the fascinating articles on the reconstruction of conciliar Catholicism in *The Jurist,* Vol. 31, No. 1 (1971), a special issue on "Co-Responsibility in the Church." And, from the Protestant side, Samuel M. Cavert,

Church Cooperation and Unity in America (New York: Association Press, 1970).

19. Decentralization and diversification of industrial bureaucracy, the power of the corporations in the Military-Industrial Complex, and the demands for community schools in urban education systems are correlative developments.

20. Paul Ramsey, *Who Speaks for the Church* (Nashville, Tennessee: Abingdon Press, 1967).

CHAPTER VIII

1. Cf., Carl Friedrich, "Authority," *A Dictionary of the Social Sciences,* ed. Gould and Kolb (New York: The Free Press, 1964), pp. 42 ff.

2. In a fascinating conversation with the well-known urban planner, Paul Opperman, he was asked what single thing was most necessary to getting creative work done in the transformation of a complex city. He replied, without hesitation, "Knowledge of the law. There are always groups, right, left and center, that try to resist or get special advantage from planners. I always won because I knew the law." After further reflection, he added, "Also a budget. Only with a budget can you accomplish anything. And, I guess the will of the community; but if the law and money are on your side you already have these." From the standpoint of the long debate between "Marxist" social theorists from Marx to the New Left with "Bourgeois" theorists from Max Weber to Talcott Parsons, Opperman's observations can be read two ways: law and budgets are the legitimizing masks of the elite to control the masses, or the societal forms of cultural ideas. I am arguing for the latter *when* held by an organized, active constituency. This accounts, I think, for the influence of Marxist ideology when it is sustained by a party better than Marxist theory does. Nor does it have the idealistic dangers that, for instance, Parsons does.

3. Max Weber, *The Protestant Ethic and the Spirit of Capitalism* (New York: Scribner's, 1958).

4. J. L. Adams, "The Prophethood of All Believers," *Taking Time Seriously* (Glencoe, Illinois: The Free Press, 1957), p. 21.

5. This is the decisive moral concern of E. Durkheim, *The Division of Labor in Society, op. cit.*

6. The legacy of Reinhold Niebuhr is the decisive contemporary example of this motif.

7. Cf. Alan Streyfeller, *Prophets, Priests, and Politicians* (Valley Forge, Pennsylvania: Judson Press, 1971).

8. Edmund N. Bacon, *Design of Cities* (New York: The Viking Press, 1967).

9. Donald Wall, *Visionary Cities: The Arcology of Paolo Soleri* (New York: Praeger, 1971). As this book goes to press, Ada Louise Huxtable reports in the *New York Times* that British authors and architects Martin Pawley and Alan Libman are moving in not incompatible directions (July 4, 1971, p. 20).

10. *Op. cit.*, p. 12.

11. "Introduction," *Natural Law* by O. Gierke (Boston: Beacon Press, 1957), p. xxvi.

12. *The New Creation as Metropolis, op. cit.*

13. *The Secular City, op. cit.*

14. *Toward an American Theology* (New York: Harper & Row, 1967).

15. *The Meaning of the City, op. cit.*

16. Other recent attempts to work on this issue may be found in the collection, "Theology in the City of Man," *Cross Currents*, Vol. IX, No. 4 (Fall, 1969).

INDEX